W9-CGV-416

Junior Worldmark Encyclopedia of the States

VOLUME 1

Junior Worldmark Encyclopedia of the

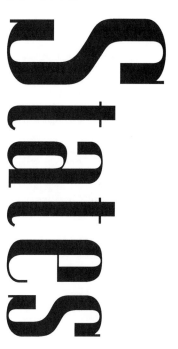

States

VOLUME **1**

Alabama to Illinois

AN IMPRINT OF GALE

an International Thomson Publishing company I(T)P®

JUNIOR WORLDMARK ENCYCLOPEDIA OF THE STATES

Timothy L. Gall and Susan Bevan Gall, *Editors*
Rosalie Wieder, *Senior Editor*
Deborah Baron and Daniel M. Lucas, *Associate Editors*
Brian Rajewski and Deborah Rutti, *Graphics and Layout*
Cordelia R. Heaney, *Editorial Assistant*
Dianne K. Daeg de Mott, Janet Fenn, Matthew Markovich,
    Ariana Ranson, and Craig Strasshofer, *Copy Editors*
Janet Fenn and Matthew Markovich, *Proofreaders*
University of Akron Laboratory for Cartographic and
    Spatial Analysis, Joseph W. Stoll, Supervisor;
    Scott Raypholtz, Mike Meger, *Cartographers*

U•X•L Staff

Jane Hoehner, *U•X•L Developmental Editor*
Carol DeKane Nagel, *Managing Editor*
Thomas L. Romig, *U•X•L Publisher*
Mary Beth Trimper, *Production Director*
Evi Seoud, *Assistant Production Manager*
Shanna Heilveil, *Production Associate*
Cynthia Baldwin, *Product Design Manager*
Barbara J. Yarrow, *Graphic Services Supervisor*
Mary Krzewinski, *Cover Designer*

Copyright © 1996
U•X•L
An Imprint of Gale Research
All rights reserved including the right of reproduction in whole or in part in any form.

Library of Congress Cataloging-in-Publication Data
Junior Worldmark encyclopedia of the states / edited by Timothy Gall
    and Susan Gall.
        p.   cm.
    Includes bibliographical references and index.
    ISBN 0-7876-0736-3 (set)
    1. United States—Encyclopedia.   I. Gall, Susan B.   II. Title.
E156.G35 1996
973'.03—dc20   95-36740
                                                               CIP

ISBN 0-7876-0736-3 (set)
ISBN 0-7876-0737-1 (vol. 1)
ISBN 0-7876-0738-X (vol. 2)
ISBN 0-7876-0739-8 (vol. 3)
ISBN 0-7876-0740-1 (vol. 4)

ITP™   U•X•L is an imprint of Gale Research
       an International Thomson Publishing Company.
       ITP logo is a trademark under license.

CONTENTS

READER'S GUIDE

Junior Worldmark Encyclopedia of the States presents profiles of the 50 states of the nation, the District of Columbia, Puerto Rico, and the U.S. dependencies, arranged alphabetically in four volumes. *Junior Worldmark* is based on the third edition of the reference work, *Worldmark Encyclopedia of the States.* The *Worldmark* design organizes facts and data about every state in a common structure. Every profile contains a map, showing the state and its location in the nation.

For this first *Junior* edition of *Worldmark,* facts were updated and many new graphical elements were added, including photographs. Recognition is due to the many tourist bureaus, convention centers, press offices, and state agencies that contributed the photographs that illustrate this encyclopedia. This edition also benefits from the work of the many article reviewers listed at the end of this Reader's Guide. The reviewers contributed insights, updates, and substantive additions that were instrumental to the creation of this work. The editors are extremely grateful for the time and effort these distinguished reviewers devoted to improving the quality of this encyclopedia.

Sources

Due to the broad scope of this encyclopedia many sources were consulted in compiling the information and statistics presented in these volumes. Of primary

importance were the following publications from the U.S. Bureau of the Census: *1990 Census of Population, 1990 Census of Manufacturers, 1992 Census of Wholesale Trade, 1992 Census of Retail Trade, 1992 Census of Service Industries,* and the *1992 Census of Agriculture.* More recent economic statistics on the labor force, income, and earnings were obtained from files posted as of January 1996 by the Economics and Statistics Administration of the U.S. Department of Commerce on *The Economic Bulletin Board,* an electronic information retrieval service. The most recent agricultural statistics on crops and livestock were obtained from files posted by the U.S. Department of Agriculture on its gopher server and its world-wide web site at http://www.econ.ag.gov. Finally, many fact sheets, booklets, and state statistical abstracts were used to update data not collected by the federal government.

Profile Features

The *Junior Worldmark* structure—40 numbered headings—allows students to compare two or more states in a variety of ways.

Each state profile begins by listing the origin of the state name, its nickname, the capital, the date it entered the union, the state song and motto, and a description of the state coat of arms. The profile also presents a picture and textual description of both the state seal and the state flag (a key to the flag color symbols appears on page xii of each volume). Next, a listing of the official state animal, bird, fish, flower, tree, gem, etc. is given. The introductory information ends with the standard time given by time zone in relation to Greenwich mean time (GMT). The world is divided into 24 time zones, each one hour apart. The Greenwich meridian, which is 0 degrees, passes through Greenwich, England, a suburb of London. Greenwich is at the center of the initial time zone, known as Greenwich mean time (GMT). All times given are converted from noon in this zone. The time reported for the state is the official time zone.

The body of each country's profile is arranged in 40 numbered headings as follows:

1 LOCATION AND SIZE. The state is located on the North American continent. Statistics are given on area and boundary length. Size comparisons are made to the other 50 states of the United States.

2 TOPOGRAPHY. Dominant geographic features including terrain and major rivers and lakes are described.

3 CLIMATE. Temperature and rainfall are given for the various regions of the state in both English and metric units.

4 PLANTS AND ANIMALS. Described here are the plants and animals native to the state.

5 ENVIRONMENTAL PROTECTION. Destruction of natural resources—forests, water supply, air—is described here. Statistics on solid waste production, hazard-ous waste sites, and endangered and extinct species are also included.

6 POPULATION. 1990 Census statistics as well as 1995 state population estimates are provided. Population density and major urban populations are summarized.

7 ETHNIC GROUPS. The major ethnic groups are ranked in percentages. Where appropriate, some description of the influence or history of ethnicity is provided.

8 LANGUAGES. The regional dialects of the state are summarized as well as the number of people speaking languages other than English at home.

9 RELIGIONS. The population is broken down according to religion and/or denominations.

10 TRANSPORTATION. Statistics on roads, railways, waterways, and air traffic, along with a listing of key ports for trade and travel, are provided.

11 HISTORY. Includes a concise summary of the state's history from ancient times (where appropriate) to the present.

12 STATE GOVERNMENT. The form of government is described, and the process of governing is summarized.

13 POLITICAL PARTIES. Describes the significant political parties through history, where appropriate, and the influential parties in the mid-1990s.

14 LOCAL GOVERNMENT. The system of local government structure is summarized.

15 JUDICIAL SYSTEM. Structure of the court system and the jurisdiction of courts in each category is provided. Crime rates as reported by the Federal Bureau of Investigation (FBI) are also included.

[16] MIGRATION. Population shifts since the end of World War II are summarized.

[17] ECONOMY. This section presents the key elements of the economy. Major industries and employment figures are also summarized.

[18] INCOME. Personal income and the poverty level are given as is the state's ranking among the 50 states in per person income.

[19] INDUSTRY. Key industries are listed, and important aspects of industrial development are described.

[20] LABOR. Statistics are given on the civilian labor force, including numbers of workers, leading areas of employment, and unemployment figures.

[21] AGRICULTURE. Statistics on key agricultural crops, market share, and total farm income are provided.

[22] DOMESTICATED ANIMALS. Statistics on livestock—cattle, hogs, sheep, etc.—and the land area devoted to raising them are given.

[23] FISHING. The relative significance of fishing to the state is provided, with statistics on fish and seafood products.

[24] FORESTRY. Land area classified as forest is given, along with a listing of key forest products and a description of government policy toward forest land.

[25] MINING. Description of mineral deposits and statistics on related mining activity and export are provided.

[26] ENERGY AND POWER. Description of the state's power resources, including electricity produced and oil reserves and production, are provided.

[27] COMMERCE. A summary of the amount of wholesale trade, retail trade, and receipts of service establishments is given.

[28] PUBLIC FINANCE. Revenues, expenditures, and total and per person debt are provided.

[29] TAXATION. The state's tax system is explained.

[30] HEALTH. Statistics on and description of such public health factors as disease and suicide rates, principal causes of death, numbers of hospitals and medical facilities appear here. Information is also provided on the percentage of citizens without health insurance within each state.

[31] HOUSING. Housing shortages and government programs to build housing are described. Statistics on numbers of dwellings and median home values are provided.

[32] EDUCATION. Statistical data on educational achievement and primary and secondary schools is given. Per person state spending on primary and secondary education is also given. Major universities are listed, and government programs to foster education are described.

[33] ARTS. A summary of the state's major cultural institutions is provided together with the amount of federal and state funds designated to the arts.

34 LIBRARIES AND MUSEUMS. The number of libraries, their holdings, and their yearly circulation is provided. Major museums are listed.

35 COMMUNICATIONS. The state of telecommunications (television, radio, and telephone) is summarized.

36 PRESS. Major daily and Sunday newspapers are listed together with data on their circulations.

37 TOURISM, TRAVEL, AND RECREATION. Under this heading, the student will find a summary of the importance of tourism to the state, and factors affecting the tourism industry. Key tourist attractions are listed.

38 SPORTS. The major sports teams in the state, both professional and collegiate, are summarized.

39 FAMOUS PEOPLE. In this section, some of the best-known citizens of the state are listed. When a person is noted in a state that is not the state of his of her birth, the birthplace is given.

40 BIBLIOGRAPHY. The bibliographic listings at the end of each profile are provided as a guide for further reading.

Because many terms used in this encyclopedia will be new to students, each volume includes a glossary and a list of abbreviations and acronyms. A keyword index to all four volumes appears in Volume 4.

Acknowledgments

Junior Worldmark Encyclopedia of the States draws on the third edition of the *Worldmark Encyclopedia of the States*. Readers are directed to that work for a complete list of contributors, too numerous to list here. Special acknowledgment goes to the government officials throughout the nation who gave their cooperation to this project.

Reviewers

The following individuals reviewed state articles. In all cases the reviewers added important information and updated facts that might have gone unnoticed. The reviewers were also instrumental in suggesting changes and improvements.

Patricia L. Harris, Executive Director, Alabama Public Library Service
Patience Frederiksen, Head, Government Publications, Alaska State Library
Jacqueline L. Miller, Curator of Education, Arizona State Capitol Museum
John A. Murphey, Jr., State Librarian, Arkansas State Library
Eugene Hainer, School Library Media Consultant, Colorado State Library
Susan Cormier, Connecticut State Library
Dr. Annette Woolard, Director of Development, Historical Society of Delaware
Reference Staff, State Library of Florida
Cheryl Rogers, Consultant, Georgia Department of Education, Public Library Services
Lorna J. T. Peck, School Library Services, Specialist, State of Hawaii Department of Education

Marcia J. Beckwith, Director, Information Services/Library, Centennial High School, Boise, Idaho

Karen McIlrath-Muskopf, Youth Services Consultant, Illinois State Library

Cordell Svengalis, Social Science Consultant, Iowa Department of Education

Marc Galbraith, Director of Reference Services, Kansas State Library

James C. Klotter, State Historian, Kentucky Historical Society

Virginia R. Smith, Head, Louisiana Section, State Library of Louisiana

Ben Keating, Division Director, Maine State Library

Patricia V. Melville, Director of Reference Services, Maryland State Archives

Brian Donoghue, Reference Librarian, Massachusetts Board of Library Commissioners

Denise E. Carlson, Head of Reference, Minnesota Historical Society

Ronnie Smith, Reference Specialist, Mississippi Library Commission

Darlene Staffeldt, Director, Statewide Library Resources, Montana State Library

Rod Wagner, Director, Nebraska Library Commission

Reference Services and Archives Staff, Nevada State Library & Archives

Kendall F. Wiggin, State Librarian, New Hampshire State Library

John H. Livingstone, Acting Assistant Commissioner and State Librarian, New Jersey State Library

Robert J. Torrez, State Historian, New Mexico State Records and Archives

R. Allan Carter, Senior Librarian, New York State Library

Staff, Information Services and State Archives Research, State Library of North Carolina

Doris Daugherty, Assistant State Librarian, North Dakota State Library

Carol Brieck and Audrey Hall, Reference Librarians, State Library of Ohio

Audrey Wolfe-Clark, Edmond, Oklahoma

Paul Gregorio, Assistant Professor of Education, Portland State University, Portland, Oregon

Alice L. Lubrecht, Acting Bureau Director, State Library of Pennsylvania

Barbara Weaver, Director, Department of State Library Services, Rhode Island

Michele M. Reid, Director of Public Services, South Dakota State Library

Dr. Wayne C. Moore, Archivist, Tennessee State Library and Archives

Douglas E. Barnett, Managing Editor, New Handbook of Texas, Texas State Historical Association

Lou Reinwand, Director of Information Services, Utah State Library

Paul J. Donovan, Senior Reference Librarian, Vermont Department of Libraries

Catherine Mishler, Head, Reference, Library of Virginia

Gayle Palmer, Senior Library Information Specialist, Washington/Northwest Collections, Washington State Library

Karen Goff, Head of Reference, West Virginia Library Commission

Richard L. Roe, Research Analyst, Wisconsin Legislative Reference Bureau

Priscilla Golden, Principal Librarian, Wyoming State Library

Staff, Washingtoniana Division, Martin Luther King Memorial Library, Washington, D.C.

Advisors

The following persons were consulted on the content and structure of this encyclopedia. Their insights, opinions, and suggestions led to many enhancements and improvements in the presentation of the material.

Mary Alice Anderson, Media Specialist, Winona Middle School, Winona, Minnesota

Pat Baird, Library Media Specialist and Department Chair, Shaker Heights Middle School, Shaker Heights, Ohio

Pat Fagel, Library Media Specialist, Shaker Heights Middle School, Shaker Heights, Ohio

Nancy Guidry, Young Adult Librarian, Santa Monica Public Library, Santa Monica, California

Ann West LaPrise, Children's Librarian, Redford Branch, Detroit Public Library, Detroit, Michigan

Nancy C. Nieman, Teacher, U.S. History, Social Studies, Journalism, Delta Middle School, Muncie, Indiana

Madeleine Obrock, Library Media Specialist, Woodbury Elementary School, Shaker Heights, Ohio

Ernest L. O'Roark, Teacher, Social Studies, Martin Luther King Middle School, Germantown, Maryland

Ellen Stepanian, Director of Library Services, Shaker Heights Board of Education, Shaker Heights, Ohio

Mary Strouse, Library Media Specialist, Woodbury Elementary School, Shaker Heights, Ohio

Comments and Suggestions

We welcome your comments on the *Junior Worldmark Encyclopedia of the States* as well as your suggestions for features to be included in future editions. Please write: Editors, *Junior Worldmark Encyclopedia of the States,* U•X•L, 835 Penobscot Building, Detroit, Michigan 48226-4094; or call toll-free: 1-800-877-4253.

Guide to State Articles

All information contained within a state article is uniformly keyed by means of a boxed number to the left of the subject headings. A heading such as "Population," for example, carries the same key numeral (6) in every article. Therefore, to find information about the population of Alabama, consult the table of contents for the page number where the Alabama article begins and look for section 6.

Introductory matter for each state includes: Origin of state name
Nickname
Capital
Date and order of statehood
Song
Motto
Flag
Official seal
Symbols (animal, tree, flower, etc.)
Time zone.

Flag color symbols

Yellow   Red   Green   Blue   Orange   Brown   White   Black

Sections listed numerically

1 Location and Size
2 Topography
3 Climate
4 Plants and Animals
5 Environmental Protection
6 Population
7 Ethnic Groups
8 Languages
9 Religions
10 Transportation
11 History
12 State Government
13 Political Parties
14 Local Government
15 Judicial System
16 Migration
17 Economy
18 Income
19 Industry
20 Labor
21 Agriculture
22 Domesticated Animals
23 Fishing
24 Forestry
25 Mining
26 Energy and Power
27 Commerce
28 Public Finance
29 Taxation
30 Health
31 Housing
32 Education
33 Arts
34 Libraries and Museums
35 Communications
36 Press
37 Tourism, Travel, and Recreation
38 Sports
39 Famous Persons
40 Bibliography

Alphabetical listing of sections

Agriculture 21
Arts 33
Bibliography 40
Climate 3
Commerce 27
Communications 35
Domesticated Animals 22
Economy 17
Education 32
Energy and Power 26
Environmental Protection 5
Ethnic Groups 7
Famous Persons 39
Fishing 23
Forestry 24
Health 30
History 11
Housing 31
Income 18
Industry 19
Judicial System 15
Labor 20
Languages 8
Libraries and Museums 34
Local Government 14
Location and Size 1
Migration 16
Mining 25
Plants and Animals 4
Political Parties 13
Population 6
Press 36
Public Finance 28
Religions 9
Sports 38
State Government 12
Taxation 29
Topography 2
Tourism, Travel, and Recreation 37
Transportation 10

Explanation of symbols

A fiscal split year is indicated by a stroke (e.g. 1994/95).
Note that 1 billion = 1,000 million = 10^9.
The use of a small dash (e.g., 1990–94) normally signifies the full period of calendar years covered (including the end year indicated).

ALABAMA

State of Alabama

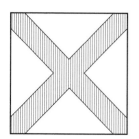

ORIGIN OF STATE NAME: Probably after the Alabama Indian tribe.
NICKNAME: The Heart of Dixie.
CAPITAL: Montgomery.
ENTERED UNION: 14 December 1819 (22d).
SONG: "Alabama."
MOTTO: *Audemus jura nostra defendere* (We dare defend our rights).
COAT OF ARMS: Two eagles, symbolizing courage, support a shield bearing the emblems of the five governments (France, England, Spain, Confederacy, US) that have held sovereignty over Alabama. Above the shield is a sailing vessel modeled upon the ships of the first French settlers of Alabama; beneath the shield is the state motto.
FLAG: Crimson cross of St. Andrew on a square white field.
OFFICIAL SEAL: Map of Alabama, including names of major rivers and neighboring states, surrounded by the words "Alabama Great Seal."
BIRD: Yellowhammer.
FISH: Tarpon.
FLOWER: Camellia.
TREE: Southern (longleaf) pine.
STONE: Marble.
MINERAL: Hematite.
TIME: 6 AM CST = noon GMT.

1 LOCATION AND SIZE

Located in the eastern south-central US, Alabama ranks 29th in size among the 50 states, with a total area of 51,705 square miles (133,915 square kilometers). Alabama extends roughly 200 miles (320 kilometers) east-west; the minimum north-south extension is 325 miles (520 kilometers). Its total boundary length is 1,044 miles (1,680 kilometers).

2 TOPOGRAPHY

Alabama is divided into four major regions: the Gulf Coastal Plain, Piedmont Plateau, Ridge and Valley section, and the Appalachian (or Cumberland) Plateau.

The largest lake wholly within Alabama is Guntersville Lake, covering about 108 square miles (280 square kilometers). The longest rivers are the Alabama, the Tennessee, and the Tombigbee. Archaeologists believe that Russell Cave, in northeastern Alabama, was the earliest site of human habitation in the southeastern US.

3 CLIMATE

Alabama's three climatic divisions are the lower coastal plain, the northern plateau, and the Black Belt and upper coastal plain, lying between the two extremes. Birmingham's temperature ranges from a normal January daily minimum of 34°F (1°C) to a normal July daily maximum of 90°F (32°C); for Mobile, the comparable minimum and maximum figures are 41°F (51°C) and 91°F (33°C). The record low temperature for the state is –27°F (–33°C), registered in 1966; the all-time high is 112°F (44°C), registered in 1925. Mobile, one of the rainiest cities in the US, recorded an average precipitation of 65 inches (165 centimeters) a year between 1951 and 1980.

4 PLANTS AND ANIMALS

Alabama was once covered by vast forests of pine, which still form the largest proportion of the state's forest growth. The state also has an abundance of poplar, cypress, hickory, oak, and various gum trees. Red cedar grows throughout the state; southern white cedar is found in the southwest; hemlock in the north.

Mammals include the white-tailed deer, bobcat, muskrat, and weasel. Alabama's birds include golden and bald eagles, osprey, and yellowhammer (the state bird). Game birds include quail, duck, and wild turkey. Freshwater fish such as bream, shad, and bass are common. Endangered or threatened animals include the American alligator, bald eagle, brown pelican, wood stork, red wolf, and Florida panther.

5 ENVIRONMENTAL PROTECTION

The Alabama Environmental Management Commission is charged with managing the state's land, air, and water resources. The most active environmental groups in the state are the Alabama Conservancy, Safe

Alabama Population Profile

Estimated 1995 population:	4,282,000
Population change, 1980–90:	3.8%
Leading ancestry group:	African American
Second leading group:	American
Foreign born population:	1.1%
Hispanic origin†:	0.6%
Population by race:	
White:	73.6%
Black:	25.3%
Native American:	0.4%
Asian/Pacific Islander:	0.5%
Other:	0.2%

Population by Age Group

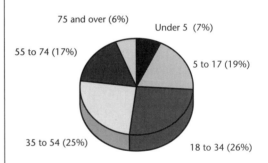

75 and over (6%)
Under 5 (7%)
55 to 74 (17%)
5 to 17 (19%)
35 to 54 (25%)
18 to 34 (26%)

Top Cities with Populations Over 25,000

City	Population	National rank	% change 1980–90
Birmingham	264,984	63	–6.5
Mobile	201,896	77	–2.1
Montgomery	192,125	83	5.2
Huntsville	163,319	108	12.1
Tuscaloosa	78,732	288	3.4
Dothan	54,787	462	9.9
Decatur	50,444	516	16.1
Gadsden	43,815	606	–10.6
Hoover	42,340	636	101.0
Florence	36,868	744	–1.6

Notes: †A person of Hispanic origin may be of any race. NA indicates that data are not available.
Sources: Economic and Statistics Administration, Bureau of the Census. *Statistical Abstract of the United States, 1994–95.* Washington, DC: Government Printing Office, 1995; Courtenay M. Slater and George E. Hall. *1995 County and City Extra: Annual Metro, City and County Data Book.* Lanham, MD: Bernan Press, 1995.

ALABAMA

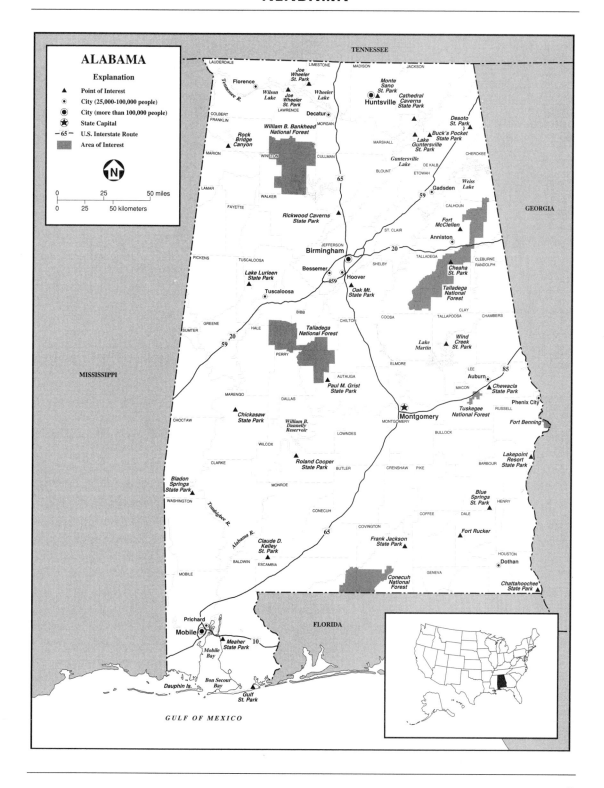

ALABAMA

Explanation

▲ Point of Interest
◉ City (25,000-100,000 people)
◉ City (more than 100,000 people)
★ State Capital
─65─ U.S. Interstate Route
▨ Area of Interest

0   25   50 miles
0   25   50 kilometers

TENNESSEE

LAUDERDALE   LIMESTONE   MADISON   JACKSON

Florence   Joe Wheeler St. Park   Monte Sano St. Park
Wilson Lake   Joe Wheeler St. Park   Wheeler Lake   Huntsville   Cathedral Caverns State Park

COLBERT   FRANKLIN   LAWRENCE   Decatur   MORGAN   MARSHALL   Desoto St. Park   Buck's Pocket State Park
William B. Bankhead National Forest   Lake Guntersville St. Park

Rock Bridge Canyon   WINSTON   CULLMAN   Guntersville Lake   DE KALB   CHEROKEE   Weiss Lake
MARION   BLOUNT   ETOWAH

LAMAR   WALKER   Gadsden   59   CALHOUN   GEORGIA

FAYETTE   Rickwood Caverns State Park   ST. CLAIR   Fort McClellen   Anniston

PICKENS   TUSCALOOSA   JEFFERSON   Birmingham   20   TALLADEGA   CLEBURNE   RANDOLPH
Bessemer   SHELBY   Cheaha St. Park
Lake Lurleen State Park   Hoover   Talladega National Forest
Tuscaloosa   459   Oak Mt. State Park

GREENE   BIBB   CHILTON   COOSA   TALLAPOOSA   CHAMBERS
SUMTER   HALE   20   Talladega National Forest   Lake Martin   Wind Creek St. Park
59   PERRY   ELMORE   CLAY   LEE   85   Auburn   Chewacla State Park

MISSISSIPPI   AUTAUGA   Paul M. Grist State Park   MACON   Phenix City
MARENGO   DALLAS   Montgomery   Tuskegee National Forest   RUSSELL   Fort Benning

Chickasaw State Park   MONTGOMERY   BULLOCK   Fort Benning
WILCOX   LOWNDES

CLARKE   Roland Cooper State Park   BUTLER   CRENSHAW   PIKE   BARBOUR   Lakepoint Resort State Park
CHOCTAW   MONROE

Bladon Springs State Park   CONECUH   Blue Springs St. Park   HENRY
WASHINGTON   COFFEE   DALE

Tombigbee R.   Alabama R.   65   COVINGTON   Fort Rucker
Claude D. Kelley St. Park   Frank Jackson State Park   HOUSTON
BALDWIN   ESCAMBIA   Dothan

MOBILE   Conecuh National Forest   GENEVA   Chattahoochee State Park

Prichard   FLORIDA
Mobile   Meaher State Park   10
Mobile Bay
Bon Secour Bay
Dauphin Is.   Gulf St. Park

GULF OF MEXICO

Photo credit: Dan Brothers, Alabama Bureau of Tourism.

Looking south, Spanish moss clings to bald cypress at Florala State Park along Lake Jackson. The 31st parallel, "Ellicott's Line," established in 1799 as the boundary between the United States and Spanish West Florida, passes through Lake Jackson.

Energy Alliance, Sierra Club, and League of Women Voters.

Nuclear power has been a source of conflict in Alabama. In 1983 one Browns Ferry reactor was ordered to shut down temporarily for inspection. In 1994, there were 13 hazardous waste sites in Alabama. There are 108 municipal land fills and 8 curbside recycling programs in the state. Air quality is generally satisfactory, and Birmingham has had no violations of ozone standard measured since 1991.

6 POPULATION

Alabama ranked 22d in population among the 50 states in 1990 with a census total of 4,040,587. By early 1995, Alabama's population will have grown to an estimated 4,282,000. Alabama has a population density of 79.6 persons per square mile (30.6 persons per square kilometer). About two out of every three Alabamians live in urban areas. First in size among Alabama's cities is Birmingham with 264,984 residents. Other major cities are Mobile, 201,896, and Montgomery, 192,125.

7 ETHNIC GROUPS

Alabama's population is largely divided between whites of English and Scotch-Irish descent and blacks descended from African slaves. The 1990 census counted about 17,000 Native Americans, mostly of Creek or Cherokee descent. The black population of Alabama in 1990 was estimated at 1,021,000, about one-fourth of the total population. As of 1990, Birmingham was 64% nonwhite, Mobile 40%, and Montgomery 43%.

In 1990, Alabama had 3,686 Asian Indians, 3,969 Koreans, and 3,529 Chinese. The population of Hispanic origin was about 25,000. Among persons reporting a single ancestry group, the leaders were Irish, 617,065, and English, 479,499.

Alabama's Cajuns, numbering perhaps 5,700, are thought to combine Anglo-Saxon, French, Spanish, Choctaw, Apache, and African ancestry. They are ethnically not related to the Cajuns of Louisiana.

8 LANGUAGES

Alabama English is mostly a Southern dialect. Alabama has experienced only minor foreign immigration, and 97.1% of all residents five years old or older speak only English at home. The three principal languages other than English spoken at home are Spanish (with 42,653 speakers), French (17,965), and German (14,603).

9 RELIGIONS

Alabama is predominantly Baptist. The first Baptist church in the state, the Flint River Church in Madison County, was organized in 1808. The major Protestant denominations are the Southern Baptist Convention, with 1,300,000 members; the United Methodist Church, with 332,000;

and Churches of Christ, with 119,000. Roman Catholics in Alabama number 137,800, and there are an estimated 8,300 Jews.

10 TRANSPORTATION

The first rail line in the state was the Tuscumbia Railroad, chartered in 1830. It made its first run, of 44 miles (71 kilometers) around the Muscle Shoals from Tuscumbia to Decatur, on 15 December 1834. As of the end of 1992, Alabama had 3,664 rail miles (5,934 kilometers) of track. As of 1993 there were 92,209 miles (148,364 kilometers) of public streets, roads, and highways. In the same year, the state had 2,136,277 registered automobiles and 1,245,737 trucks.

Thanks to the Tennessee Valley Authority, the Tennessee River has been transformed since the 1930s into a year-round navigable waterway. The 234-mile (377-kilometer), $2-billion Tennessee-Tombigbee project, which opened in 1985, provided a new barge route from the Midwest to the Gulf of Mexico. This was not only the largest civilian engineering project in the US during the early 1980s, but it was also by far the largest earth-moving project in US history.

Mobile, on the Gulf of Mexico, is Alabama's only international port. It was the 14th busiest in the nation in 1991, handling 13.5 million tons of exports and 7.0 million tons of imports. Alabama's largest and busiest facility is Birmingham Municipal Airport, which boarded 932,512 passengers during 1991.

Photo credit: Dan Brothers, Alabama Bureau of Tourism.

Having made ports of call at Florence and Decatur, a day of steamboating aboard the Delta Queen draws to a close on the waters of Lake Guntersville. Steamboat transportation was extremely important to Alabama's cotton merchants in the mid-1800s.

11 HISTORY

Moundville (near Tuscaloosa) is one of the most important Native American Mound Builder sites in the southeastern US. This site includes 20 "platform mounds" for Native American buildings, dating from 1200 to 1500. When the first Europeans arrived, half the inhabitants of present-day Alabama were members of either the Creek tribe or smaller groups living under Creek control.

During the 16th century, five Spanish expeditions entered or explored the region now called Alabama. The most extensive was that of Hernando de Soto, whose army marched from the Tennessee Valley to the Mobile Delta in 1540. In 1702, two French naval officers established Ft. Louis de la Mobile, the first permanent European settlement in Alabama. Mobile remained in French hands until 1763, when it was turned over to the British under the terms of the Treaty of Paris.

A British garrison held Mobile during the American Revolution until it was captured in 1780 by the forces of Spain, an ally of the rebellious American colonists. Spanish control of Mobile lasted until the city was again seized during the War of 1812, this time by American troops. West Florida, including Mobile, was the only territory added to the US as a result of that war.

At the start of the 19th century, Native Americans still held most of present-day Alabama. War broke out in 1813 between American settlers and a Creek faction known as the Red Sticks, who were determined to resist the advancing whites. After General Andrew Jackson and his Tennessee militia crushed the Red Sticks in 1814 at the Battle of Horseshoe Bend in central Alabama, he forced the Creek to sign a treaty ceding some 40,000 square miles (103,600 square kilometers) of land to the US, thereby opening about three-fourths of the present state to white settlement.

Statehood

From 1814 onward, pioneers, caught up by what was called "Alabama fever," poured into the state. They came from the Carolinas, Virginia, Georgia, Tennessee, and Kentucky looking for opportunities in what Andrew Jackson called "the best unsettled country in America." In 1817, Alabama became a territory; on 2 August 1819, a state constitution was adopted. On the following 14 December, Alabama was admitted to statehood.

Alabama seceded from the Union in January 1861 and shortly thereafter joined the Confederacy. Montgomery served as capital of the Confederacy until May, when the seat of government was moved to Richmond, Virginia. During the Confederacy's dying days in the spring of 1865, federal troops swept through Tuscaloosa, Selma, and Montgomery. Estimates of the number of Alabamians killed in the

Civil War range from 25,000 upward. During Reconstruction, Alabama was under military rule until readmitted to the Union in 1868.

Cotton remained the foundation of the Alabama economy in the late 19th and early 20th centuries. However, with the abolition of slavery it was now raised by sharecroppers. Alabama also attempted to create a "New South" in which agriculture would be balanced by industry. In the 1880s and 1890s, at least 20 Alabama towns were touted as ironworking centers. Birmingham, founded in 1871, became the New South's leading industrial center.

Civil Rights

During the 1950s and 1960s, national attention focused on civil rights demonstrations in Alabama, including the Montgomery bus boycott of 1955, the Birmingham and University of Alabama demonstrations of 1963, and the voting rights march from Selma to Montgomery in 1965. The leading opponents were Dr. Martin Luther King, Jr., head of the Southern Christian Leadership Conference, and Governor George C. Wallace, who was against racial integration. These black protests and the sometimes violent reactions to them—such as the 1963 bombing of a church in Birmingham in which four young black girls were killed—helped influence the US Congress to pass the Civil Rights Act of 1964 and the Voting Rights Act of 1965.

The civil rights era brought other momentous changes to Alabama. New racial attitudes among most whites have contributed to a vast improvement in the climate of race relations since 1960. Hundreds of thousands of black voters are now an important force in state politics. Blacks attend school, colleges, and universities of their choice and enjoy equal access to all public facilities. In 1984 there were 314 black elected officials, including 25 mayors, 19 lawmakers in the Alabama state legislature, and an associate justice of the state supreme court. In 1990, 704 blacks held elective office.

12 STATE GOVERNMENT

Alabama's legislature consists of a 35-seat senate and a 105-seat house of representatives, all of whose members are elected at the same time for four-year terms. Elected executive officials include the governor and lieutenant-governor (separately elected), secretary of state, attorney general, treasurer, and auditor. The governor is limited to a maximum of two consecutive terms.

A bill becomes a law when it is passed by a majority of both houses and is either signed by the governor or left unsigned for six days while the legislature is in session, or passed over the governor's veto by a majority of the elected members of each house. The governor may "pocket veto" a measure submitted fewer than five days before adjournment by not signing it within ten days after adjournment.

13 POLITICAL PARTIES

The major political parties in Alabama are the Democratic and Republican parties, each affiliated with the national party organization. The Republicans are weak below the federal-office level.

During the 20th century, the Democratic Party has commanded practically every statewide office, major and minor. In the 1992 presidential elections, 48% of the vote went to Republican George Bush; 41% to Democrat Bill Clinton; and 11% to independent Ross Perot. Alabama's delegation of US Representatives in 1994 consisted of 4 Democrats and 4 Republicans. The state legislature in 1994 consisted of 27 Democrats and 8 Republicans in the State Senate, and 81 Democrats and 23 Republicans in the State House. Minority elected officials in 1992 included 702 blacks. There were 9 women serving in the state legislature and in the executive branch in 1993.

Alabama Presidential Vote by Political Parties, 1948–92

YEAR	ALABAMA WINNER	DEMOCRAT	REPUBLICAN
1948	Thurmond (SRD)	—	40,930
1952	Stevenson (D)	275,075	149,231
1956	Stevenson (D)	279,542	195,694
1960	*Kennedy (D)	318,303	236,110
1964	Goldwater (R)	—	479,085
1968	Wallace (AI)	195,918	146,591
1972	*Nixon (R)	256,923	728,701
1976	*Carter (D)	659,170	504,070
1980	*Reagan (R)	636,730	654,192
1984	*Reagan (R)	551,899	872,849
1988	*Bush (R)	549,506	815,576
1992	Bush (R)	690,080	804,283

*Won US presidential election.

14 LOCAL GOVERNMENT

Alabama has 67 counties, 440 municipalities, and at least 497 special districts. Counties are governed by county commissions, usually consisting of three to seven commissioners, elected by district. Until the late 1970s, the most common form of municipal government was the commission, whose members are elected

Photo credit: Dan Brothers, Alabama Bureau of Tourism.

Birmingham's most famous Civil Rights landmark, Sixteenth Street Baptist Church, is just across the street from the Civil Rights Institute. On 15 September 1963, a fatal bomb explosion at the church horrified the city and the nation and became a turning point in the Civil Rights Movement.

either at-large or by district. Partly in response to court orders requiring district elections in order to permit the election of more black officials, there has since been a trend toward the mayor-council form.

15 JUDICIAL SYSTEM

The high court of Alabama is the supreme court, consisting of a chief justice and eight associate justices, all elected for staggered six-year terms. It issues opinions on constitutional issues and hears cases appealed from the lower courts. The court of civil appeals has exclusive appeals jurisdiction in all suits involving sums up to $10,000. This court's three judges are elected for six-year terms, and the one who has served the longest is the presiding judge. The five judges of the court of criminal appeals are also elected for six-year terms; those judges choose the presiding judge by majority vote.

Circuit courts, which included 40 districts and 127 judgeships in 1994, have exclusive original jurisdiction over civil actions involving sums of more than $5,000, and over criminal prosecutions involving felony offenses. They also have original jurisdiction and appeals jurisdiction over most cases from district and municipal courts.

A new system of district courts replaced county and juvenile courts as of January 1977, staffed by judges who serve six-year terms. Municipal court judges are appointed by the municipality. Alabama had an FBI Crime Index rate in 1994 of 4,903 crimes per 100,000 population. At the end of 1994, 19,573 prisoners were held in state and federal prisons in Alabama.

16 MIGRATION

Since the Civil War, migration to Alabama has been slight. Many blacks left Alabama from World War I through the 1960s, and the proportion of blacks fell from 35% in 1940 to 25.3% in 1990. Following the civil rights revolution, more blacks chose to remain in the state, and some who had gone elsewhere returned. Overall, Alabama lost as many as 944,000 residents through migration between 1940 and 1970 but enjoyed a net gain from migration of over 143,000 between 1970 and 1990. As of 1990, about 76% of Alabamians were born in the state.

17 ECONOMY

Cotton dominated Alabama's economy from the mid-19th century to the 1870s, when large-scale industrialization began. Although Alabama's prosperity has increased, particularly in recent decades, the state still lags in wage rates and per capita income. One factor that has hindered the growth of the state's economy is declining investment in resource industries owned by large corporations outside the state. Between 1974 and 1983, manufacturing grew at little more than half the rate of all state goods and services. The 1980–82 recession hit the state economy harder than the nation as a whole: 39,000 jobs were lost in manufacturing alone, and real output in manufacturing fell by 10.5%.

18 INCOME

Alabama's per capita (per person) income in 1994 was $17,925, for a rank of 40th among the 50 states. In 1993, 17.4% of all Alabamians were living below the federal poverty level. Total personal income rose to $75.6 billion in 1994, an increase of 5.8%.

19 INDUSTRY

Alabama's industrial boom, which began in the 1870s, quickly transformed Birmingham into the leading industrial city in the South, producing pig iron more cheaply than its northern US and English competitors. By the late 1970s, the older smokestack industries were clearly in decline, but Birmingham received a boost in 1984 when US Steel announced it would spend $1.3 billion to make its Fairfield plant the newest fully integrated steel mill in the nation.

As of 1994, the principal employers among industry groups were printing and publishing, rubber and plastics, furniture and furnishings, non-electrical machinery, and transportation equipment. In 1994, manufacturing was estimated to account for 21.6% of all wage and salary employment.

20 LABOR

Alabama's civilian labor force in 1994 numbered 2,031,000. Alabama's total employment was 1,909,000, yielding an unemployment rate of 6%. As of 1994, 13.9% of the state's workers were union members versus 15.5% of all US workers who were union members.

21 AGRICULTURE

Alabama ranked 26th among the 50 states in agricultural income in 1994, with $2.9 billion. There was considerable diversity in Alabama's earliest agriculture. By the mid-19th century, however, cotton had taken over. Diversification began early in the 20th century, a trend accelerated by the destructive effects of the boll weevil on cotton growing. As of 1993 there were some 46,000 farms in Alabama, occupying approximately 9.8 million acres (4 million hectares), or roughly 30% of the state's land area.

In 1994, Alabama ranked fourth in the US in production of peanuts, with 446,000,000 pounds. Exports of peanuts and peanut products from Alabama were valued at $30.7 million in 1994, third among the states. The 1994 cotton crop of 740,000 bales was tenth highest in the nation. Other crops (and their national rankings) included sweet potatoes, 79,800,000 pounds (5th); pecans, 4,000,000 pounds (6th); and fresh tomatoes, 46,200,000 pounds (11th). Cullman County accounted for 10% of the state's agricultural sales in 1992.

Photo credit: Dan Brothers, Alabama Bureau of Tourism.

Sculpted in Italy and dedicated in 1919, the Boll Weevil Monument in Enterprise is thought to be the world's only statue commemorating an insect pest. The "boll weevil" was not added to the top of the cast lead statue until 1948.

22 DOMESTICATED ANIMALS

The principal livestock-raising regions of Alabama are the far north, the southwest, and the Black Belt. Livestock and products accounted for $2.1 billion in 1994, or 74% of all agricultural receipts. During 1994, production of cattle accounted for 10.7% of all agricultural receipts. At the close of 1994, there were 1,780,000 cattle and 280,000 hogs on Alabama farms and ranches. In addition, there were 36,000 milk cows in 1994.

Alabama is a leading producer of chickens, broilers, and eggs. Broiler production in 1994 accounted for 49.7% of Alabama's agricultural receipts. Exports of poultry and poultry products were fourth among the states, at $189.3 million. Egg production accounted for 7% of agricultural receipts in 1994.

23 FISHING

Alabama's commercial fish catch was 23,689,000 pounds in 1992. The principal fishing port is Bayou La Batre, which brought in about 16,200,000 pounds, 18th highest in the nation. Catfish farming is of growing importance. As of 1 July 1993, there were 260 catfish farms (down from 370 in 1990), covering 17,500 acres of water surface. There were 102 processing and wholesaling plants with a combined total of about 1,500 employees in 1991. The US Fish and Wildlife Service spent over $2.3 million for the Sport Fish Restoration Program in 1991.

24 FORESTRY

Forestland in Alabama, predominantly pine, covers 21,900,000 acres (8,645,000 hectares). This is nearly 3% of the nation's total, and 67% of the state's land area. Nearly all of that was classified as commercial timberland, 95% of it privately owned. Four national forests covered a gross area of 1,272,017 acres (516,404 hectares) in 1993, of which 48% was privately held.

25 MINING

In 1994, Alabama's nonfuel mineral industry mined and processed an estimated $576 million worth of mineral commodities. Alabama produced 4.8 million short tons of cement valued at $226.3 million, 2 billion metric tons of clay worth $27 million, 13.1 million short tons of sand and gravel valued at $52.7 million, and 29 million short tons of crushed stone worth $178.1 million. The state ranked 17th nationally in total mineral production, 11th in mineral output, and 24th in metal production.

26 ENERGY AND POWER

Electrical generating plants in Alabama produced a total of 85 billion kilowatt hours of electricity in 1991. About half came from private sources (the Alabama Power Company and Alabama Electric Cooperative), with most of the remainder from the Tennessee Valley Authority, which also owned three of the state's five nuclear reactors.

Significant petroleum finds in southern Alabama date from the early 1950s. The 1991 output was 18,637,000 barrels; proven reserves as of 31 December 1991 totaled 43,000,000 barrels. During the same year, 165.8 billion cubic feet of natural gas were extracted, from 3,392 wells, leaving reserves of 5,414 billion cubic feet. Coal production reached 25,451,000 tons in 1992, eighth among the states, of which all was bituminous. Coal reserves in 1992 totaled 4.7 billion tons, two-thirds bituminous and one-third lignite.

27 COMMERCE

With sales that totaled $3.2 billion, Alabama ranked 27th among the 50 states in wholesale trade in 1992. That year, Alabama ranked 24th in retail trade, with sales of $29 billion. In 1992, service establishments generated $14.9 billion in receipts and ranked 26th in the nation.

Alcoholic beverages, except for beer, are sold in ABC (Alcoholic Beverage Control) stores, run by the state. Prohibition of alcoholic beverages is by local option; 26 of the 67 counties were dry in 1994, but some dry counties had wet cities (cities that allowed alcoholic beverages). Alabama exported $3.6 billion worth of goods in 1992 (26th in the US).

28 PUBLIC FINANCE

The Division of the Budget within the Department of Finance prepares and administers the state budget, which the governor submits to the legislature for amendment and approval. The state's fiscal year runs from 1 October through 30 September. As of mid-1994, the total debt of Alabama state government was $1.443 billion, or $357.03 per capita (per person).

29 TAXATION

Per capita (per person) tax revenues of all state and local governments in Alabama were $1,328 in 1990. This was less than the revenues of every other state except Arkansas and Mississippi. Alabama's receipts from property taxes ($163 per capita) were the lowest in the nation. The state tax burden ($945 per capita) in 1990 was 43d among the states.

As of the end of 1994, the personal income tax, which is designated for education, ranged from 2% to 5%, depending on income and marital status. The tax on corporate net income was 5% for most enterprises, but 6% for financial institutions. The state also imposed a sales tax of 4%; localities might charge up to an additional 3%. Alabama residents paid $10.8 billion in federal taxes in 1992.

30 HEALTH

Alabama's infant death rate for the 12 months ending with February 1994, 9.8 per 1,000 live births, was one of the highest in the US. The state's overall death rate in 1991, 979.8 deaths per 100,000 population, included a death rate from heart disease of 322.2 per 100,000, compared to the national rate of 285.9.

Alabama had 137 hospitals in 1991; there were 23,660 beds. The average expense to hospitals in the state for care in 1991 was $673 per inpatient day, close to 17% below the US average. Alabama had 7,705 physicians in 1991. The 1992 rate of 183 physicians per 100,000 population was 40th among the states.

31 HOUSING

In July 1993, there were an estimated 1,715,000 housing units in Alabama. A total of 16,105 new privately owned units valued at $1,147 million were authorized in 1993. During 1992/93, Alabama received $290.1 million in aid from the US Department of Housing and Urban Development (HUD), including $49.9 million in HUD community development block grants. In 1990, the median home value was $53,700. Median monthly costs for owners (with a mortgage) and renters in 1990 were $555 and $325, respectively.

32 EDUCATION

Alabama spends less than almost any other state on its school system. Its per capita expenditure ($700) on education placed it 48th among the states in 1993. In 1990, 66.9% of Alabamians age 25 and older were high school graduates, the third-lowest rate in the nation. Approximately ten percent of adult Alabamians had no education beyond the eighth grade.

The total enrollment in Alabama's public schools as of December during the 1993/94 school year was 726,024. Of these, 527,373 attended schools from kindergarten through grade eight, and 198,651 attended high school. In fall 1993, estimated enrollment in nonpublic schools was 35,000.

As of 1993/94, there were 64 institutions of higher education in Alabama, 48 public and 16 private. The largest state universities are Auburn University, with a fall 1993 enrollment of 21,363, and the three University of Alabama campuses. The latter's main campus in Tuscaloosa has an enrollment of 19,480; Birmingham, 15,913; and Huntsville, 8,232. Tuskegee University, founded as a normal and industrial school in 1881 under the leadership of Booker T. Washington, became one of the nation's most famous black colleges. Its fall 1993 enrollment was 3,371. The fall 1993 total enrollment in institutions of higher education was 233,300.

Photo credit: Dan Brothers, Alabama Bureau of Tourism.

The W.C. Handy Music Festival in Florence won a 1994 Regional Designation Award in the Arts by the Cultural Olympiad of Atlanta. The festival was so named to honor the musical genius of W.C. Handy, the "Father of the Blues."

33 ARTS

The Alabama Council on the Arts and Humanities, established by the legislature in 1967, provides aid to local nonprofit arts organizations. There were 70 local arts councils in 1980. From 1987 to 1991, federal and state arts funding amounted to $12,510,407.

The Alabama Shakespeare Festival State Theater performs in Montgomery and also tours. The festival has been attended by over one million people. It has also generated $9.4 million and 337 jobs for the city of Montgomery. The Birmingham Festival of Arts was founded in 1951, and the city's Alabama School of Fine Arts has been state-supported since 1971. The arts have brought $53.9 million to Birmingham along with 515 full time jobs.

34 LIBRARIES AND MUSEUMS

As of 1993/94, Alabama had 20 county and multi-county regional library systems. Alabama public libraries had a combined total of 7,202,586 volumes in 1993/94, when the total circulation was 15,224,803. The Amelia Gayle Gorgas Library of the University of Alabama had 1,661,003 volumes; the Birmingham Public and Jefferson County Free Library had 19 branches and 954,553 volumes. The Alabama Department of History and Archives Library, at Montgomery, has special collections on Alabama history and the Civil War.

Collections on aviation and space exploration in Alabama's libraries, particularly its military libraries, may be the most extensive in the US outside of Washington, D.C. Memorabilia of Werner von Braun are in the library at the Alabama Space and Rocket Center at Huntsville. Also, the Redstone Arsenal's Scientific Information Center holds some 240,000 volumes and 1,800,000 technical reports.

Alabama had 74 museums in 1994. The most important art museum is the Birmingham Museum of Art. Russell Cave National Monument has an archaeological exhibit. In Florence is the W.C. Handy Home; at Tuscumbia is Helen Keller's birthplace, Ivy Green.

35 COMMUNICATIONS

In March 1993, 92.6% of Alabama's 1,587,000 occupied housing units had telephones. During 1993, Alabama had 284 operating radio stations (151 AM, 133 FM) and 41 television stations, of which 9 were noncommercial educational broadcast stations. In 1993, ten large cable systems served the state.

36 PRESS

The oldest Alabama newspaper still in existence in the state is the *Mobile Register,* founded in 1813. As of 1994, Alabama had 13 morning dailies; 15 evening dailies; and 22 Sunday papers. The leading daily, the *Birmingham News,* had a 1994 circulation of 212,529.

37 TOURISM, TRAVEL, AND RECREATION

A top tourist attraction is the Alabama Space and Rocket Center at Huntsville, home of the US Space Camp. Among the many antebellum houses and plantations to be seen in the state are Magnolia Grove (a state shrine) at Greensboro; Gaineswood and Bluff Hall at Demopolis; Arlington in Birmingham; Oakleigh at Mobile; Sturdivant Hall at Selma; and Shorter Mansion at Eufaula.

The celebration of Mardi Gras in Mobile, which began in 1704, predates that in New Orleans and now occupies several days before Ash Wednesday. The state fair is held at Birmingham every October.

During 1994, tourists visited Alabama's four national park sites, which include Tuskegee Institute National Historic Site and Russell Cave National Monument, an almost continuous archaeological record of human habitation from at least 7000 BC to about AD 1650.

During 1991, an estimated 6,084,000 tourists visited Alabama's 22 state parks which cover a total of 47,000 acres (19,270 hectares).

38 SPORTS

There are no major league professional sports teams in Alabama. There is a minor league baseball club at Birmingham. Two major professional stock car races, the Winston 500 and Talladega 500, in May and July respectively, are held at Alabama International Motor Speedway in Talladega. Dog racing was legalized in Mobile in 1971. Four of the major hunting-dog competitions in the US are held annually in the state.

Football reigns supreme among collegiate sports, especially at the University of Alabama, which finished number one in 1961, 1965 (with Michigan State), 1978 (with USC), 1979, and 1992, and is a perennial top-ten entry. The Blue-Gray game, an all-star contest, is held at Montgomery on Christmas Day, and the Senior-South game is played in Mobile.

Boat races include the Lake Eufaula Summer Spectacular Boat Race in August, and the Dixie Cup Regatta in Guntersville in July. The Alabama Sports Hall of Fame is located at Birmingham.

39 FAMOUS ALABAMIANS

Alabama's most widely known political figure is George Corley Wallace (b.1919), who served as governor 1963–67 and 1971–79, and was elected to a fourth term in 1982. Wallace, an outspoken opponent of racial desegregation in the 1960s, was a candidate for the Democratic presidential nomination in 1964 and 1972. While campaigning in Maryland's Democratic presidential primary on 15 May 1972, Wallace was shot and paralyzed from the waist down by a would-be assassin.

Civil rights leader Martin Luther King, Jr. (b.Georgia, 1929–68), winner of the Nobel Peace Prize in 1964, first came to national prominence as leader of the Montgomery bus boycott of 1955. He also led demonstrations at Birmingham in 1963 and at Selma in 1965. His widow, Coretta Scott King (b.1927) is a native Alabamian.

Helen Keller (1880–1968), deaf and blind as the result of a childhood illness, was the first such multihandicapped person to earn a college degree; she later became a world famous author and lecturer.

40 BIBLIOGRAPHY

Barnard, William D. *Dixiecrats and Democrats: Alabama Politics, 1942–1950.* Tuscaloosa, Ala.: University of Alabama Press, 1974.

Carter, Dan T. *Scottsboro: A Tragedy of the American South.* Baton Rouge: Louisiana State University Press, 1969.

Marks, Henry S., and Marsha Marks. *Alabama Past Leaders.* Huntsville, Ala.: Strode, 1981.

Martin, David L. *Alabama's State and Local Government.* Tuscaloosa, Ala.: University of Alabama Press, 1985.

Rosengarten, Theodore. *All God's Dangers: The Life of Nate Shaw.* New York: Knopf, 1974.

ALASKA

State of Alaska

ORIGIN OF STATE NAME: From the Aleut world *alakshak,* meaning "peninsula" or "mainland."
NICKNAME: Land of the Midnight Sun.
UNOFFICIAL NICKNAME: The Last Frontier.
CAPITAL: Juneau.
ENTERED UNION: 3 January 1959 (49th).
SONG: "Alaska's Flag."
MOTTO: North to the Future.
FLAG: On a blue field, eight gold stars form the Big Dipper and the North Star.
OFFICIAL SEAL: In the inner circle symbols of mining, agriculture, and commerce are depicted against a background of mountains and the northern lights. In the outer circle are a fur seal, a salmon, and the words "The Seal of the State of Alaska."
BIRD: Willow ptarmigan.
FISH: King salmon.
FLOWER: Wild forget-me-not.
TREE: Sitka spruce.
GEM: Jade.
MINERAL: Gold.
SPORT: Dogteam racing (mushing).
TIME: 3 AM Alaska Standard Time, 2 AM Hawaii-Aleutian Standard Time = noon GMT.

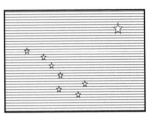

1 LOCATION AND SIZE

Situated at the northwest corner of the North American continent, Alaska is separated by Canadian territory from the conterminous 48 states. Alaska is the largest of the 50 states, with a total area of 591,004 square miles (1,530,699 square kilometers). Land takes up 570,833 square miles (1,478,456 square kilometers) and inland water 20,171 square miles (52,243 square kilometers). Alaska is more than twice the size of Texas, the next-largest state, and occupies 16% of the total US land area; the east-west extension is 2,261 miles (3,639 kilometers); the maximum north-south extension is 1,420 miles (2,285 kilometers).

Alaska is bounded on the north by the Arctic Ocean and Beaufort Sea; on the east by Canada's Yukon Territory and province of British Columbia; on the south by the Gulf of Alaska, Pacific Ocean, and Bering Sea; and on the west by the Bering Sea, Bering Strait, Chukchi Sea, and Arctic Ocean.

Alaska's many offshore islands include St. Lawrence, St. Matthew, Nunivak, and the Pribilof group in the Bering Sea;

Kodiak Island in the Gulf of Alaska; and the Aleutian Islands in the Pacific.

The total boundary length of Alaska is 8,187 miles (13,176 kilometers), including a general coastline of 6,640 miles (10,686 kilometers); the tidal shoreline extends 33,904 miles (54,563 kilometers). Alaska's geographic center is about 60 miles (97 kilometers) northwest of Mt. McKinley. The northernmost point in the US—Point Barrow, at 71°23′30″N, 156°28′30″w—lies within the state of Alaska, as does the westernmost point— Cape Wrangell on Attu Island in the Aleutians, at 52°55′30″N, 172°28′E. Little Diomede Island, belonging to Alaska, is less than 2 miles (3 kilometers) from Big Diomede Island, belonging to Russia.

2 TOPOGRAPHY

Topography varies sharply among the six distinct regions of Alaska. In the southeast is a narrow coastal panhandle cut off from the main Alaskan land mass by the St. Elias Range. This region, featuring numerous mountain peaks of 10,000 feet (3,000 meters) in elevation, is paralleled by the Alexander Archipelago. South-central Alaska, which covers a 700-mile (1,100-kilometer) area along the Gulf of Alaska, includes the Kenai Peninsula and Cook Inlet, a great arm of the Pacific penetrating some 200 miles (320 kilometers) to Anchorage. The southwestern region includes the Alaska Peninsula, filled with lightly wooded, rugged peaks, and the 1,700-miles (2,700-kilometers) sweep of the Aleutian islands, barren masses of volcanic origin. Western Alaska extends from Bristol Bay to the Seward Peninsula, an

Alaska Population Profile

Estimated 1995 population:	634,000
Population change, 1980–90:	36.9%
Leading ancestry group:	German
Second leading group:	English
Foreign born population:	4.5%
Hispanic origin†:	3.2%
Population by race:	
White:	75.5%
Black:	4.1%
Native American:	15.6%
Asian/Pacific Islander:	3.6%
Other:	1.2%

Population by Age Group

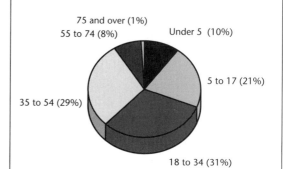

75 and over (1%)
55 to 74 (8%)
Under 5 (10%)
5 to 17 (21%)
35 to 54 (29%)
18 to 34 (31%)

Top Cities with Populations Over 25,000

City	Population	National rank	% change 1980–90
Anchorage	245,866	65	29.8
Fairbanks	33,221	840	36.2
Juneau	28,364	979	37.0

Notes: †A person of Hispanic origin may be of any race. NA indicates that data are not available.
Sources: Economic and Statistics Administration, Bureau of the Census. *Statistical Abstract of the United States, 1994–95.* Washington, DC: Government Printing Office, 1995; Courtenay M. Slater and George E. Hall. *1995 County and City Extra: Annual Metro, City and County Data Book.* Lanham, MD: Bernan Press, 1995.

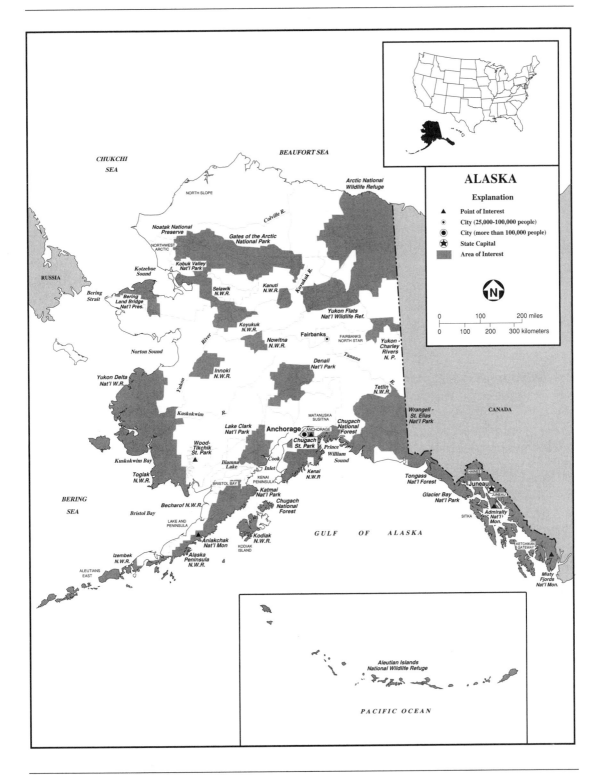

immense tundra dotted with lakes and containing the deltas of the Yukon and Kuskokwim rivers, the longest in the state at 1,875 miles (3,017 kilometers) and 680 miles (1,094 kilometers), respectively. Interior Alaska extends north of the Alaska Range and south of the Brooks Range, including most of the drainage of the Yukon and its major tributaries, the Tanana and Porcupine rivers. The Arctic region extends from Kotzebue, north of the Seward Peninsula, east to Canada.

The 11 highest mountains in the US—including the highest in North America, Mt. McKinley (20,320 feet—6,194 meters), located in the Alaska Range—are in the state, which also contains half the world's glaciers; the largest, Malaspina, covers more area than the entire state of Rhode Island. Ice fields cover 5% of the state. Alaska has more than 3 million lakes larger than 20 acres (8 hectares), and more than one-fourth of all the inland water wholly within the US lies inside the state's borders. The largest lake is Iliamna, occupying about 1,100 square miles (2,850 square kilometers).

3 CLIMATE

Americans who called Alaska "Seward's icebox" when it was first purchased from the Russians were unaware of the variety of climatic conditions within its six topographic regions. Although minimum daily winter temperatures in the Arctic region of the state and in the Brooks Range average –20°F (–29°C) and the ground at Point Barrow is frozen permanently to 1,330 feet (405 meters), summer maximum daily temperatures in the Alaskan lowlands average above 60°F (16°C) and have been known to exceed 90°F (32°C). The southeastern region is moderate, ranging from a daily average of 30°F (–1°C) in January to 56°F (13°C) in July; the south-central zone has a similar summer range, but winters are somewhat harsher. The Aleutian Islands have chilly, damp winters and rainy, foggy weather for most of the year; western Alaska is also rainy and cool. The all-time high for the state was 100°F (38°C), recorded at Ft. Yukon on 27 June 1915; the reading of –79.8°F (–62°C) registered at Prospect Creek Camp, in the northwestern part of the state, on 23 January 1971 is the lowest temperature ever officially recorded in the US.

Juneau receives an average of 53 inches (135 centimeters) of precipitation each year. The average annual snowfall there is 104 inches (264 centimeters).

4 PLANTS AND ANIMALS

Life zones in Alaska range from grasslands, mountains, and tundra to thick forests, in which Sitka spruce (the state tree), western hemlock, tamarack, white birch, and western red cedar predominate.

Mammals abound in the wilderness. Reindeer and elk inhabit coastal islands. Moose are found mainly in the southcentral and interior parts of the state. There are at least 13 large caribou herds that migrate across the state. Kodiak, polar, black, and grizzly bears, Dall sheep, and an abundance of small mammals are also found. The sea otter and musk ox have been successfully reintroduced. Round Island, along the north shore of Bristol Bay, has the world's largest walrus

An active glacier in Glacier Bay.

rookery. North America's largest population of bald eagles nests in Alaska, and whales migrate annually to the icy bays. Pristine lakes and streams are famous for trout and salmon fishing. In all, 386 species of birds, 430 fishes, 105 mammals, 7 amphibians, and 3 reptiles have been found in the state. Endangered species include the Eskimo curlew, American and Arctic peregrine falcons, Aleutian Canada goose, and short-tailed albatross; numerous species considered endangered in the conterminous US remain common in Alaska.

5 ENVIRONMENTAL PROTECTION

Alaska's number one environmental health problem is the unsafe water and sanitation facilities in over 135 of Alaska's communities—mostly Alaska Native villages. The people of these communities must carry their water from streams or watering points to their homes; people must use "honey buckets" or privies for disposal of human waste; and solid waste lagoons are usually a collection of human waste, trash, and junk, infested with flies and other carriers of disease.

Recent oil spills in Alaska have highlighted a need for better prevention and response abilities, and since 1989 these capabilities have been increased through stronger laws and more clearly defined roles among all the various governments and communities.

Mining throughout the state and timber harvesting largely in the southern areas continue to be areas of concern for environmental protection, as do winter violations of air quality standards for carbon monoxide in Anchorage and Fairbanks.

6 POPULATION

Alaska, with a land area one-fifth the size of the conterminous US, ranked 49th in population in 1990 with a census figure of 550,043. Regions of settlement and development constitute less than 0.001% of Alaska's total land area. The population density was 1 person per square mile (0.4 persons per square kilometer) in 1990, and Alaska had surpassed Wyoming's population total. The increase of 36.9% from 1980 to 1990 made Alaska the second-fastest growing state during the period (behind only Nevada), and the Census Bureau estimated a population of 634,000 for 1995.

The Alaska gold rush of the 1890s resulted in a population boom from 32,052 in 1890 to 63,592 a decade later; by the 1920s, however, when mining had declined, Alaska's population had decreased to 55,036. The region's importance to US national defense during the 1940s led to a rise in population from 72,524 to 128,643 during that decade. Oil development, especially the construction of the Alaska pipeline, brought a 78% population increase between 1960 and 1980. Almost all of this gain was from migration; as of 1990, over 60% of all state residents had been born in another state. The state's population is much younger than that of the nation as a whole (the median age was only 31.5 in 1990), and only 9% of all Alaskans were 55 years of age or older in 1990. Alaska is also one of the few states where men outnumber women.

Alaska's population is 67.5% urban. About half of all state residents live in and around Anchorage, which has a population of 245,866. Other leading urban areas are Fairbanks, 33,221, and Juneau, 28,364.

7 ETHNIC GROUPS

Indians—primarily Athapaskan, Tlingit, Haida, and Tsimshian living along the southern coast—number around 34,000. Eskimos (42,024) and Aleuts (10,244), the other native people, live mostly in scattered villages to the north and northwest. Taken together, Alaskan natives numbered about 86,000 or 15.6% of the population.

Blacks number around 22,000, or 4.1% of the population. Among those of Asian and Pacific Islands origin are 8,584 Filipinos, 3,009 Japanese, and 4,349 Koreans. Out of Alaska's total population, about 18,000 individuals are of Hispanic origin, with 6,888 of those claiming Mexican ancestry. Foreign-born persons number approximately 25,000, or 4.4% of the population.

8 LANGUAGES

From the Tlingit, Haida, and Tsimshian groups of lower Alaska almost no language influence has been felt, save for *hooch* (from Tlingit *hoochino*); but some native words have escaped into general usage, notably Eskimo *mukluk* and Aleut *parka*. Native place-names abound: Skagway and Ketchikan (Tlingit), Kodiak and Katmai (Eskimo), and Alaska and Akutan (Aleut).

Almost 88% of the population five years old and older speaks only English in the home. Other major languages spoken in the home, and the number of people speaking them, include various Native American, Alaskan, and Aleut languages, 26,780; Spanish, 10,020; and Tagalog, 5,124.

9 RELIGIONS

The largest religious organization in the state is the Roman Catholic Church, which has over 45,000 members. Southern Baptists constitute the largest Protestant denomination, with 29,000 members. Other major groups are the Church of Jesus Christ of Latter-day Saints (Mormons), 15,700; Assembly of God, 8,800; Presbyterians, 6,300; and Episcopalians, 7,540.

Many Aleuts were converted to the Russian Orthodox religion during the 18th century, and small Russian Orthodox congregations are still active on the Aleutian Islands, in Kodiak and southeastern Alaska, and along the Yukon River.

10 TRANSPORTATION

Alaska had no rail service until 1923, when the Alaska Railroad linked Seward, Anchorage, and Fairbanks. This railroad of 470 route miles (756 kilometers) is still the only one in the state and is not directly connected to any other North American line (although rail-barge service provides access to the rest of the US rail network); it was federally operated until 1985, when it was bought by the state government for $22.3 million. The line handled over 5.1 million tons of freight in 1991, mostly nonmetallic minerals (35%), petroleum (28%), and coal (26%).

The Alaska Highway, which extends 1,523 miles (2,451 kilometers) from Dawson Creek, British Columbia, to Fairbanks, is the only road link with the rest of the US. Only 13,849 miles (22,283 kilometers) of roads were in use as of 1993, including 2,541 miles (4,088 kilometers) of roads in national parks and forests. During the same year, the state had 489,004 registered vehicles and 437,696 licensed drivers. The state's major ports, Nikishka and Anchorage, handled 6,181,693 and 2,309,056 tons of cargo, respectively, in 1991. Valdez, the terminus of the Trans-Alaska Pipeline, handled 99.6 million tons, almost entirely crude oil. It was the fourth-busiest US port.

Air travel is the primary means of trans-state transportation, with several bush carriers serving the remote communities. There are approximately 10,000 active pilots and 6,600 active aircraft registered in the state, with about 995,000 hours flown—3.3% of the nation's total. Anchorage International Airport, the state's largest, carries over 1,300,000 passengers and 317,000 tons of freight annually. Alaska has a total of 545 air facilities.

Photo credit: Susan D. Rock.

A shopping and business district in Juneau.

[11] HISTORY

At some time between 10,000 and 40,000 years ago, the ancestors of all of America's aboriginal peoples trekked over a land bridge that connected northeastern Siberia with northwestern America. These early hunter-gatherers dispersed, eventually becoming three distinct groups: Aleut, Eskimo, and Indian.

Ages passed before overseas voyagers rediscovered Alaska. Separate Russian parties led by Aleksei Chirikov and Vitas Bering (who had sailed in 1728 through the strait that now bears his name) landed in Alaska in 1741. In 1784, the first permanent Russian settlement was established on Kodiak Island: 15 years later, the Russian American Company was granted a monopoly over the region. Its manager, Aleksandr Baranov, established Sitka as the company's headquarters. In 1802, the Tlingit Indians captured Sitka but two years later lost the town and the war with the Russian colonizers. Increasingly, the imperial Russian government viewed the colonies as a drain on the treasury. In 1867, as a result of the persistence of Secretary of State William H. Seward, a devoted American expansionist, Russia agreed to sell its American territories to the US for $7,200,000. From 1867 until the first Organic Act of 1884, which provided for a federally appointed governor, Alaska was administered first by the US Army, then by the US Customs Service.

The Gold Rush

The pace of economic development quickened after the discovery of gold in 1880 at Juneau. But it was the major strike in Canada's Klondike region in 1898 that sparked a mass stampede to the Yukon Valley and other regions of Alaska, including the Arctic.

Subsequent development of the fishing and timber industries increased Alaska's prosperity and prospects, although the region suffered from a lack of transportation facilities. A significant achievement came in 1914 when construction started on the Alaska Railroad connecting Seward, a new town with an ice-free port, with Anchorage and Fairbanks. Congress granted territorial status to the region in 1912, and the first statehood bill was introduced in Congress four years later.

Mineral production declined sharply after 1914. Population declined too, and conditions remained depressed through the 1920s, although gold mining was helped by a rise in gold prices in 1934. World War II provided the next great economic impetus for Alaska; the Aleutian campaign following the Japanese invasion of the islands, though not as pivotal as the combat in other areas of the Pacific, did show American policymakers that Alaska's geography was in itself an important resource.

Statehood

The US government built the Alaska Highway and many other facilities, including docks, airfields, and an extension of the Alaska Railroad. Population soared as thousands of civilian workers and military personnel moved to the territory. The Alaska Statehood Act was adopted by Congress in June 1958 and ratified by Alaska voters that August. On 3 January 1959, President Dwight Eisenhower signed the proclamation that made Alaska the 49th state.

In 1971, the Native Claims Settlement Act provided an extensive grant to the state's natives but also precipitated a long federal-state controversy over land allocations. A major oil field was discovered in 1968, and in 1974, over the opposition of many environmentalists, construction began on the 789-mile (1,270-kilometer) Trans-Alaska Pipeline from Prudhoe Bay to Valdez.

The state's dependence on oil—82% of its revenue came from oil industry taxes and royalties—became a disadvantage when overproduction in the Middle East drove the price of oil down from $36 a barrel at the peak of Alaska's oil boom in 1980-81 to $13.50 a barrel in 1988. In 1986, the state's revenues had declined by two-thirds. Alaska lost 20,000 jobs between 1985 and 1989.

On 24 March 1989, the *Exxon Valdez*, a 987-foot oil tanker, hit a reef and ran aground. The tanker spilled 11 million gallons of crude oil. The oil eventually contaminated 1,285 miles of shoreline, fouling Prince William Sound and its wildlife sanctuary, the Gulf of Alaska, and the Alaska Peninsula. In the settlement of the largest environmental suit in US history brought by the state and federal governments, Exxon was fined $1.025 billion in civil and criminal penalties.

12 STATE GOVERNMENT

Under Alaska's first and only constitution—adopted in 1956, effective since the time of statehood, and amended 19 times by the end of 1983—the house of representatives consists of 40 members elected for two-year terms; the senate has 20 members elected for staggered four-year terms. The minimum age is 21 for a representative, 25 for a senator; legislators must have resided in the state for at least three years before election and in the district at least one year.

Alaska's executive branch, modeled after New Jersey's, features a strong governor who appoints all cabinet officers (except the commissioner of education) and judges subject to legislative confirmation. The lieutenant governor is the only other elected executive. The governor must be at least 30 years of age and must have been a US citizen for seven years and an Alaska resident for seven years. The term of office is four years, and the governor is limited to two consecutive terms. The qualifications for the lieutenant governor are the same as for the governor.

After a bill has been passed by the legislature, it becomes law if it is: signed by the governor; left unsigned for 15 days (Sundays excluded) while the legislature is in session or for 20 days after it has adjourned; or passed by a two-thirds vote of the combined houses over a gubernatorial veto (to override a veto of an appropriations bill requires a three-fourths vote). Constitutional amendments require a two-thirds vote of the legislature and ratification by the electorate.

13 POLITICAL PARTIES

When Congress debated the statehood question in the 1950s, it was assumed that Alaska would be solidly Democratic, but this expectation has not been borne out; as of 1994, of 306,440 registered voters, only 15% were Democrats, while 22% were Republican, and 59% were unaffiliated. In presidential elections since 1968, Alaskans have voted Republican seven consecutive times. Alaskans gave George Bush 40% of the vote in 1992, while Bill Clinton received 30% and independent Ross Perot garnered 28%. Alaska's state legislature consisted of 10 Democrats and 10 Republicans in the state senate, and 22 Democrats and 17 Republicans and 1 Independent in the state house.

Alaska Presidential Vote by Major Political Parties, 1960–92

YEAR	ALASKA WINNER	DEMOCRAT	REPUBLICAN
1960	Nixon (R)	29,809	30,953
1964	*Johnson (D)	44,329	22,930
1968	*Nixon (R)	35,411	37,600
1972	*Nixon (R)	32,967	55,349
1976	Ford (R)	44,058	71,555
1980	*Reagan (R)	41,842	186,112
1984	*Reagan (R)	62,007	138,377
1988	*Bush (R)	72,584	119,251
1992**	Bush (R)	78,294	102,000

* Won US presidential election.

** Independent candidate Ross Perot received 73,481 votes.

14 LOCAL GOVERNMENT

Unlike most other states, Alaska has no counties. Instead, the needs of its small, scattered population were met in 1995 by 16 boroughs (covering over 40% of the state) governed by elected assemblies; the rest of the state was considered an unorganized borough. As of 1995 there were 145 cities, most of them governed by elected mayors and councils. Juneau, Sitka, and Anchorage, known as Alaska's three unified municipalities, have consolidated city and borough functions.

15 JUDICIAL SYSTEM

The supreme court, consisting of a chief justice and 4 associate justices, hears appeals for civil matters from the 15 superior courts, whose 30 judges in 1994 were organized among the four state judicial districts, and for criminal matters from the 3-member court of appeals. The superior court has original jurisdiction in all civil and criminal matters, and it hears appeals from the district court. The lowest court is the district court, of which there are 56 in four districts.

All judges are appointed by the governor from nominations made by the Judicial Council, but are thereafter subject to voter approval; supreme court justices serve terms of 10 years; court of appeals and superior court judges, 6 years; and district judges, 4 years. In 1994, the crime rate was 5,708.1 crimes per 100,000 population. Alaska has no capital punishment statute. There were 3,068 inmates of state and federal prisons at the end of 1993. Alaska had 2,196 practicing attorneys in 1994.

16 MIGRATION

The earliest immigrants to North America, more than 10,000 years ago, likely came to Alaska via a land bridge across what is now the Bering Strait. The Russian fur traders who arrived during the 1700s found Aleuts, Eskimos, and Indians already established there. Despite more than a century of Russian sovereignty over the area, however, few Russians came, and those that did returned to the mother country with the purchase of Alaska by the US in 1867.

Virtually all other migration to Alaska has been from the continental US—first during the gold rush of the late 19th century, and most recently during the oil boom of the 1970s. Between 1970 and 1983, Alaska's net gain from migration was 78,000, but from 1985 to 1990, Alaska suffered a net loss from migration of over 37,500.

Urbanization increased with migration during the 1980s; the urban population increased from 64.5% in 1980 to 67.5% of the total population in 1990. In the 1980s, migration added 36,000 people to the state, or 34% of the total population increase. Only 34% of the 1990 population was born within the state, a lower percentage than any other state except Florida and Nevada.

17 ECONOMY

When Alaska gained statehood in 1959, its economy was almost totally dependent on the US government. Fisheries, limited mining (mostly gold and gravel), and some lumber production made up the balance.

That all changed with development of the petroleum industry during the 1970s. Construction of the Trans–Alaska Pipeline brought a massive infusion of money and people into the state.

The collapse of oil prices in the mid-1980s hit Alaska hard. But by 1990, a recovery was underway.

Commercial fishing is one of the foundations of the Alaska economy. The seafood industry had wholesale values of more than $3 billion in 1990, and Alaska's fishery accounts for 50% of the total annual US catch.

The value of Alaska's forest products grew from $248 million in 1986 to $641 million in 1990. Log exports began to decline in 1990 and are expected to drop 50% by 1997 as the supply of timber shrinks.

In 1992, Alaska workers were distributed by industry as follows: 73,300 in government; 53,700 in services; 47,900 in wholesale and retail trade; 22,600 in transportation and utilities; 18,000 in manufacturing; 10,700 in finance, insurance, and real estate; 10,600 in mining; and 10,300 in construction.

18 INCOME

Alaska boasts the tenth highest per capita (per person) income in the US: $23,395 in 1994. Total personal income rose to $14.2 billion in 1994, up 3.7%.

Living costs are high: in 1993, Anchorage's typical family living costs were 33% above the US urban average, and costs in some other Alaskan cities were much higher. A total of 9.1% of all Alaskans were living below the federal poverty level in 1993.

19 INDUSTRY

Alaska's small but growing manufacturing sector is centered on petroleum refining and the processing of lumber and food products, especially seafood. Petroleum accounted for 39% of the gross state product of $23.7 billion in 1993. That year, fish products and timber accounted for 50% and 21% of Alaskan exports, respectively.

Five of Alaska's ten top employers are engaged in the petroleum industry: ARCO Alaska, VECO, BP Exploration, Alyeska Pipeline Service, and Alaska Petroleum Contractors.

20 LABOR

Following completion of the Trans-Alaska Pipeline in 1977, the state entered a period of high unemployment that lasted through the end of the decade and into the 1980s and 1990s. Of the 305,000 in the civilian labor force in 1994, 24,000 were unemployed, for a rate of 7.8%.

In 1994, 19.3% of Alaskan workers were union members. The median wage rate was $11.50 per hour for production workers in 1993.

21 AGRICULTURE

Hampered by a short growing season and frequent frosts, Alaska has very limited commercial agriculture. Farm income in 1994 was only $27.7 million, the lowest of all states. Greenhouse and nursery

Photo credit: Alaska Division of Tourism.

Mt. McKinley (20,320 feet—6,194 meters) is the tallest mountain in North America.

items, hay, and potatoes are the main commodities produced. In 1992 there were about 540 farms and 960,000 acres (238,0000 hectares) in farms; the leading farming region is the Matanuska Valley, northeast of Anchorage.

22 DOMESTICATED ANIMALS

Dairy and livestock products account for about 22% of Alaska's agricultural income. Alaska had 9,900 cattle and 1,700 sheep at the beginning of 1995. In 1991, an estimated 13.3 million pounds of milk, valued at $2.7 million, were produced by 1,000 milk cows. Meat and poultry production is negligible by national standards.

23 FISHING

Alaska was the leading fishing state in terms of earnings and in the total weight of catch in 1992. The salmon catch, the staple of the industry, amounted to 729 million pounds of fish and over $311 million in 1991. Pollock, formerly ignored for its commercial value, accounted for 55% of the total weight of the 1991 catch. Crab, a major export item, had recently declined in availability; the shellfish harvest, however, was over 400 million pounds in 1991 (rebounding from under 100 million pounds in 1984), with snow crab accounting for 89% of the volume and 65% of the value of shellfish harvested that year. In all, Alaska's commercial catch in 1992 totaled over 5.6 billion pounds, valued at $1.5 billion. In that year, Kodiak ranked third among US fishing ports in value of catch, with $90 million. Alaska had 416 processing and wholesale plants with an average of about 11,700 employees during 1991, as well as a commercial fishing fleet of 17,580 boats and vessels that year.

There are over 354,000 licensed sport anglers (64% of the state's total population) in Alaska.

24 FORESTRY

Alaska's timber resources are vast, but full-scale development of the industry awaits fundamental land-use decisions at the federal and state levels. In the early 1990s, Alaska had 28 million acres (11.48 million hectares) of commercial timberland. It is estimated Alaska has 49.4 billion cubic feet of harvestable timber. Alaska contains the nation's largest natural forests, Tongass in the southeast (17.4 million acres—7 million hectares) and Chugach along the Gulf Coast (6.6 million acres—2.7 million hectares).

Lumbering and related industries employed about 5,295 workers in 1991. The product value of the wood products is $600-800 million per year.

25 MINING

The Bureau of Mines estimated the 1994 value for Alaska nonfuel mineral production at $429 million, about 13% more than the $378 million reported in 1993. Most of the increase was due to gains in the values of crushed stone, gold, lead, sand and gravel, silver, and zinc.

State estimates show that about 9,600 people were employed in all aspects of the mineral industry in 1994.

26 ENERGY AND POWER

As of 1993, Alaskan production of crude oil was 24% of the nation's total, and second only to that of Texas. Of the 577 million barrels produced, 97% came from the vast North Shore fields and 3% from the Cook Inlet area. The Trans-Alaska Pipeline, which runs 789 miles (1,270 kilometers) from the North Slope oil fields to the port of Valdez on the southern coast, carries 1,600,000 barrels of crude oil a day. Proven reserves in Alaska total 6 billion barrels, or about one-quarter of national reserves.

Natural gas production in 1993 was 430 billion cubic feet, 7th among states. Proved reserves are 9.5 trillion cubic feet. Electric power production totaled over 4.6 billion kilowatt hours in 1993; installed capacity was nearly 1.7 million kilowatts, and almost all generating facilities were government-owned. Alaska also had proved coal reserves totaling 6.1 billion tons in 1992. Production of coal in 1992 was 1,527,000 tons, from a single mine at Healy. Alaska's total consumption of energy per capita was 1,040.4 million Btu, over three times greater than the national average.

27 COMMERCE

Sales from wholesale trade in 1992 amounted to $3.6 billion, 49th among the states, and retail sales exceeded $5.4 billion (48th) in 1993. More than half of all retail sales were in the Anchorage metropolitan area. Food stores accounted for 24.5% of all retail sales, followed by eating and drinking places, 12.6%; automotive dealers and gasoline service stations, 18%; department stores, 11.2%, and others, 33.7%. Service establishments had receipts of $2.8 billion in 1992, 45th among the states.

Over $1.3 billion worth of imports and $5.1 billion worth of exports pass through the Anchorage customs district yearly. Exports of manufactured goods exceed $3.2 billion. One-third of Alaska's manufactured goods are exported to other countries, the highest ratio of all the states, with paper and food products the leading items. Alaska is the leading fish-exporting state and the largest exporter of salmon.

28 PUBLIC FINANCE

Alaska's annual budget is prepared by the Division of Budget and Management, within the Office of the Governor, and submitted by the governor to the legislature for amendment and approval. The fiscal year runs from 1 July through 30 June.

As of 1993, the outstanding debt of Alaska was over $4.4 billion, or about $7,400 per capita (per person).

29 TAXATION

The huge sums generated by the sale of oil leases and by oil and gas royalties make Alaska's tax structure highly unusual. Government derives 85% of its revenue from oil, and local governments, 65%. There is no state sales tax, but some localities impose a sales tax, as well as a property tax. The corporate tax rate in 1994 ranged from 1% on the first $10,000 of taxable income to 9.4% on amounts over $90,000. Other taxes include ones on alcoholic beverages, motor fuels and vehicles, estates, cigarettes, insurance companies, and fisheries. In April 1980, the state legislature abolished the personal income tax; the business tax was ended in 1979. Nevertheless, Alaska by far led all states in 1992 in per capita (per person) state tax burden, with $2,730.

30 HEALTH

Alaska's birthrate of 20 per 1,000 population in 1992 was second only to Utah's. The infant mortality rate of 6.7 per 1,000 live births for the year ending with February 1994 was below the national average. The abortion ratio was 222 per 1,000 births in 1992.

Alaska's overall death rate of 391.8 per 100,000 population in 1992 was less than half the US rate, but the death rate from accidents (60.9 per 100,000) was the highest in the US and almost twice the national rate, and the suicide rate of 15.3 was above the national average. The commercial fishing industry has one of the highest occupational fatality rates in Alaska; during 1991 and 1992 the annual occupational fatality rate for the fishing industry was 200 per 100,000 workers. The fatality rate for the shellfish industry was 530 per 100,000. The death rate of 18.4 per 100,000 for cerebrovascular diseases was significantly lower than the national rate of 56.4, due to the relative youth of the state's population.

Alaska's 16 community hospitals in 1993 had 1,300 beds and 37,300 admissions; hospital personnel included 3,583 nurses and 820 physicians. The average daily expense to Alaskan hospitals per inpatient amounted to $1,136, more than all but three other states. Over 13% of the state's residents did not have health insurance in 1993.

31 HOUSING

Despite the severe winters, housing designs in Alaska do not differ notably from those in other states. Builders do usually provide thicker insulation in walls and ceilings, but the high costs of construction have not encouraged more energy-efficient adaptation to the environment. In 1980, the state legislature passed several measures to encourage energy conservation in housing and in public buildings. In native villages, traditional dwellings like the half-buried huts of the Aleuts have long since given way to conventional, low-standard housing.

In 1993, there were an estimated 243,000 housing units, 85% of which were occupied. From 1970 to 1978, 43,009 building permits were issued, as construction boomed during the years of pipeline building. As of 1990, only 87.5% of Alaska's housing units had complete plumbing facilities, the lowest proportion of all states. In 1993, the state authorized 1,657 new privately-owned housing units, valued at $228.4 million. The median house value was $94,400 in 1990, down 22.1% from 1980 after adjusting for inflation. The median monthly cost for an owner-occupied unit with a mortgage was $1,059 in 1990 (fourth highest in the US); the median rent was $559 per month.

32 EDUCATION

As of 1991, 87% of the population 25 years or older had completed high school. Alaska spent $7,263.65 per public school pupil during the 1991/92 school term. Enrollment in public schools was 119,202 for the 1992/93 school term. Private school enrollment was 4,581 in 1993/94.

The University of Alaska is the state's leading higher educational institution. The main campus at Fairbanks, established in 1917, had 5,072 students in 1993, while the Anchorage campus had 13,519. Private institutions included two colleges with four-year programs, a theological seminary, and Alaska Pacific University. The University of Alaska's Rural Education Division has a network of education centers and offers 90 correspondence courses in 22 fields of study.

33 ARTS

The Council on the Arts sponsors tours by performing artists, supports artists' residences in the schools, aids local arts projects, and purchases the works of living Alaskans for display in state buildings.

By 1992, there were 250 arts-related associations in Alaska and 32 local art groups. Fairbanks, Juneau, and Anchorage have symphony orchestras, and Anchorage has a civic opera.

34 LIBRARIES AND MUSEUMS

Alaska public libraries had an estimated combined book stock of 1,780,826 and a circulation of 3,425,225 in 1991; facilities are located in seven boroughs and in most larger towns. Anchorage had the largest public library system, with four branches and 476,804 volumes in 1991. Also notable are the State Library in Juneau and the library of the University of Alaska at Fairbanks.

Alaska had 39 museums in 1994. The Alaska State Museum in Juneau offers an impressive collection of native crafts and Alaskan artifacts. Sitka National Historical Park features Indian and Russian items, and the nearby Museum of Sheldon Jackson College holds important native collections. Noteworthy historical and archaeological sites include the Totem Heritage Center in Ketchikan. Anchorage has the Alaska Zoo.

35 COMMUNICATIONS

Considering the vast distances traveled and the number of small, scattered communities, the US mail is a bargain for Alaskans. In March 1993, 90.4% of the state's 191,000 residences had telephones. There were 86 radio stations (41 AM, 45 FM) in 1993, along with 16 television stations (5 noncommercial educational).

36 PRESS

One of Alaska's seven daily newspapers and two of its four Sunday newspapers are in Anchorage. The *Anchorage Daily News* (mornings) in 1994 had a daily circulation of 45,628 and a Sunday circulation of 103,831. The *Tundra Times,* also published in Anchorage, is a statewide weekly devoted to native concerns. The University of Alaska Press is the state's main academic publisher.

37 TOURISM, TRAVEL, AND RECREATION

With thousands of miles of unspoiled scenery and hundreds of mountains and lakes, Alaska has vast tourist potential. An estimated 900,000 travelers visited Alaska in 1992. Alaska's tourism industry was valued at $1.1 billion in 1992.

One of the most popular tourist destinations is Glacier Bay National Monument. In 1991, 6,815,000 visitors went to state parks and recreation areas in Alaska. Alaska's state and national parks, preserves, historical parks, and monuments totaled 52.9 million acres (21.7 million hectares) in 1994. Licenses were held by 184,826 fishers and 174,433 hunters who were state residents in 1991.

38 SPORTS

There are no major league professional sports teams in Alaska; Anchorage, however, has a minor league basketball franchise. Sports in Alaska generally revolve around the outdoors, including skiing, fishing, hiking, mountain biking, and camping. Perhaps the biggest sporting event in the state is the Iditarod Trail Sled Dog Race, covering 1,159 miles from Anchorage to Nome. The race is held in March, and men and women compete against each other. With a $50,000 purse, it is the richest sled dog race in the world.

Photo credit: Susan D. Rock.

A pair of Huskies hitched to a sled team wait for the signal to start the Iditarod Trail Sled Dog Race—a long, strenuous race across Alaska.

39 FAMOUS ALASKANS

Alaskan's best-known officeholder was Ernest Gruening (b.New York, 1887–1974), a territorial governor from 1939 to 1953 and US senator from 1959 to 1969. Outstanding historical figures include Vitus Bering (b.Denmark, 1680–1741), a seaman in Russian service who commanded the discovery expedition in 1741, and Aleksandr Baranov (b.Russia, 1746–1819), the first governor of Russian America. Secretary of State William H. Seward (b.New York, 1801–72), was instrumental in the 1867 purchase of Alaska, and ranks as the state's "founding father," although he never visited the region.

40 BIBLIOGRAPHY

Alaska, State of. Department of Commerce and Economic Development. Division of the Economic Enterprises. *The Alaska Economy.* Vol. 7, Juneau, 1979.

Alaska, State of. Department of Education. Division of Libraries, Archives, and Museums. *Alaska Blue Book 1993–94.* Juneau, 1994.

Brooks, Alfred Hulse. *Blazing Alaska's Trails.* Fairbanks: University of Alaska Press, 1972.

Hunt, William R. *North of 53°: The Wild Days of the Alaska-Yukon Mining Frontier.* New York: Macmillan, 1974.

Naske, Claus M. *A History of Alaska Statehood.* Lanham, Md.: University Press of America, 1985.

Naske, Claus M., and Herman E. Slotnick. *Alaska: A History of the 49th State.* Grand Rapids, Mich.: Eerdmans, 1979.

ARIZONA

State of Arizona

ORIGIN OF STATE NAME: Probably from the Pima or Tohono O'Odham word *arizonac,* meaning "place of small springs."

NICKNAME: The Grand Canyon State.

CAPITAL: Phoenix.

ENTERED UNION: 14 February 1912 (48th).

SONG: "Arizona."

MOTTO: *Ditat Deus* (God enriches).

FLAG: A copper-colored five-pointed star symbolic of the state's copper resources rises from a blue field; six yellow and seven red segments radiating from the star cover the upper half.

OFFICIAL SEAL: Depicted on a shield are symbols of the state's economy and natural resources, including mountains, a rising sun, and a dam and reservoir in the background, irrigated farms and orchards in the middle distance, a quartz mill, a miner, and cattle in the foreground, as well as the state motto. The words "Great Seal of the State of Arizona 1912" surround the shield.

BIRD: Cactus wren.

FLOWER: Blossom of the saguaro cactus.

TREE: Paloverde.

OFFICIAL NECKWEAR: Bola tie.

TIME: 5 AM MST = noon GMT. Arizona does not observe daylight savings time.

1 LOCATION AND SIZE

Located in the Rocky Mountains region of the southwestern US, Arizona ranks sixth in size among the 50 states. The total area of Arizona is 114,000 square miles (295,260 square kilometers). Arizona extends about 340 miles (547 kilometers) east-west; the state's maximum north-south extension is 395 miles (636 kilometers). Arizona's total boundary length is 1,478 miles (2,379 kilometers).

2 TOPOGRAPHY

Arizona is a state of extraordinary topographic diversity and beauty. The Colorado Plateau, which covers two-fifths of the state in the north, is a dry highland region characterized by deep canyons. The most notable is the Grand Canyon, a vast gorge more than 200 miles (320 kilometers) long, up to 18 miles (29 kilometers) wide, and more than 1 mile (1.6 kilometers) deep. Also within this region are the Painted Desert and Petrified Forest.

The Mogollon Rim separates the northern plateau from a central region of alternating basins and ranges. The Sonora Desert, in the southwest, contains the lowest point in the state, 70 feet (21 meters) above sea level. The Colorado is the state's major river. Arizona has few natural lakes, but there are several large artificial lakes formed by dams.

3 CLIMATE

Arizona has a dry climate. Average daily temperatures at Yuma, in the southwestern desert, range from 43°F to 67°F (6°C to 19°C) in January and from 81°F to 106°F (27°C to 41°C) in July. The maximum recorded temperature was 127°F (53°C), registered at Parker on 7 July 1905; the minimum, –40°F (–40°C), was set at Hawley Lake on 7 January 1971.

Annual precipitation ranges from 3 inches (8 centimeters) in the extreme southwest to between 25 and 30 inches (63 to 76 centimeters) at the highest elevations of the state. Snow, sometimes as much as 100 inches (254 centimeters) of it, falls on the highest peaks each winter.

4 PLANTS AND ANIMALS

The desert is known for many varieties of cacti, from the saguaro, whose blossom is the state flower, to the cholla and widely utilized yucca. Desert flowers include the night-blooming cereus. Among medicinal desert plants is the jojoba, also harvested for its oil-bearing seeds. Trees include spruce, fir, juniper, ponderosa pine, oak, and piñon.

Arizona's native animals range from desert species of lizards and snakes to the deer, elk, and antelope of the northern highlands. Prairie dog "towns" dot the northern regions. Rattlesnakes are abundant, and the desert is rife with reptiles such as the collared lizard. Native birds

Arizona Population Profile

Estimated 1995 population:	4,149,000
Population change, 1980–90:	34.8%
Leading ancestry group:	German
Second leading group:	English
Foreign born population:	7.6%
Hispanic origin†:	18.8%
Population by race:	
White:	80.8%
Black:	3.0%
Native American:	5.6%
Asian/Pacific Islander:	1.5%
Other:	9.1%

Population by Age Group

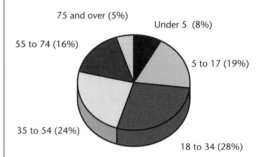

75 and over (5%)
Under 5 (8%)
55 to 74 (16%)
5 to 17 (19%)
35 to 54 (24%)
18 to 34 (28%)

Top Cities with Populations Over 25,000

City	Population	National rank	% change 1980–90
Phoenix	1,012,230	8	24.5
Tucson	415,079	35	22.6
Mesa	296,645	52	89.0
Glendale	156,165	112	52.4
Tempe	142,139	124	32.9
Scottsdale	137,022	136	47.1
Chandler	100,173	199	204.6
Yuma	61,047	394	29.4
Peoria	55,958	449	313.2
Flagstaff	48,132	533	32.0

Notes: †A person of Hispanic origin may be of any race. NA indicates that data are not available.
Sources: Economic and Statistics Administration, Bureau of the Census. *Statistical Abstract of the United States, 1994–95.* Washington, DC: Government Printing Office, 1995; Courtenay M. Slater and George E. Hall. *1995 County and City Extra: Annual Metro, City and County Data Book.* Lanham, MD: Bernan Press, 1995.

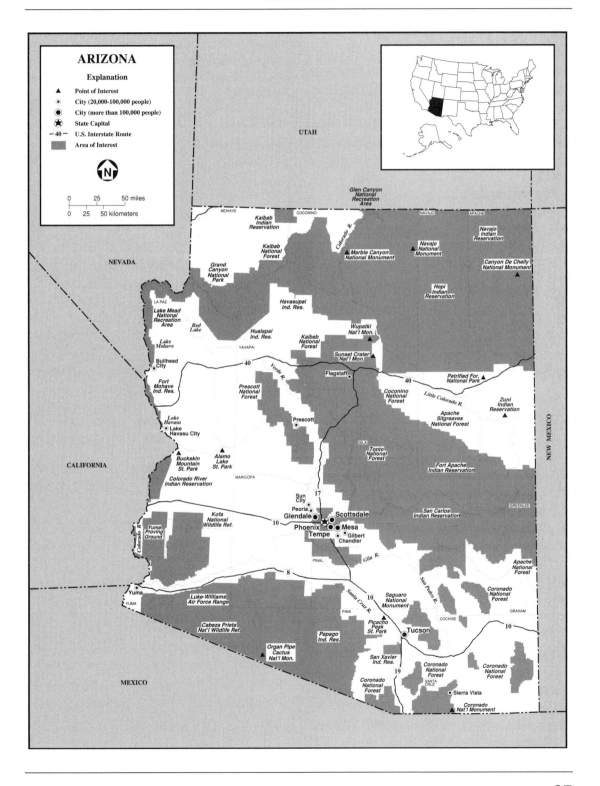

Organ Pipe Cactus.

include the thick-billed parrot, white pelican, and cactus wren (the state bird). Arizona counts the osprey, desert tortoise, spotted bat, and Gila monster among its threatened wildlife.

5 ENVIRONMENTAL PROTECTION

Aside from Phoenix, whose air quality is poorer than that of most other US cities, Arizona has long been noted for its clear air, open lands, and beautiful forests. Legislation enacted in 1980 attempts to allocate water use among cities, mining, and agriculture. As of 1994, Arizona had 10 hazardous waste sites and 85 municipal landfills. Some 13 communities had curbside recycling programs.

6 POPULATION

Arizona ranked 24th in the US, with a 1990 census population of 3,665,228, 34.8% more than in 1980. Arizona's population growth rate has been one of the nation's highest for two decades. The state estimate for 1995 was 4,149,000.

Arizonans 55 years of age or older increased to 21% in 1992, reflecting the state's continuing popularity among retirees. Despite its rapid population growth, Arizona still had a population density of only 32.3 persons per square mile (12.4 persons per square kilometer) in 1990. Three out of four Arizonans live in metropolitan areas. The largest cities are Phoenix, with a 1992 population of 1,012,230; Tucson, 415,079; Mesa, 296,645; and Glendale, 156,165. Phoenix was the nation's eighth-largest city in 1992.

7 ETHNIC GROUPS

Arizona has by far the nation's greatest expanse of Native American lands. The largest single American Indian nation, the Navajo, has a registered reservation population exceeding 96,000 in Arizona. This group is located primarily in the northeastern part of the state. After the Navajo, the leading tribes are the Tohono O'Odham in the south, Apache in the east, and Hopi in the northeast. Altogether, over 255,000 Arizonans report having primarily Native American ancestry.

The southern part of Arizona has most of the state's largest ethnic majority, which consists of a Hispanic population estimated at 668,000 (18.8% of the population). The bulk of Hispanics are of Mexican origin. There are over 111,000 black Americans in Arizona. Filipinos, Chinese, Japanese, and other Asian and Pacific Island peoples make up 1.5% of the population.

8 LANGUAGES

The linguistic influence of Arizona's Tohono O'Odham, Pima, Apache, Navajo, and Hopi tribes is almost totally limited to some place-names, including Arizona itself. Most borrowed Indian words are derived from the Nahuatl speech of the Mexican Aztecs—for example, *coyote, chili, mesquite,* and *tamale.*

English in the state is a blend of North Midland and South Midland dialects without clear regional differences. Over 2,674,000 Arizonans—79.2% of all residents five years old and older—speak only English at home. Other languages spoken at home, and the number of people speaking them, include Spanish, 478,234; various Native American languages, 110,559; and German, 21,344.

9 RELIGIONS

The state has over 655,000 Catholics. The Church of Jesus Christ of Latter-day Saints (Mormons) constitutes the second-largest Christian denomination with about 200,000 known Mormons. Other major denominations include the Southern Baptist Convention, 163,000; and the United Methodist Church, 60,000. Arizona's estimated Jewish population approaches 71,000, nearly all of whom live in the Phoenix or Tucson metropolitan areas.

10 TRANSPORTATION

There was a total of 1,855 rail miles (2,985 kilometers) of railroad track in 1992, with ten railroads operating in the state. Amtrak provides limited passenger service. The total number of riders in the state was 105,242 in 1991/92. In 1993, the state had 55,763 miles (89,723 kilometers) of public streets and roads. Interstate highways in Arizona totaled 1,189 miles (1,913 kilometers). Of the 2,891,589 motor vehicles registered in that year, 2,068,438 were passenger automobiles. Arizona had 183 airports and 89 heliports in 1991. The leading air terminal was Phoenix Sky Harbor International Airport, which handled 10,972,232 arriving and departing passengers (seventh highest in the nation).

11 HISTORY

It is believed that by AD 500, early inhabitants of present-day Arizona had acquired a basic agriculture from what is now Mexico. They were divided into several cultures—the Anasazi, the Mogollon, and the Hohokam. For reasons unknown—a devastating drought is the most likely explanation—these cultures were in decay and the population much reduced by the 14th century. Two centuries later, when the first Europeans arrived, most of the natives were living in simple shelters in fertile river valleys, dependent on hunting, gathering, and small-scale farming for subsistence. The Hopi were the oldest group, their roots reaching back to the Anasazi.

Photo credit: Arizona Office of Tourism.

Montezuma Castle National Monument.

The Spanish presence in Arizona involved exploration, missionary work, and settlement. Between 1539 and 1605, four expeditions crossed the land, followed by Franciscan and Jesuit missionaries. The Spanish military outpost, or *presidio*, established at Tubac on the Santa Cruz River in 1752 was the first major European settlement in Arizona. The end of the 18th century and the beginning of the 19th were periods of relative peace on the frontier.

When Mexico revolted against Spain in 1810, the Arizona settlements were not affected. However, with the outbreak of the Mexican War in 1846, two US armies marched across the region. The California gold rush of 1849 saw thousands of Americans pass along the Gila River. In 1850, most of present-day Arizona became part of the new US Territory of New Mexico; the southern strip was added by the Gadsden Purchase in 1853.

The outbreak of the Civil War in 1861 saw the declaration of southern Arizona as Confederate territory. A small Confederate force entered Arizona in 1862 but was driven out by a volunteer Union army from California. On 24 February 1863,

President Abraham Lincoln signed into law the Organic Act of Arizona, a measure creating the new Territory of Arizona.

Statehood

The development of rich gold mines along the lower Colorado River and in the interior mountains attracted both people and money to Arizona, as did the discovery of silver in Tombstone and other districts in the late 1870s. Phoenix, established in 1868, grew steadily as an agricultural center, eventually becoming the state capital in 1889. On 14 February 1912, Arizona entered the Union as the 48th State.

World War I spurred the expansion of the copper industry, intensive agriculture, and livestock production, but the 1920s brought depression: banks closed, mines shut down, and agricultural production declined. To revive the economy, local citizens pushed highway construction, tourism, and the resort business. Arizona also shared in the general distress caused by the Great Depression of the 1930s and received large amounts of federal aid for relief and recovery.

Prosperity returned during World War II as camps for military training, prisoners of war, and displaced Japanese-Americans were built throughout the state. Arizona emerged from World War II a modern state. Wartime industries spawned an expanding peacetime manufacturing boom that soon provided the principal source of income, followed by tourism, agriculture, and mining.

During the 1950s, the political scene changed. Arizona Republicans captured the governorship, gained votes in the legislature, won congressional seats, and brought a viable two-party system to the state. The rise of Barry Goldwater of Phoenix to national prominence further encouraged Republican influence. Meanwhile, air conditioning changed lifestyles, prompting a significant migration to the state.

Arizona politics in recent years have been rocked by the discovery of corruption in high places. In 1988, Governor Evan Mecham was impeached on two charges of official misconduct. In 1989, two senators, John McCain and Dennis DeConcini, were indicted for influencing federal bank regulators on behalf of Lincoln Savings and Loan Association. Lincoln's president, Charles Keating Jr., had contributed large sums to the senators' re-election campaigns. In 1990, Peter MacDonald, the leader of the Navajo Nation, was convicted in the Navajo Tribal Court of soliciting $400,000 in bribes and kickbacks.

12 STATE GOVERNMENT

Legislative authority is vested in a 30-member senate and a 60-member house of representatives. All senators and representatives serve two-year terms and are chosen at the general election in November of each even-numbered year. Chief executive officials elected statewide include the governor, secretary of state, treasurer, attorney general, state mine inspector, and superintendent of public instruction, all of whom serve four-year terms.

Bills may originate in either house of the legislature and must be passed by both houses and approved by the governor in order to become law. A two-thirds vote in each house is necessary to override the governor's veto. Under the initiative procedure, legislation and proposed constitutional amendments can be placed on the ballot by petition.

13 POLITICAL PARTIES

Conservative Republican Senator Barry Goldwater, who was first elected in 1952 and won the Republican presidential nomination in 1964, led the Republican party to dominance in Arizona politics in the post-World War II period. Arizonans gave the most votes to Republican presidential candidates in every election from 1952 through 1992. Several Arizona Republicans were appointed to high office during the Nixon years. Democrat and former governor Bruce Babbitt was named Secretary of the Interior for the Clinton administration in 1992.

Arizonans reelected Republican Fife Symington as governor in 1994. Following the November 1994 election, Arizona's delegation of US Representatives went from three Democrats and three Republicans to one Democrat and five Republicans, reflecting the nationwide shift to the Republican party that year.

14 LOCAL GOVERNMENT

Arizona is divided into 15 counties. Local governmental units include towns, cities, and charter cities. Towns generally follow the council-mayor form of government. In all, there were 598 local government units in 1992, of which 86 were municipal governments. Each of the 22 Indian reservations in Arizona has a tribal council or board with members elected by the people.

15 JUDICIAL SYSTEM

The supreme court is the highest court in Arizona and has administrative responsibility over all other courts in the state. The court of appeals is organized in two

Arizona Presidential Vote by Political Party, 1948–92

YEAR	ELECTORAL VOTE	ARIZONA WINNER	DEMOCRAT	REPUBLICAN	PROGRESSIVE
1948	4	*Truman (D)	95,251	77,597	3,310
1952	4	*Eisenhower (R)	108,528	152,042	—
1956	4	*Eisenhower (R)	112,880	176,990	—
1960	4	Nixon (R)	176,781	221,241	—
1964	5	Goldwater (R)	237,753	242,535	—
					AMERICAN IND.
1968	5	*Nixon (R)	170,514	266,721	46,573
					AMERICAN
1972	6	*Nixon (R)	198,540	402,812	21,208
1976	6	Ford (R)	295,602	418,642	7,647
1980	6	*Reagan (R)	246,843	529,688	18,784
1984	7	*Reagan (R)	333,854	681,416	10,585
1988	7	*Bush (R)	454,029	702,541	13,351
					IND. (Perot)
1992	8	Bush (R)	543,086	572,086	353,741

*Won US presidential election.

geographical divisions which together have 18 judges. The superior court is the general trial court of the state; there must be at least one superior court judge in every Arizona county.

Counties are divided into precincts, each of which has a justice court. Every incorporated city and town has a police court. According to the FBI Crime Index of 1994, Arizona had a crime rate of 7,924.6 per 100,000 population. In 1993 federal and state institutions held 17,811 prisoners at year-end.

16 MIGRATION

In the 1980s, half of Arizona's total population increase was from migration; about 530,000 persons moved there during that time. By 1990, only 34.2% of state residents had been born in Arizona; only three other states had a lower proportion. Arizona showed a net gain of 296,449 immigrants from 1985 to 1990. Mexico is the main source of foreign immigrants.

17 ECONOMY

Federal sources estimated the value of manufacturing shipments in 1991 at $22.9 billion. In 1992, the value of production from mining was almost $3.2 billion; and from agriculture (including livestock), $1.8 billion. Leading products include electronic components from the manufacturing sector, copper from the mining sector, and cattle and cotton from the farming sector.

18 INCOME

In 1994, Arizona ranked 37th among the 50 states with a per capita (per person) income of $19,153. Total personal income rose to $78.1 billion in 1994, up 8.7%. In 1993, about 15.4% of the population was below the federal poverty level.

19 INDUSTRY

Manufacturing, which has grown rapidly since World War II, became the state's leading economic activity in the 1970s. The major manufacturing centers are the Phoenix and Tucson areas. Principal industries include machinery, electrical and electronic equipment (computers, semiconductors, communication equipment), aircraft equipment, food products, and printing and publishing. Military equipment accounts for much of the output.

20 LABOR

In 1994, the civilian labor force totaled 1,988,000, and 7.9% were union members. The unemployment rate was 6.4% in 1994. Arizona's employment distribution in 1991 consisted of 2.6% in agriculture; 0.9% in mining; 5.1% in construction; 11.3% in manufacturing; 4.7% in transportation, communications, and utilities; 4.9% in wholesale trade; 19.7% in retail trade; 6.1% in finance, insurance, and real estate; 25.6% in services; and other, 19.1%.

21 AGRICULTURE

In 1994 there were about 7,400 farms covering 35 million acres (14.1 million hectares), or about 48% of the state's total area. The average size of 5,173 acres (2,094 hectares) per farm was by far the highest in the US. Farm marketings in 1994 amounted to over $1.8 billion, 56% from crops. About 95% of all farmland is

Photo credit: Arizona Office of Tourism.

Sheep herding in Monument Valley.

dependent on irrigation provided by dams and water projects. Cotton is the leading cash crop in Arizona. In 1994 the state produced 1,870,000 bales of cotton lint accounting for 16.4% of Arizona's agricultural receipts. In 1994, Arizona ranked second in the nation in lemon production and third for broccoli, cauliflower, lettuce, cantaloupes, oranges, tangerines, and grapefruit. Lettuce accounted for 9.8% of the state's agricultural receipts in 1994, or 16.5% of national lettuce production value. Although lemon production made up only 3.5% of the state's agricultural receipts in 1994, Arizona's lemons accounted for 25% of national production value for that crop.

22 DOMESTICATED ANIMALS

The total inventory of cattle was 830,000 in 1994. In 1994, the state had 145,000 sheep and 170,000 hogs. Marketings of livestock and products amounted to $824 million in 1994. Cattle production accounted for 25% of the states's agricultural receipts in 1994; dairy products, 14.9%.

23 FISHING

Arizona has no commercial fishing. The state's lakes and mountain streams lure the state's 417,000 licensed sport fishermen and are an increasingly important tourist attraction.

24 FORESTRY

Arizona's forests are more valuable for soil conservation and recreation than for lumber. In 1990 there were 19,595,000 acres (7,930,000 hectares) of forestland in Arizona, 25% of the state's area. National forests covered nearly 12 million acres (5 million hectares) as of 1990.

25 MINING

Arizona leads the nation in nonfuel mineral production value, thanks to the state's copper industry. In 1994 the value of the state's natural mineral production exceeded $3.3 billion. Production figures for principal minerals are as follows: copper, 1.1 million metric tons; sand and gravel, 26 million short tons; gold, 6,156 kilograms; and crushed stone, 6 million short tons. Arizona was the second largest producer of molybdenum in the United States in 1992, trailing only Colorado.

26 ENERGY AND POWER

In 1993, Arizona produced 68 billion kilowatt hours of electric power. Hydroelectric plants accounted for 18% of power output. Three nuclear power plants generated 32% of the total output. In 1993, the state marketed 196 billion cubic feet of natural gas. Coal production in 1992 was 12,512,000 short tons, all of it from two surface mines.

27 COMMERCE

In 1992, wholesale sales in Arizona totaled $28 billion. Retail sales in 1993 reached $34 billion. Service establishments reported receipts of $18.6 billion in 1992.

Goods worth $5.11 billion were exported in 1992.

28 PUBLIC FINANCE

Government revenues for 1992/93 were $9,380 million, while expenditures for the same period were $9,379.5 million. As of 1993, Arizona's total outstanding debt was $3 billion, or $774 per person.

29 TAXATION

State tax receipts in 1993 came to over $5.3 billion. Arizona has a state sales tax, with the retail sales tax rate at 5%. An estate tax, luxury tax, insurance premium tax, and transport fuel tax are also levied. The state also receives tax revenue from collections of the general property tax and the motor-vehicle license tax, and it has a lottery.

30 HEALTH

The percentage of deaths from accidents and suicide in 1992 was above average, while the death rate for heart disease and cardiovascular diseases was low. Serious public-health problems include tuberculosis and San Joaquin Valley fever (coccidioidomycosis), especially among Native Americans. In 1991 there were 93 hospitals, with 13,595 beds, and the average payment to a hospital for care provided per inpatient day was $1,091 in 1993. In 1993, there were 7,606 nonfederal physicians and 27,000 nurses practicing in the state. In 1993, 20% of the population was without health insurance.

31 HOUSING

In July 1993, Arizona had an estimated 1,743,000 units of year-round housing. The median value of a home in Arizona was $80,100 in 1990. An owner-occupied unit with a mortgage had a median monthly cost of $769 in 1990; the median cost for a rental unit was $438. In 1993, 38,656 new units were authorized.

32 EDUCATION

In 1993, Arizona spent an average of $4,140 per pupil on primary and secondary schooling. This amount ranks 44th among the states in per pupil spending. In 1992/93, enrollment at public schools was 732,306. There were 35,062 public-school teachers in 1993. Private schools enrolled 37,033 students in 1992/93. The leading public higher educational institutions are the University of Arizona at Tucson and Arizona State University at Tempe. As of 1993, the state had 12 colleges and universities and 17 community colleges, with a total enrollment of 291,985.

33 ARTS

Arizona has traditionally been a center for Native American folk arts and crafts, which are displayed at museums throughout the state. Modern Arizona artists are featured at the Tucson Museum of Art and the Yuma Art Center. Phoenix and Tucson have symphony orchestras, and the Arizona Opera Company performs in both cities.

34 LIBRARIES AND MUSEUMS

In 1991/92, Arizona's public libraries had a combined book stock of 7.4 million volumes, and total circulation was 26 million. Spending on libraries per capita (per person) was $16.90 in 1991/92. Arizona has more than 103 museums and historic sites. Attractions in Tucson include the Arizona State Museum, the Flandreau Planetarium, and the Gene C. Reid Zoological Park. Phoenix's facilities include the Heard Museum (anthropology and primitive art), Arizona Mineral Resources Museum, and Desert Botanical Garden. Archaeological and historical sites include the cliff dwellings at the Canyon De Chelly. The town of Tombstone was the site of the famous gunfight at the O. K. Corral in the early 1880s.

35 COMMUNICATIONS

Almost 94% of the homes in Arizona had telephones in March 1993. There were 153 radio stations broadcasting in Arizona in 1993 (70 AM and 83 FM). The state also had 25 television stations in 1993. Six large cable television systems were providing service in 1993.

36 PRESS

As of 1994 there were 7 morning dailies, 13 evening dailies, and 54 weekly newspapers. Leading dailies (with 1994 daily circulation figures) include the *Arizona Republic* (363,125); the *Arizona Daily Star* (88,413); the *Gazette* (86,216); and *The Citizen* (52,378). Among the most notable magazines and periodicals published in Arizona are *Arizona Highways*, *Phoenix Magazine*, *Phoenix Living*, and *Arizona Living*, devoted to the local and regional lifestyle.

Navajo children, Monument Valley.

37 TOURISM, TRAVEL, AND RECREATION

Tourism and travel is a leading industry in Arizona, accounting for nearly $6.8 billion in revenue. There are 22 national parks and monuments located entirely within Arizona. By far the most popular is Grand Canyon National Park, which has 4.2 million visitors per year. Petrified Forest National Park and Saguaro National Monument are also popular national parks. Popular for sightseeing and shopping are the state's Indian reservations, particularly those of the Navajo and Hopi.

38 SPORTS

There are two major league professional teams in Arizona, both in Phoenix: The Cardinals of the National Football League, and the Suns of the National Basketball Association. The Arizona Diamondbacks of Major League Baseball will begin play by 1997, and the Winnipeg Jets of the National Hockey League are scheduled to move to Phoenix after the 1995/96 season. Several major league baseball teams hold spring training in Arizona. Phoenix and Tucson have entries in the Pacific Coast League, the Firebirds and the Toros, respectively. There is also horse racing, dog racing, and auto racing; rodeos are held throughout the state. Both Arizona State and the University of Arizona joined the Pacific 10 Conference in 1978. College football's Fiesta Bowl is held annually at Sun Devil Stadium in Tempe.

39 FAMOUS ARIZONANS

Although Arizona entered the Union relatively late, many of its citizens have achieved national prominence, especially since World War II. William H. Rehnquist (b.Wisconsin, 1924) was appointed associate justice of the US Supreme Court in 1971 and chief justice in 1986. In 1981 Sandra Day O'Connor (b.Texas, 1930) became the first woman to serve on the Supreme Court. Barry Goldwater (b.1909), son of a pioneer family, was elected to the US Senate in 1952, won the Republican presidential nomination in 1964, and returned to the Senate in 1968. Morris K. Udall (b.1922), first elected to the US House of Representatives in 1960, contended for the Democratic presidential nomination in 1976.

Also important to the state's history and development were Chiricahua Apache leaders Cochise (1812?–74) and Geronimo (1829–1909), who fought against the Army and avoided capture in the Southwest for over two decades. Wyatt Earp (b.Illinois, 1848–1929) was a legendary lawman of Tombstone during the early 1880s. César Chávez (1927–93) was a well-known activist for migrant workers and president of the United Farm Workers of America.

A writer whose name has been associated with Arizona is Zane Grey (b.Ohio, 1875–1939), who wrote many of his western adventure stories in his summer home near Payson. Well-known performing artists from Arizona include singer Linda Ronstadt (b.1946). Joan Ganz Cooney (b.1929), president of the Children's Television Workshop, was one of the creators of the award-winning children's program, *Sesame Street*.

40 BIBLIOGRAPHY

Alampi, Gary, ed. *Gale State Rankings Reporter.* Detroit: Gale Research Inc., 1994.

Arizona: Its People and Resources. 2d ed., rev. Tucson: University of Arizona Press, 1972.

Faulk, Odie B. *Arizona: A Short History.* Norman: University of Oklahoma Press, 1970.

ARKANSAS

State of Arkansas

ORIGIN OF STATE NAME: French derivation of *Akansas* or *Arkansas,* a name given to the Quapaw Indians by other tribes.

NICKNAME: The Land of Opportunity.

CAPITAL: Little Rock.

ENTERED THE UNION: 15 June 1836 (25th).

SONG: "Arkansas."

MOTTO: *Regnat populus* (The people rule).

COAT OF ARMS: In front of an American eagle is a shield displaying a steamboat, plow, beehive, and sheaf of wheat, symbols of Arkansas's industrial and agricultural wealth. The angel of mercy, the goddess of liberty encircled by 13 stars, and the sword of justice surround the eagle, which holds in its talons an olive branch and three arrows, and in its beak a banner bearing the state motto.

FLAG: On a red field, 25 stars on a blue band border a white diamond containing the word "Arkansas" and four blue stars.

OFFICIAL SEAL: Coat of arms surrounded by the words "Great Seal of the State of Arkansas."

BIRD: Mockingbird.

FLOWER: Apple blossom.

TREE: Pine.

GEM: Diamond.

INSECT: Honeybee.

TIME: 6 AM CST = noon GMT.

1 LOCATION AND SIZE

Located in the western south-central US, Arkansas ranks 27th in size among the 50 states. The total area of Arkansas is 53,187 square miles (137,754 square kilometers). Arkansas extends about 275 miles (443 kilometers) east-west and 240 miles (386 kilometers) north-south. The total boundary length of Arkansas is 1,168 miles (1,880 kilometers).

2 TOPOGRAPHY

The Boston Mountains in the northwest and the Ouachita Mountains in the west-central region constitute Arkansas's major uplands. Aside from the Arkansas River valley, the state's lowlands belong to the Mississippi Alluvial Plain and the Gulf Coastal Plain. The highest elevation in Arkansas, at 2,753 feet (839 meters), is Magazine Mountain. The state's lowest point, at 55 feet (17 meters), is on the Ouachita River in south-central Arkansas.

Arkansas's largest lake is the artificial Lake Ouachita, covering 63 square miles (163 square kilometers); Lake Chicot, in southeastern Arkansas, is the state's largest natural lake, with a length of 18 miles

(29 kilometers). Principal rivers include the Mississippi, the Arkansas, and the Red, White, Ouachita, and St. Francis rivers, all of which drain south and southeast into the Mississippi. Numerous springs are found in Arkansas, including Mammoth Springs, one of the largest in the world, with a flow rate averaging nine million gallons an hour. Crowley's Ridge, a unique strip of hills formed by sedimentary deposits and windblown sand, lies west of the St. Francis River.

3 CLIMATE

Arkansas has a temperate climate, warmer and more humid in the southern lowlands than in the mountainous regions. At Little Rock, the normal daily temperature ranges from 40°F (4°C) in January to 81°F (27°C) in July. A record low temperature of –29°F (–34°C) was set on 13 February 1905 at the Pond weather station, and a record high of 120°F (49°C) on 10 August 1936 at the Ozark station.

Average yearly precipitation is approximately 45 inches (114 centimeters) in the mountainous areas and greater in the lowlands. Little Rock receives an annual average of 49 inches (124 centimeters). Snowfall in the capital averages 5.4 inches (13.7 centimeters) a year.

4 PLANTS AND ANIMALS

Arkansas has at least 2,600 native plants, and there are many adopted exotic species. Cypresses, water oak, hickory, and ash grow in the Mississippi Valley, while Crowley's Ridge is thick with tulip trees and beeches. A forest belt of oak, hickory, and pine stretches across south-central

Arkansas Population Profile

Estimated 1995 population:	2,473,000
Population change, 1980–90:	2.8%
Leading ancestry group:	Irish
Second leading group:	German
Foreign born population:	1.1%
Hispanic origin†:	0.8%
Population by race:	
White:	82.7%
Black:	15.9%
Native American:	0.5%
Asian/Pacific Islander:	0.5%
Other:	0.4%

Population by Age Group

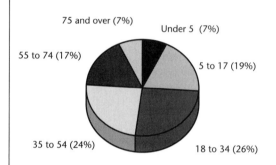

75 and over (7%)
Under 5 (7%)
55 to 74 (17%)
5 to 17 (19%)
35 to 54 (24%)
18 to 34 (26%)

Top Cities with Populations Over 25,000

City	Population	National rank	% change 1980–90
Little Rock	176,870	99	10.9
Fort Smith	73,949	309	1.6
North Little Rock	62,328	387	–4.0
Pine Bluff	57,675	422	0.9
Jonesboro	48,617	547	47.6
Fayetteville	46,071	574	15.0
Hot Springs	33,653	826	–9.3
Springdale	32,782	848	27.7
Jacksonville	30,645	917	NA
Conway	30,177	933	30.0

Notes: †A person of Hispanic origin may be of any race. NA indicates that data are not available.
Sources: Economic and Statistics Administration, Bureau of the Census. *Statistical Abstract of the United States, 1994–95.* Washington, DC: Government Printing Office, 1995; Courtenay M. Slater and George E. Hall. *1995 County and City Extra: Annual Metro, City and County Data Book.* Lanham, MD: Bernan Press, 1995.

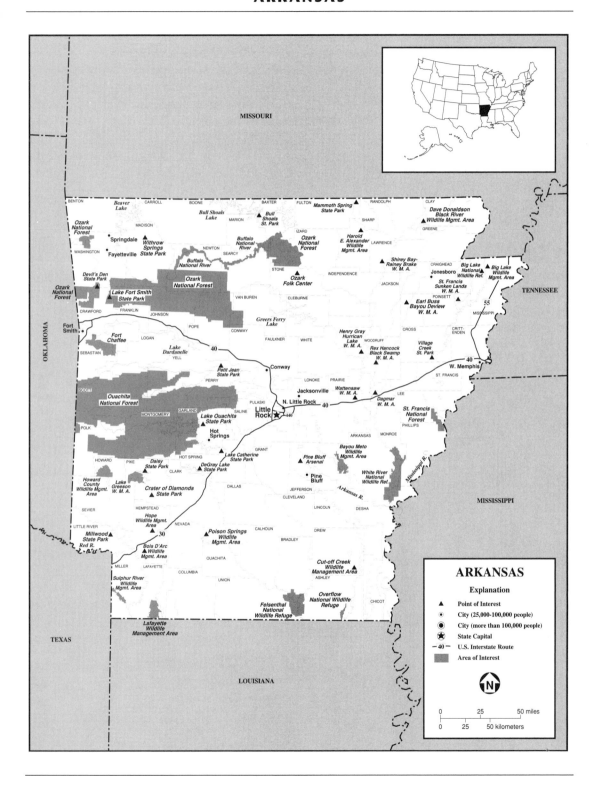

ARKANSAS

Explanation

▲ Point of Interest

⊙ City (25,000-100,000 people)

◉ City (more than 100,000 people)

★ State Capital

—40— U.S. Interstate Route

▨ Area of Interest

and southwestern Arkansas. The state has at least 26 native varieties of orchid, and the passion flower is abundant.

Arkansas's native animals include mink, armadillo, white-tailed deer, and eastern chipmunk. Black bears roam the swamp and mountain regions. Among 300 native birds are such game birds as the eastern wild turkey, mourning dove, and bobwhite quail. Among local fish are catfish, gar, and the unusual paddle fish. The Arkansas Game and Fish Commission lists the leopard darter and fat pocketbook pearly mussel as threatened species. The peregrine falcon and American alligator are among those listed as endangered.

5 ENVIRONMENTAL PROTECTION

Arkansas spent 1.15% of its budget ($18.45 per person) on the environment and natural resources in fiscal year 1991/92. In 1987, the state adopted what is believed to be the first "eco-region" water quality standards in the nation; they are based on individual characteristics within each of six district eco-regions of the state, as opposed to having blanket standards that apply statewide. There are 64 municipal landfills in the state and 2 curbside recycling programs. Arkansas has 12 hazardous waste sites.

6 POPULATION

At the time of the 1990 census, Arkansas had a population of 2,350,725 (33d in the US). Estimates for 1995 showed Arkansas with 2,473,000 residents. The average population density was 45 persons per square mile (17 persons per square kilometer). The Census Bureau estimates that the population will be 2,509,000 in 2000.

Over 40% of all state residents lived in metropolitan areas in 1992. The largest city in Arkansas is Little Rock, which had a 1992 population of 176,870. Other major cities in 1992 included Fort Smith, 73,949; North Little Rock, 62,328; Pine Bluff, 57,675; and Fayetteville, 46,071.

7 ETHNIC GROUPS

Arkansas's population is predominantly white, composed mainly of descendants of immigrants from the British Isles. The largest minority group consists of black Americans, numbering 374,000, or 15.9% of the population, followed by Native Americans, 13,000 (0.5%). About 20,000 Arkansans are of Hispanic origin. The 1990 census listed 1,788 Vietnamese, 1,575 Chinese, 2,166 Filipinos, 1,202 Asian Indians, and 754 Japanese.

8 LANGUAGES

Arkansas English is essentially a blend of Southern and South Midland speech, with South Midland dominating the mountainous northwest and Southern the southeastern agricultural areas. A few place-names—such as Arkansas itself, Choctaw, Caddo, and Ouachita—attest to the one-time presence of Native Americans, mostly members of the Caddoan tribes, in the Territory of Arkansas.

About 2,125,900 Arkansans—97.2% of the residents five years old or older—speak only English at home. The most common other languages spoken at home are Spanish (27,351 people), German (7,059), and French (8,210).

9 RELIGIONS

The largest denomination in Arkansas is the Southern Baptist Convention, which has over 617,000 members. Other leading Protestant groups are the United Methodist Church, with 197,402 members and the Baptist Missionary Association of America, with 78,121. The Roman Catholic population of Arkansas numbers 73,000 and the estimated Jewish population is 2,400.

10 TRANSPORTATION

As of 1992, Arkansas was served by four major railroads and had 2,477 rail miles (3,985 kilometers) of track. In 1991/92, the number of Arkansas Amtrak riders amounted to 29,601. By 1993, Arkansas had 77,192 miles (124,202 kilometers) of public roads, streets, and highways. During the same year, 986,955 automobiles and 535,058 trucks were registered in Arkansas. In 1993, private and commercial automobiles in the state came only to 40 per every 100 residents, fewer than in any other state.

Development of the Arkansas River, completed during the early 1970s, made the waterway commercially navigable all the way to Tulsa, Oklahoma. In 1991, Arkansas had 166 airports. The principal airport in the state, Adams Field at Little Rock, boarded 932,424 passengers in that year.

11 HISTORY

Foremost among the Native American tribes in Arkansas were the Quapaw, an agricultural people who had migrated to southern Arkansas in the early 16th century; the Caddo, fighters from Texas; the warlike Osage; and the Choctaw and Chickasaw of the northeast. Another prominent tribe, the Cherokee, arrived in the early 19th century, after federal and state authorities had driven them westward. Nearly all these tribes had been expelled to what is now Oklahoma by the time Arkansas became a state.

The first Europeans to set foot in Arkansas were Spaniards, led by Hernando de Soto in 1541. More than 100 years later, in 1673, a small band of Frenchmen led by Jacques Marquette, a Jesuit missionary, and Louis Jolliet, a fur trader and explorer, ended their voyage down the Mississippi at the mouth of the Arkansas River. Nine years later, the French explorer Robert Cavelier, Sieur de la Salle, claimed all the Mississippi Valley for his king, Louis XIV.

Statehood

In 1762 France ceded the territory to Spain. Restored to France in 1800, the territory was sold to the US in the Louisiana Purchase of 1803. After first becoming part of the Missouri Territory, Arkansas gained territorial status in its own right in 1819. The territorial capital was moved from Arkansas Post to Little Rock in 1821. By 1835, Arkansas Territory had a population of 52,240, including 9,838 slaves. It was admitted to the Union in 1836 as a slave state, paired with the free

The Old State House in Little Rock.

state of Michigan in accordance with the Missouri Compromise.

Increasing numbers of slaves were brought into the largely agricultural state as the cultivation of cotton spread. Arkansas, like the rest of the South, was headed for secession, although it waited to commit itself until the Civil War had begun. There was considerable Union sentiment in the state, but pro-Union sympathies crumbled after Confederate guns fired on Fort Sumter, South Carolina. On 6 May 1861, at a convention held in Little Rock, Arkansans voted 69–1 to secede.

By September 1863, the Union Army had taken Little Rock, and the Capital was moved to Washington, in Hempstead County, until the conclusion of hostilities in 1865. Like virtually all white southerners, Arkansas's white majority hated the postwar Reconstruction government. In 1874 the white Democratic majority adopted a new state constitution, throwing out the carpetbagger constitution of 1868.

Modernization

Industrialization, urbanization, and modernization did not come to Arkansas until after the depression of the 1930s. Following World War II, the state became the first in the South to racially integrate its public colleges and universities. Little

Rock's school board decided in 1954 to comply with the US Supreme Court's racial desegregation decision. Nevertheless, in September 1957, Governor Orval E. Faubus called out the National Guard to block the integration of Central High School at Little Rock. US President Dwight D. Eisenhower enforced a federal court order to integrate the school by sending in federal troops. Faubus, then in his second term, was elected to a third term and then to three more.

The contrast between Faubus and his successor could not have been greater. Winthrop Rockefeller, millionaire heir of a famous family, moved to Arkansas from New York in the early 1950s, establishing himself as a gentleman rancher and building a Republican Party organization in one of the most strongly Democratic states in the Union. In 1966, Rockefeller became the first Republican governor of Arkansas since Reconstruction. He helped bring a new image and spirit to the state.

Rockefeller's successors have continued his progressive approach. Governor Bill Clinton, who became United States President in 1992, introduced investment tax credits to help corporations modernize their facilities and thereby to create jobs. Clinton also signed a "bare bones" health insurance law which dropped state requirements for some of the more costly coverages and thus made health insurance affordable for small businesses.

He increased spending for education and passed legislation requiring competency tests for teachers. But Clinton remained hampered in his efforts to increase government spending because the state constitution requires that any increase in the state income tax obtain approval of two-thirds of the Legislature. Arkansas continues to rank among the poorest states in the nation, with a per capita (per person) income in 1994 of only $16,817 (49th among the states).

12 STATE GOVERNMENT

Arkansas's legislature, the general assembly, consists of a 35-member senate and a 100-member house of representatives. Senators serve four-year terms; representatives serve for two years. A bill passed by both houses of the legislature becomes law if: it is signed by the governor; the governor's veto is overridden by a majority of all elected members of each house; or the bill is neither signed nor returned by the governor within five days when the legislature is in session.

13 POLITICAL PARTIES

Republicans ruled during Reconstruction, which ended in Arkansas after the election of 1872. During the 1890s, as in the rest of the South, Democrats succeeded in passing laws imposing segregation and disenfranchising blacks as well as poor whites.

Although elected to the governorship as a progressive in 1954, Democrat Orval Faubus took a segregationist stand on racial matters in 1957. Faubus's successor, progressive Republican Winthrop Rockefeller, was followed by three more progressives, all Democrats: Dale Bumpers, David Pryor, and Bill Clinton. In a major upset, Clinton was defeated in 1980 by

Republican Frank White, but Clinton recaptured the statehouse in 1982 and won reelection in 1984, 1986, and 1990. Clinton ran for and won the US presidency in 1992. On 8 November 1994, Democratic governor Jim Guy Tucker was one of the few of his party nationwide to resist a Republican landslide.

As of 1994, both of Arkansas's senators—Dale Bumpers and David Pryor—were Democrats. Arkansas's US Representatives in 1994 included two Republicans and two Democrats. Following the November 1994 elections, the state legislature had 30 Democrats and 5 Republicans in the state senate, and 89 Democrats and 11 Republicans in the state house.

14 LOCAL GOVERNMENT

There are 75 counties in Arkansas, ten of them with two county seats. Each county is governed by a quorum court, consisting of 9–15 justices of the peace, elected for two-year terms. Elected county executives, who serve two-year terms, include the sheriff, assessor, coroner, treasurer, and county judge.

15 JUDICIAL SYSTEM

Arkansas's highest court is the supreme court, consisting of a chief justice and six associate justices, elected for staggered eight-year terms. An appeals court of six judges, also elected for eight-year terms, was established in 1978. Other courts include the circuit courts (law) and the chancery courts (equity).

Arkansas had an FBI Crime Index rate of 4,798.7 per 100,000 population in 1994. In December 1993 there were 8,625 prisoners in state and federal correctional institutions.

Arkansas Presidential Vote by Political Parties, 1948–92

YEAR	ARKANSAS WINNER	DEMOCRAT	REPUBLICAN	STATES' RIGHTS DEMOCRAT
1948	*Truman (D)	149,659	50,959	40,068
1952	Stevenson (D)	226,300	177,155	—
				CONSTITUTION
1956	Stevenson (D)	213,277	186,287	7,008
				NAT'L STATES' RIGHTS
1960	*Kennedy (D)	215,049	184,508	28,952
1964	*Johnson (D)	314,197	243,264	2,965
				AMERICAN IND.
1968	Wallace (AI)	188,228	190,759	240,982
				AMERICAN
1972	*Nixon (R)	199,892	448,541	2,887
1976	*Carter (D)	498,604	267,903	—
				LIBERTARIAN
1980	*Reagan (R)	398,041	403,164	8,970
1984	*Reagan (R)	388,646	534,774	2,2221
1988	*Bush (R)	349,237	466,578	3,297
				IND. (Perot)
1992	*Clinton (D)	505,823	337,324	99,132

* Won US presidential election.

The state capitol building in Little Rock.

16 MIGRATION

During the depression years of the 1930s and afterwards, Arkansas lost much of its farm population to migration, and many blacks left the state for the industrial cities of the Midwest and the east and west coasts. The net loss from migration totaled 919,000 between 1940 and 1970.

Between 1970 and 1980, however, the state gained 180,000 residents through migration, as the Ozarks became one of the fastest-growing rural areas in the US. Net migration from 1985 to 1990 amounted to a gain of nearly 36,600. As of 1990, just over two-thirds of all Arkansans had been born in the state.

17 ECONOMY

Not until the 1950s did Arkansas enjoy significant success in attracting industry, thanks in large part to the efforts of Winthrop Rockefeller. By the mid-1990s, Arkansas's principal industries had become manufacturing, dominated by lumber and wood products companies; agriculture; and forestry. Four Fortune 500 firms are headquartered in Arkansas: Tyson Foods, Inc., Riceland Foods, Murphy Oil, and Hudson Foods. Six Fortune Service 500 companies also have their headquarters in Arkansas.

18 INCOME

Total personal income for Arkansas increased by 6.4% to $41.2 billion in

1994. In 1994, Arkansas ranked 49th among the 50 states in per capita (per person) income, with $16,817. An estimated 20% of the population was living below the federal poverty level in 1993.

19 INDUSTRY

Manufacturing in Arkansas is diverse, ranging from blue jeans to bicycles, though resource industries such as rice processing and woodworking still play a major role. The total value of shipments of manufactured goods in 1991 was over $31 billion.

20 LABOR

Arkansas's civilian labor force totaled 1,207,000 in 1994. About 1,142,000 Arkansans were employed and 65,000 unemployed, for an overall unemployment rate of 5.3% in 1994. In that year, 7.9% of workers were union members.

21 AGRICULTURE

Farm marketings in Arkansas were nearly $5.3 billion in 1994 (11th in the US). The state is the nation's leading producer of rice and is among the leaders in cotton and soybeans. These three crops together accounted for 35.4% of agricultural receipts in 1994. Confined mainly to slaveholding plantations before the Civil War, cotton farming became more widespread in the postwar period. As elsewhere in the South, sharecropping by tenant farmers predominated well into the 20th century, until modernization gradually brought an end to the system.

During 1994, Arkansas produced 115,600,000 bushels of soybeans; 40,480,000 bushels of wheat; and 18,375,000 bushels of sorghum for grain. The rice harvest in 1994 was nearly 8.1 billion pounds; the cotton crop in 1994 was 1,760,000 bales.

22 DOMESTICATED ANIMALS

Poultry farms are found throughout Arkansas, but especially in the northern and western regions. Livestock and products accounted for over $3.1 billion in farm marketings in 1994. Arkansas was the top-ranked broiler-producing state in the US in 1994, accounting for 34.5% of the state's agricultural receipts. During the same year, cattle production amounted to 6.4% of agricultural receipts. The livestock inventory in 1994 included 25,806,000 chickens, 2,010,000 cattle, and 770,000 hogs.

23 FISHING

Fish farming is an important part of the state's economy. As of 1993, the state ranked first in the US in minnow farming and second only to Mississippi in catfish farming. As of 1 July 1993, there were 150 catfish operations covering 18,800 acres of water surface.

24 FORESTRY

Forestland comprised 17,864,000 acres (7,324,240 hectares), or 53% of the state's total land area, in 1990. The southwest and central plains, the state's timber belt, constitute one of the most concentrated sources of yellow pine in the US. Three national forests in Arkansas covered a total of 2,478,454 acres (1,002,998 hectares) in 1990.

25 MINING

The US Bureau of Mines estimate of the value of mineral production in Arkansas in 1994 was $392 million. In 1992, 23,100,000 short tons of crushed stone were produced, valued at $109,000,000; 158,145,000 kilograms of bromine worth $79,073,000; and 8,761,000 short tons of sand and gravel with a value of $37,789,000.

26 ENERGY AND POWER

As of 1993, Arkansas's power production totaled 38 billion kilowatt hours. Arkansas has two nuclear power plants that generate 35.5% of the state's electric power. During 1993, 10 million barrels of crude petroleum were produced, leaving proven reserves of 70,000,000 barrels. Production of natural gas was 196 billion cubic feet, with 1.7 trillion cubic feet of reserves remaining. About 37,000 tons of bituminous coal are mined each year.

27 COMMERCE

Arkansas ranked 30th in the US in wholesale trade sales during 1992, with total sales of $28 billion. Retail establishments recorded $33.8 billion in sales in 1993 (21st in the US). Service establishments had receipts of $18.6 billion (22d in the nation).

28 PUBLIC FINANCE

Under the 1874 constitution, state expenditures may not exceed revenues. For the fiscal year ending 30 June 1993, revenues for the General Fund were $5,487.4 million and expenditures were $5,077.5 million.

29 TAXATION

As of 1993, Arkansas's state tax revenue per capita (per person) was $2,319, the 31st lowest in the US. In 1994, the state sales tax was 4.5%. City and county property taxes in Arkansas are among the lowest in the nation. Arkansas's outstanding debt totaled $1.9 billion, or $777 per capita.

30 HEALTH

In 1992 Arkansas's incidence of cerebrovascular disease—84.5 per 100,000 population—led the US. Death rates from heart disease, cancer, accidents, motor vehicle accidents, homicide, and suicide also exceeded the national average. Arkansas's 87 community hospitals had 11,000 beds in 1993. Hospital expenses for services provided in 1993—$678 per inpatient day and $4,585 per stay—were among the lowest in the US. In 1993, the state had 3,908 nonfederal physicians and 14,000 nurses. Almost 20% of the population was without health insurance in 1993.

31 HOUSING

In mid-1993, there were an estimated 1,018,000 housing units in Arkansas. In 1990, the median value of a home in Arkansas was $46,300, lower than in 47 other states, and down 6.3% from 1980 after adjusting for inflation. The median monthly cost for an owner-occupied unit (including a mortgage) was $514; a rental unit had a median monthly cost of $328 in 1990.

32 EDUCATION

In 1990, 68.7% of all Arkansans 25 years of age and older were high school graduates. In 1983, in an effort to raise the quality of education in Arkansas, the state legislature approved a comprehensive program that included smaller classes, more high school level courses, and competency tests for teachers. Public school enrollment in 1993 totaled 443,000. In 1993 the state spent an average of $3,838 per pupil on primary and secondary education, 48th among the 50 states. In 1993, Arkansas had 20 public and private four-year colleges and universities, of which the largest was the University of Arkansas at Fayetteville. Arkansas also has 12 two-year colleges, 6 vocational-technical schools, 5 technical institutes, and 13 technical colleges.

33 ARTS

Little Rock is the home of the Arkansas Symphony and the Arkansas Arts Center. The best-known center for traditional arts and crafts is the Ozark Folk Center at Mountain View. The Arkansas Folk Festival is held there during two weekends in April. From 1987 to 1991, arts funding in Arkansas amounted to $7,712,411.

34 LIBRARIES AND MUSEUMS

During 1988, Arkansas had 32 county or regional library systems and 14 municipal libraries. That year, public libraries held a total of 4,593,882 volumes and circulation amounted to 7,527,061. There were 71 museums in 1994 and a number of historic sites. Principal museums include the

Photo credit: Wleck Photo DataBase.

Canoeing on the Buffalo River in the Buffalo National River Park.

Arkansas Arts Center and the Museum of Science and History, both at Little Rock.

35 COMMUNICATIONS

In March 1993, 88.6% of the state's homes had telephones, one of the lowest rates in the nation. There were 228 radio stations (90 AM, 138 FM) and 23 television stations. Cable television service was supplied by four large systems in 1993.

36 PRESS

The first newspaper in Arkansas, the *Arkansas Gazette* (established in 1819), was the state's most widely read and influential journal until it ceased publication in 1991. In 1994 there were 9 morning dailies, 17 evening papers, and 14 Sunday papers. The leading dailies (with 1994 circulations) are the *Southwest Times Record* (44,330) and the *Arkansas Democrat Gazette* (177,403).

37 TOURISM, TRAVEL, AND RECREATION

During 1992, tourists spent over $2.7 billion in Arkansas. In 1991, the 44 state parks had 6,949,000 visitors. Leading attractions are the mineral waters and recreational facilities at Hot Springs, Eureka Springs, Mammoth Spring, and Heber Springs. The Crater of Diamonds, near Murfreesboro, is the only known public source of natural diamonds in North America. For a fee, visitors may hunt for diamonds and keep any they find. More than 100,000 diamonds have been found in the area since 1906.

Photo credit: The White House.

President of the United States, Bill Clinton. Clinton was born in Hope, Arkansas, and was elected governor of Arkansas in 1978. He won reelection in 1982, 1984, 1986, and 1990.

38 SPORTS

Arkansas has no major league professional sports teams. The Razorback football team of the University of Arkansas won the Orange Bowl in 1978 and the Bluebonnet Bowl in 1982. The men's basketball team won or shared the Southwest Conference championship in 1977, 1978, 1979, 1981, 1982, and 1994.

39 FAMOUS ARKANSANS

Arkansas has produced one president of the United States, William Jefferson Clinton (b. 1946). Clinton, a Democrat, defeated incumbent George Bush in the 1992 presidential election. Clinton's wife is the former Hillary Rodham (b. Illinois 1947).

Hattie W. Caraway (b. Tennessee, 1878–1950), was the first woman elected to the US Senate, serving from 1931 to 1945. Senator John L. McClellan (1896–1977), investigated organized labor and organized crime. Senator J. William Fulbright (b. Missouri, 1905) was chairman of the Senate Foreign Relations Committee. General Douglas MacArthur (1880–1964) was supreme commander of Allied forces in the Pacific during World War II and in Korea.

Orval E. Faubus (b.1910) served six terms as governor (a record), and drew international attention during the 1957 integration crisis at Little Rock Central High School. Winthrop Rockefeller (b.New York, 1917–73) was Faubus's most prominent successor. Bill Clinton, at the time of his election in 1978, was the nation's youngest governor.

John H. Johnson (b.1918), publisher of the nation's leading black-oriented magazines—*Ebony, Jet,* and others—is an Arkansan, as is Helen Gurley Brown (b.1922), editor of *Cosmopolitan*. John Gould Fletcher (1886–1950) was a Pulitzer Prize-winning poet. Other Arkansas writers include Maya Angelou (b.Missouri, 1928) and Eldridge Cleaver (b.1935).

Arkansas planter Colonel Sanford C. Faulkner (1803–74) is credited with having written the well-known fiddle tune "The Arkansas Traveler" and its accompanying dialogue. Perhaps the best-known country music performers are Johnny Cash (b.1932) and Glen Campbell (b.1938). Film stars Dick Powell (1904–63) and Alan Ladd (1913–64) were also Arkansans.

Notable Arkansas sports personalities include football coach Paul "Bear" Bryant (1913–83); Brooks Robinson (b.1937), considered by some the best-fielding third baseman in baseball history; Lou Brock (b.1939), who holds the record for the most stolen bases; and star pass-catcher Lance Alworth (b.Mississippi, 1940).

40 BIBLIOGRAPHY

Alampi, Gary, ed. *Gale State Rankings Reporter.* Detroit: Gale Research Inc., 1994.

Angelou, Maya. *I Know Why the Caged Bird Sings.* New York: Bantam, 1971.

Ashmore, Harry S. *Arkansas: A Bicentennial History.* New York: Norton, 1978.

Fletcher, John Gould. *Arkansas.* Chapel Hill: University of North Carolina Press, 1947.

CALIFORNIA

State of California

ORIGIN OF STATE NAME: Probably from the mythical island California in a 16th-century romance by Garci Ordónez de Montalvo.

NICKNAME: The Golden State.

CAPITAL: Sacramento.

ENTERED UNION: 9 September 1850 (31st).

SONG: "I Love You California."

MOTTO: Eureka (I have found it).

FLAG: The flag consists of a white field with a red star at upper left and a red stripe and the words "California Republic" across the bottom; in the center, a brown grizzly bear walks on a patch of green grass.

OFFICIAL SEAL: In the foreground is the goddess Minerva; a grizzly bear stands in front of her shield. The scene also shows the Sierra Nevada, San Francisco Bay, a miner, a sheaf of wheat, and a cluster of grapes, all representing California's resources. The state motto and 31 stars are displayed at the top. The words "The Great Seal of the State of California" surround the whole.

COLORS: Yale blue and golden yellow.

ANIMAL: California grizzly bear (extinct).

BIRD: California valley quail.

FISH: California golden trout.

FLOWER: Golden poppy.

TREE: California redwood.

ROCK: Serpentine.

MINERAL: Native gold.

GEMSTONE: Benitoite.

REPTILE: California desert tortoise.

INSECT: California dog-face butterfly (flying pansy).

MARINE MAMMAL: California gray whale.

FOSSIL: California saber-toothed cat.

TIME: 4 AM PST = noon GMT.

1 LOCATION AND SIZE

Situated on the Pacific coast of the southwestern US, California is the nation's third-largest state (after Alaska and Texas). The total area of California is 158,706 square miles (411,048 square kilometers). California extends about 350 miles (560 kilometers) east-west; its maximum north-south extension is 780 miles (1,260 kilometers).

The eight Santa Barbara islands lie from 20 to 60 miles (32–97 kilometers) off California's southwestern coast. The small islands and islets of the Farallon group are about 30 miles (48 kilometers) west of San Francisco Bay. The total boundary length of the state is 2,050 miles (3,299 kilometers).

2 TOPOGRAPHY

California is the only state in the US with an extensive seacoast, high mountains, and deserts. The state's extreme physical diversity is best illustrated by the fact that Mt. Whitney (14,495 feet—4,418 meters), the highest point in the continental US, is situated no more than 80 miles (129 kilometers) from the lowest point in the entire country, Death Valley (282 feet, or 86 meters, below sea level). California has 41 mountains exceeding 10,000 feet (3,050 meters). The mean elevation of the state is about 2,900 feet (900 meters).

California's principal geographic regions are the Sierra Nevada in the east, the Coast Ranges in the west, the Central Valley between them, and the Mojave and Colorado deserts in the southeast. The mountain-walled Central Valley is drained by the state's two principal rivers, the Sacramento River in the north and the San Joaquin River in the south. The Coast Ranges mountain system, extending more than 1,200 miles (1,900 kilometers) alongside the Pacific, is drained by the Klamath, Eel, Russian, Salinas, and other rivers.

The Salton Sea, in the Imperial Valley of the southeast, is the state's largest lake, occupying 374 square miles (969 square kilometers). The California coast is indented by two magnificent natural harbors, San Francisco Bay and San Diego Bay, and two smaller bays, Monterey and Humboldt. Two groups of islands lie off

California Population Profile

Estimated 1995 population:	32,398,000
Population change, 1980–90:	25.7%
Leading ancestry group:	Mexican
Second leading group:	German
Foreign born population:	21.7%
Hispanic origin†:	25.8%
Population by race:	
White:	69.0%
Black:	7.4%
Native American:	0.8%
Asian/Pacific Islander:	9.6%
Other:	13.2%

Population by Age Group

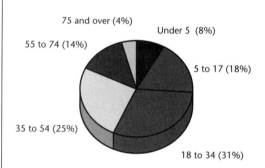

75 and over (4%)
Under 5 (8%)
55 to 74 (14%)
5 to 17 (18%)
35 to 54 (25%)
18 to 34 (31%)

Top Cities with Populations Over 25,000

City	Population	National rank	% change 1980–90
Los Angeles	3,489,779	2	17.5
San Diego	1,148,851	6	26.8
San Jose	801,331	11	24.3
San Francisco	728,921	13	6.6
Long Beach	438,771	31	18.8
Sacramento	382,816	39	34.0
Fresno	376,130	40	62.3
Oakland	373,219	42	9.7
Santa Ana	288,024	55	44.2
Anaheim	274,162	58	21.5

Notes: †A person of Hispanic origin may be of any race. NA indicates that data are not available.
Sources: Economic and Statistics Administration, Bureau of the Census. *Statistical Abstract of the United States, 1994–95.* Washington, DC: Government Printing Office, 1995; Courtenay M. Slater and George E. Hall. *1995 County and City Extra: Annual Metro, City and County Data Book.* Lanham, MD: Bernan Press, 1995.

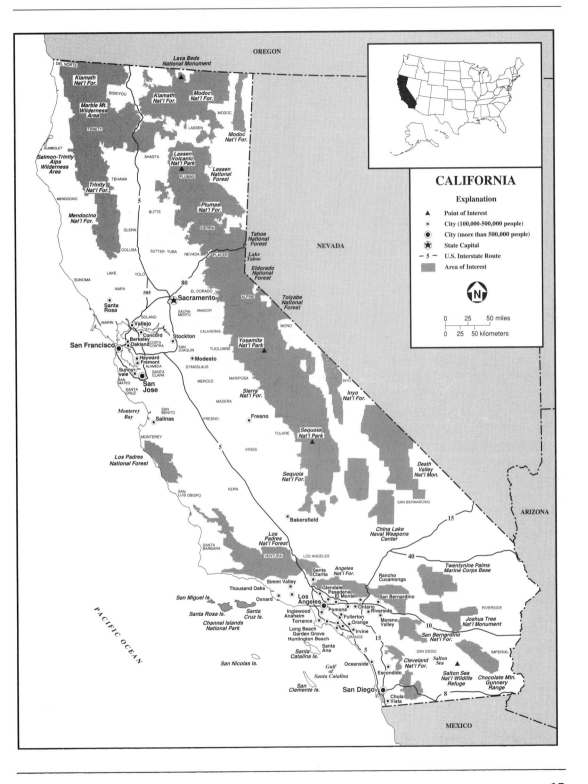

CALIFORNIA

Explanation

▲ Point of Interest
⊙ City (100,000-500,000 people)
◉ City (more than 500,000 people)
★ State Capital
– 5 – U.S. Interstate Route
▨ Area of Interest

the California shore: the Santa Barbara Islands and the rocky Farallon Islands. Because water is scarce in the southern part of the state, more than 1,000 dams and reservoirs have been built in California. By 1993, there were 1,336 reservoirs in the state.

The San Andreas Fault extends from north of San Francisco Bay for more than 600 miles (970 kilometers) southeast to the Mojave Desert. This is a major active earthquake zone and was responsible for the great San Francisco earthquake of 1906.

3 CLIMATE

California has four main climatic regions. Mild summers and winters prevail in central coastal areas, where temperatures are steadier than practically anywhere else in the US. In the area between San Francisco and Monterey, for example, the difference between average summer and winter temperatures is seldom more than 10°F (6°C). Mountainous regions are characterized by milder summers and colder winters, with markedly low temperatures at high elevations. The Central Valley has hot summers and cool winters, while the Imperial Valley is marked by very hot, dry summers, with temperatures frequently exceeding 100°F (38°C).

Average annual temperatures for the state range from 47°F (8°C) in the Sierra Nevada to 73°F (23°C) in the Imperial Valley. The highest temperature ever recorded in the US was 134° (57°C), registered in Death Valley on 10 July 1913. The state's lowest temperature was –45°F (–43°C),

recorded on 20 January 1937 at Boca, near the Nevada border.

Los Angeles has an average January minimum temperature of 47°F (8°C) and an average July maximum of 83°F (28°C). Sacramento's January minimums average 37°F (3°C), with July maximums of 93°F (34°C). Annual precipitation varies from only 2 inches (5 centimeters) in the Imperial Valley to 68 inches (173 centimeters) at Blue Canyon, near Lake Tahoe.

4 PLANTS AND ANIMALS

The state's six life zones are the lower Sonoran (desert); upper Sonoran (foothill regions and some coastal lands); transition (coastal areas and moist northeastern counties); and the Canadian, Hudsonian, and Arctic zones, comprising California's highest elevations.

Plant life in the arid climate of the lower Sonoran zone features native cactus, mesquite, and paloverde. The Joshua tree *(Yucca brevifolia)* is found in the Mojave Desert. Flowering plants include the dwarf desert poppy and a variety of asters. Fremont cottonwood and valley oak grow in the Central Valley. The upper Sonoran zone includes the unique chaparral belt, with forests of small shrubs, stunted trees, and herbaceous plants. The golden poppy *(Eschscholtzia californica)*—the state flower—also flourishes in this zone.

The transition zone includes most of the state's forests, with such magnificent specimens as the redwood *(Sequoia sempervirens)* and "big tree" or giant sequoia *(Sequoia gigantea),* among the oldest living things on earth (some are believed to

Photo credit: Corel Corporation.

The General Sherman tree in the Sequoia National Forest.

be at least 4,000 years old). Characteristic wildflowers include varieties of mariposa, tulip, and tiger and leopard lilies.

The high elevations of the Canadian zone contain abundant Jeffrey pine, red fir, and lodgepole pine. Just below the timberline, in the Hudsonian zone, grow the whitebark, foxtail, and silver pines. At approximately 10,500 feet (3,200 meters) begins the Arctic zone, a treeless region whose plantlife includes a number of wildflowers, including Sierra primrose, yellow columbine, alpine buttercup, and alpine shooting star. Among the numerous plant species found in California that are federally classified as endangered are the Contra Costa wallflower, Antioch Dunes evening primrose, and San Clemente Island larkspur.

Mammals found in the deserts of the lower Sonoran zone include the jackrabbit, kangaroo rat, squirrel, and opossum. The Texas night owl, roadrunner, and various species of hawk are common birds, and reptiles include the sidewinder and horned toad. The upper Sonoran zone is home to such mammals as the antelope, brown-footed woodrat, and ring-tailed cat. Birds of this zone include the California thrasher and California condor.

Animal life is abundant amid the forests of the transition zone. Colombian black-tailed deer, black bear, gray fox, cougar, and bobcat are found. Garter snakes and rattlesnakes are common, and birds include the kingfisher, chickadee, towhee, and hummingbird.

Mammals of the Canadian zone include the mountain weasel, snowshoe hare, and several species of chipmunk. Birds include the blue-fronted jay and Sierra hermit thrush. Birds become scarcer as one ascends to the Hudsonian zone. Principal mammals of this region are also visitors from other zones, though the Sierra coney and white-tailed jackrabbit make their homes here.

Aquatic life in California is abundant. Many trout species are found, among them rainbow, golden, and Tahoe. Migratory species of salmon are also common. Deep-sea life-forms include sea brass, yellowfin tuna, barracuda, and several types of whale. Native to the cliffs of northern California are seals, sea lions, and many types of shorebirds.

Joint efforts by state and federal wildlife agencies have established an ambitious—if somewhat controversial—recovery program to revitalize the dwindling population of the majestic condor, the largest bird native to the US. As of 1990, some 72 California plants and animals were on the federal endangered list. These include the California gray whale (the official state marine mammal), salt marsh harvest mouse, bald eagle, California least tern, San Francisco garter snake, and Owens River pupfish. All seven butterflies listed as endangered on the federal list are California species. Among threatened animals are the Paiute cutthroat

trout, and Southern sea otter. California has a total of 290,821 acres (117,6791 hectares) of National Wildlife Refuges.

5 ENVIRONMENTAL PROTECTION

In 1892, naturalist John Muir and other wilderness lovers founded the Sierra Club. This group, with other private groups of conservationists, has been influential in saving the Muir Woods and other stands of redwoods from the lumbermen's axes. State land-reclamation programs have been important in providing new agricultural land and controlling flood damage.

California's primary resource problem is water: the southern two-thirds of the state accounts for about 75% of annual water consumption but only 30% of the supply. Water has been diverted from the Sierra Nevada snow runoff and from the Colorado River to the cities and dry areas largely by means of aqueducts. Some 700 miles (1,100 kilometers) of aqueducts have been constructed in federal and state undertakings.

Air pollution has been a serious problem since July 1943, when heavy smog enveloped Los Angeles for the first time. In 1960, the state legislature passed the first automobile antismog law in the nation, requiring that all cars be equipped with antismog exhaust devices within three years. The city's smog problem has since been reduced to a manageable level, but pollution problems still persist there and in other California cities.

In 1972, the state legislature enacted stringent controls on toxic waste disposal.

California has also been a leader in recycling waste products—for example, using acid waste from metal-processing plants as a soil additive in citrus orchards. California has 96 hazardous waste sites, more than all states except New Jersey and Pennsylvania.

6 POPULATION

About 12% of all Americans live in California, which ranks first in population among the 50 states. Los Angeles is the second most populous city in the US and Los Angeles County ranks first in population among all US counties.

At the 1990 census, the population of 29,760,021 was 49.6% male and 50.4% female. The population density in 1985 was 165 persons per square mile (64 persons per square kilometer); by 1990, the density was 190.8 persons per square mile (73.3 persons per square kilometer). The estimated population for 1995 was 32,398,000. In 1992, 18% of all Californians were over 55.

In 1990, California was second only to New Jersey in the proportion of residents living in metropolitan areas, more than 95%. In 1992 Los Angeles had a population of 3,489,779; San Diego, 1,148,851; San Jose, 801,331; San Francisco, 728,921; Long Beach, 438,771; and Oakland, 373,219. In the same year, the Los Angeles-Anaheim-Riverside urban complex was the second most populous metropolitan area in the US (after New York City).

7 ETHNIC GROUPS

At least 32% of all foreign-born persons in the US live in California. The state has the nation's largest populations of those born in: Mexico, the Philippines, Canada, Germany, the United Kingdom, Korea, Vietnam, China, El Salvador, India, Japan, Taiwan, Guatemala, Iran, Laos, Hong Kong, Peru, France, Cambodia, Honduras, and Thailand. California also has the most Native Americans and Asian Indians, more blacks than any state except New York, more Eskimos and Aleuts than any state except Alaska, and more native Hawaiians than any state except Hawaii.

The westward movement of American settlers in the third quarter of the 19th century, followed by Germans, Irish, North Italians, and Italian Swiss immigrants, overshadowed but did not obliterate California's Spanish heritage. In 1990, 7,688,000 (25.8%) of the state's residents were of Hispanic origin, more than any other state and 34% of the US total. The majority of these Hispanics—5,322,170—were Mexican-Americans. As of 1990, there were also 113,548 Puerto Ricans, 143,017 Guatemalans, and 300,102 Salvadorans. Nearly 50% of all Mexican-Americans in the US are farm laborers.

California had 2,846,000 Asians and Pacific Islanders in 1990, over 39% of the US total. In 1990, the state's Chinese population was 641,250, more than double that of New York State and by far the highest in the US. The nation's oldest and largest Chinatown is in San Francisco. In 1990 there were 353,251 Japanese-Americans in California. After their removal from their homes and internment during World War II, most Japanese, deprived of their landholdings, entered urban occupations. Many dispersed to other regions of the country.

While the Chinese and Japanese communities in California are the oldest in the state, they were not the most populous in 1990. This distinction was held by the Filipino community, which numbered 709,599 that year. There were also 260,822 Koreans, 242,946 Vietnamese, 112,560 Asian Indians, 43,418 native Hawaiians, 26,444 Samoans, and 19,820 Guamanians.

Native Americans numbered around 242,000 in 1990, of whom 1,854 were Eskimos and 1,091 were Aleuts. Los Angeles has more Native Americans than any other US city. Black Americans constitute a smaller proportion of California's population than of the nation's as a whole: less than 8% in 1990.

8 LANGUAGES

As in much of the West, California English is a combination of the eastern dialects and subdialects brought by the continuing westward migration from the eastern states. The interior valley is Midland-oriented, but generally, in both northern and southern California, Northern speech is dominant.

Boonville, a village about 100 miles (160 kilometers) north of San Francisco, is notorious for "Boontling," a local dialect contrived in the mid-19th century by Scotch-Irish settlers who wanted privacy and freedom from obscenities in their conversation.

Now declining in use, Boontling has about 1,000 vocabulary replacements of usual English words, together with some unusual pronunciations.

California's large foreign-language populations have posed major educational problems. In 1974, a landmark San Francisco case, *Lau v. Nichols,* brought a decision from the US Supreme Court that children who do not know English should not thereby be handicapped in school, but should receive instruction in their native tongue while learning English.

In 1990, 18,764,213 Californians—or 68.5% of the population five years old or over—reported speaking only English at home. Other languages spoken at home included the following:

Spanish	5,478,712
Chinese	575,447
Tagalog	464,644
Vietnamese	233,074
Other various Indo-European	231,654
Korean	215,845
Japanese	174,451
German	165,962
French	132,657
Indic	119,318
Italian	111,133
Portuguese	78,232
Arabic	73,738
Mon-Khmer	59,622
Russian	44,978
Other various West-Germanic	34,433
Greek	32,889

9 RELIGIONS

In the early 20th century, many dissident sects sprang up, including such organizations as Firebrands for Jesus, the Psychosomatic Institute, the Mystical Order of Melchizedek, the Infinite Science Church, and Nothing Impossible, among many others. Canadian-born Aimee Semple

Photo credit: Jeff Hyman.

Gateway to Chinatown Plaza, Los Angeles.

McPherson, who preached her Foursquare Gospel during the 1920s at the Angelus Temple in Los Angeles, was typical of the many charismatic preachers of new doctrines who gave—and still give—California its exotic religious flavor. Since World War II, religions such as Zen Buddhism and Scientology have won enthusiastic followings, along with various cults devoted to self-discovery and self-improvement.

Nevertheless, the large majority of religious Californians continue to follow traditional faiths. In 1990, there were 7,142,067 Roman Catholics and 4,524,337 known Protestants. The largest non-Catholic Christian denominations were the Church of Jesus Christ of Latter-day Saints (Mormon) with 533,741 members; Southern Baptist, 504,516; United Methodist, 266,306; Presbyterian, 258,854; American Baptist, 184,723; Assembly of God, 263,059; Episcopal, 178,263; and the Lutheran Church-Missouri Synod, 143,987. In 1990, the Jewish population was estimated at 918,935, nearly two-thirds of whom lived in the Los Angeles metropolitan area.

10 TRANSPORTATION

California has—and for decades has had—more motor vehicles than any other state, and ranks second only to Texas in interstate highway mileage. A complex 5,400-mile (8,700-kilometer) network of

Photo credit: Robert Holmes.

The Golden Gate Bridge, San Francisco.

Southern Pacific, and Union Pacific. Amtrak passenger trains connect the state's major population centers. In 1991–92, the number of riders throughout the state totaled 5,727,530.

Urban transit began in San Francisco in 1861 with horse-drawn streetcars. Cable-car service was introduced in 1873; a few cable cars are still in use, mainly for the tourist trade. The 71-mile (114-kilometer) Bay Area Rapid Transit System, or BART, connects San Francisco with Oakland.

In Los Angeles, competition from buses—which provided greater mobility, but aggravated the city's smog and congestion problems—forced the trolleys to end service in 1961.

The Pasadena Freeway, the first modern expressway in California, opened in 1941. During the 1960s and 1970s, the state built a complex toll-free highway network tying in with the federal highway system, and costing more than $10 billion. Local, state, and federal authorities combined spent almost $7.8 billion on California highways in 1992, with $1.8 billion of that amount for maintenance.

Los Angeles County claims more automobiles, more miles of streets, and more intersections than any other US city. The 8-mile (13-kilometer) San Francisco–Oakland Bay Bridge was completed in 1936. The next year saw the opening of the magnificent Golden Gate Bridge, which at 4,200 feet (1,280 meters) was the world's longest suspension bridge until 1964.

In 1993, California had 169,201 miles (272,244 kilometers) of public roads and

urban freeways is one of the engineering wonders of the modern world—but the traffic congestion in the state's major cities during rush hours may well be the worst in the country.

The Central Pacific–Union Pacific transcontinental railroad was finished in 1869. The railroads dominated transportation in the state until motor vehicles came into widespread use in the 1920s.

As of 1992, California had 6,530 rail miles (10,506 kilometers) of track. Class I railroads operating within the state in 1991 included Santa Fe, Burlington Northern, registered 22,823,712 motor vehicles—about 55 for every 100 state residents. In that year, California also led the nation in number of traffic injuries (315,184); pedestrian fatal injuries (850); and vehicular fatalities (4,163). Yet the state's death rate per 100,000 vehicle miles—1.7—was slightly less than the US average.

In 1991, the port at Long Beach handled 52.8 million tons of cargo, for a total value of over $48.8 billion. The port at Los Angeles handled just over 47 million tons. Other main ports are Richmond, Oakland, and San Francisco. California has 547 airports and 360 heliports. California's most active air terminal—and the nation's third most active—is Los Angeles International Airport, which handles over 200,000 departing passenger aircraft and boards over 18,000,000 passengers each year.

11 HISTORY

The region now known as California has been populated for at least 10,000 years, and possibly far longer. On the eve of European discovery, at least 300,000 Native Americans lived there. This large population was divided into no fewer than 105 separate tribes or nations speaking at least 100 different languages and dialects. In general, the California tribes depended for their survival on hunting, fishing, and gathering the abundant natural food resources. The basic unit of political organization was the village community, consisting of several small villages, or the family unit.

European contact with California began in 1533 when Hernán Cortés, Spanish conqueror of the Aztecs, sent a naval expedition northward along the western coast of Mexico in search of new wealth. The expedition led to the discovery of Baja California (now part of Mexico). On 28 September, Juan Rodriquez Cabrillo landed at the bay now known as San Diego, thus becoming the first European discoverer of Alta (or Upper) California.

European interest in the Californias declined in the succeeding decades, and California remained for generations on the fringe of European activity in the New World. Spanish interest in California revived during the late 18th century. Because rival colonial powers were becoming increasingly aggressive, Spain decided to establish permanent settlements in the north. Over the next half-century, the 21 missions established by Catholic Franciscans along the Pacific coast from San Diego to San Francisco formed the core of Hispanic California.

The principal concern of the missionaries was to convert the Native Americans to Christianity. They were also taught to perform a wide variety of new tasks: making bricks, tiles, pottery, shoes, saddles, wine, candles, and soap; herding horses, cattle, sheep, and goats; and planting, irrigating, and harvesting. In addition to transforming the way of life of these native Californians, the missions also reduced their number by introducing new diseases.

Spanish control of California ended with the successful conclusion of the Mexican Revolution in 1821. For the next quarter-century, California was a province of the independent nation of Mexico.

During the Mexican period, California attracted a considerable minority of immigrants from within the US. The first organized group to cross the continent for the purpose of settlement in California was the Bidwell-Bartleson party of 1841. Subsequent groups of overland pioneers included the ill-fated Donner party of 1846, whose members, stranded by a snowstorm near the Sierra Nevada summit, resorted to cannibalism so that 47 of the 87 travelers could survive.

Gold Rush

Following the 1846–48 Mexican War, resulting from a dispute over the Texas border, Mexico ceded California and other territories to the US. Mexico received $15 million and the settlement by the US of some $3 million in claims by Mexican citizens. Just nine days before the treaty ending the war was signed, James Wilson Marshall discovered gold along the American River in California. The news of the gold discovery, on 24 January 1848, soon spread around the globe, and a massive rush of people poured into the region. By the end of 1848, about 6,000 miners had obtained $10 million worth of gold. In 1852, the peak year of production, about $80 million in gold was mined in the state.

California's census population quadrupled during the 1850s, reaching nearly 380,000 by 1860, and continued to grow at a rate twice that of the nation as a whole in the 1860s and 1870s. One of the most serious problems facing California in the early years of the gold rush was the absence of government. The US Congress, deadlocked over the slavery controversy, failed to provide any form of legal government for California from the end of the Mexican War until its admission as a state in the fall of 1850. Taking matters into their own hands, 48 delegates gathered at a constitutional convention in Monterey in September 1849 to draft a fundamental law for California. To the surprise of many, the convention decided by unanimous vote to exclude slavery from the region. California soon petitioned Congress for admission as a state, having bypassed the preliminary territorial stage. On 9 September 1850, President Millard Fillmore signed the admission bill, and California became the 31st state to enter the union.

Statehood

The early years of statehood were marked by racial discrimination and considerable ethnic conflict. The Native American population declined from an estimated 150,000 in 1845 to less than 30,000 by 1870. In 1850, the state legislature enacted a foreign miners' license tax, aimed at eliminating competition from Mexican and other Latin American miners. The 25,000 Chinese who replaced the Mexicans as the state's largest foreign minority—making up about a tenth of the state's population by 1852—soon became the target of a new round of discrimination. The legislature enacted new taxes aimed at Chinese miners and passed an immigration tax on the Chinese as well.

Controversy also centered on the status of the Mexican *ranchos*, those vast estates created by the Mexican government that totaled more than 13 million acres (5 million hectares) by 1850. In the early years of statehood, thousands of squatters took up residence on the rancho lands. By the time the legal title to the property was confirmed by federal commissions and courts—a process which often took as long as 17 years—the original occupants were often bankrupt and benefited little from the decision.

Despite the population boom during the gold rush, California remained isolated from the rest of the country until completion of the transcontinental railroad in 1869. In the late 19th century, California's economy became more diversified. The early dependence on gold and silver mining was overcome through the development of large-scale irrigation projects and the expansion of commercial agriculture. The population of southern California boomed in the 1880s, fueled by the success of the new citrus industry, an influx of invalids seeking a warmer climate, and a railroad rate war between the Southern Pacific and the newly completed Santa Fe.

Early 20th Century

During the early 20th century, California's population growth became increasingly urban. Between 1900 and 1920, the population of the San Francisco Bay area doubled, while residents of metropolitan Los Angeles increased fivefold. On 18 April 1906, San Francisco's progress was interrupted by the most devastating earthquake ever to strike California. The quake and the fires that raged for three days killed at least 452 people, razed the city's business section, and destroyed some 28,000 buildings. The survivors immediately set to work to rebuild the city, and completed about 20,000 new buildings within three years. By 1920, the populations of the two urban areas of Los Angeles and San Francisco were roughly equal.

During the first half of the 20th century, California's population growth far outpaced that of the nation as a whole because of the new economic opportunities it offered. In the early 1920s, major discoveries of oil were made in the Los Angeles Basin, and for several years during the decade, California ranked first among the states in production of crude oil.

During the 1930s hundreds of thousands of refugees streamed into the state from the dust bowl of the southern Great Plains. The film industry, which offered at least the illusion of prosperity to millions of Americans, continued to prosper during the nationwide economic depression. By 1940 there were more movie theaters in the US than banks, and the films they showed were almost all California products.

During World War II, the enormous expansion of military installations, shipyards, and aircraft plants attracted millions of new residents to California. The war years also saw an increase in the size and importance of ethnic minorities. By 1942, only Mexico City had a larger urban Mexican population than Los Angeles. During the war, more than 93,000 Japanese-Americans in California—most of whom were US citizens and

American-born—were interned in "relocation centers" throughout the Far West.

Post–World War II

California continued to grow rapidly during the postwar period, as agricultural, aerospace, and service industries provided new economic opportunities. Politics in the state were influenced by international tensions, and the California legislature expanded the activities of its Fact-Finding Committee on Un-American Activities. Blacklisting became common in the film industry. The early 1950s saw the rise to the US vice-presidency of Richard Nixon, whose early campaigns capitalized on fears of Communism.

At the beginning of 1963, California (according to census estimates) became the nation's most populous state. By 1970, however, California's growth rate had slowed considerably. Economic opportunity gave way to recessions and high unemployment. Pollution of air and water called into question the quality of the California environment. The traditional romantic image of California was overshadowed by reports of mass murders, bizarre religious cults, extremist social and political movements, and racial and campus unrest.

In 1968, Richard Nixon became the first native Californian to be elected a US president. Both Ronald Reagan, governor of the state from 1967 to 1975, and Edmund G. Brown, Jr., elected governor in 1974 and reelected in 1978, were active candidates for the US presidency in 1980.

Reagan was the Republican presidential winner that year and in 1984.

1980s–90s

Assisted by the Reagan administration's military build-up, which invested billions of dollars in California's defense industry, the state's economy rebounded in the early and mid-1980s. By the late 1980s and early 1990s, however, a recession and cuts in military spending combined to produce a dramatic economic decline. In 1992, the state's unemployment rate climbed to 10.1%. Jobs in the California aerospace and manufacturing sector dropped by 24%.

California's economic woes were matched by civil disorders. In 1991, an onlooker released a seven-minute videotape which showed a group of Los Angeles police officers beating a black motorist, Rodney King, with nightsticks, at the conclusion of a high-speed freeway chase. The four officers who had been charged with unnecessary brutality were then acquitted (in a jury trial that took place in a mostly white suburb). The verdict set off riots in South Central Los Angeles that killed 60 people and caused an estimated $1 billion in property damage.

In the late 1980s and early 1990s, California was also hit by two severe earthquakes. The first, which struck the San Francisco area in 1989, caused the collapse of buildings, bridges, and roadways. As many as 270 people were killed and 100,000 houses were damaged. In 1994, an earthquake measuring 6.7 on the Richter scale occurred 20 miles northwest of downtown Los Angeles, leaving 680,000 people without electricity and causing $13–20 million in property damage.

In 1994, anger over illegal immigration led to passage of Proposition 187, which would bar illegal aliens from welfare, education, and nonemergency health services. Passage of the measure prompted immediate challenges in the courts by the opposition, and the issue has not been resolved.

12 STATE GOVERNMENT

The California legislature consists of a 40-member senate and an 80-member assembly. Senators are elected to four-year terms, half of them every two years, and assembly members are elected to two-year terms. Bills, which may be introduced by either house, are referred to committees, and must be read before each house three times. Legislation must be approved by an absolute majority vote of each house, except for appropriations bills, certain urgent measures, and proposed constitutional amendments, which require a two-thirds vote for passage. A governor's veto may be overridden by two-thirds majority votes in both houses.

Constitutional amendments and proposed legislation may also be placed on the ballot through the initiative procedure. For a constitutional amendment, petitions must be signed by at least 8% of the number of voters who took part in the last gubernatorial election; for statutory measures, 5%. In each case, a simple majority vote at the next general election is required for passage.

Officials elected statewide include the governor and lieutenant governor (who run separately), secretary of state, attorney general, controller, treasurer, and superintendent of public instruction. Each serves a four-year term. As chief executive officer of the state, the governor is responsible for the state's policies and programs, appoints department heads and members of state boards and commissions, serves as commander in chief of the California National Guard, may declare states of emergency, and may grant executive clemency to convicted criminals.

The lieutenant governor acts as president of the senate and may assume the duties of the governor in case of the latter's death, resignation, impeachment, inability to discharge the duties of the office, or absence from the state.

13 POLITICAL PARTIES

As the state with the largest number of US representatives (52 in 1992) and electoral votes (54) California plays a key role in national and presidential politics. As of 1994, California had 15,101,673 registered voters, including 7,410,914 Democrats, or 49% of all voters; 5,593,555 Republicans, or 37%; and 2,097,204 unaffiliated, or 14%. Even with an advantage in voter registration, however, the Democrats managed to carry California in presidential elections only three times between 1948 and 1992. Also, during the same period only two Democratic governors—Edmund G. "Pat" Brown (in 1958 and 1962) and his son, Edmund G. "Jerry" Brown, Jr. (in 1974 and 1978)—were elected.

Three times Californians gave their presidential electoral votes to a California Republican, Richard Nixon, though they turned down his bid for governor in 1962. They elected one former film actor, Republican George Murphy, as US senator in 1964, and another actor, Republican Ronald Reagan, as governor in 1966 and 1970 and as president in 1980 and 1984. Democratic nominee Bill Clinton won 46% of the popular vote in 1992, while incumbent George Bush received 33% and Independent Ross Perot picked up 20.6%.

Political third parties have had remarkable success in California since the days of the secretive, anti-foreign, anti-Catholic, Native American Party. The latter was called the Know-Nothing party because members were instructed to say they "knew nothing" when asked what they stood for. They elected one of their leaders, J. Neely Johnson, as governor in 1855. The most impressive third-party triumph came in 1912, when the Progressive Party's presidential candidate, Theodore Roosevelt, and his vice-presidential nominee, Governor Hiram Johnson, defeated both the Republican and Democratic candidates among state voters. During the depression year of 1934, the Socialist Party leader and novelist Upton Sinclair won the Democratic nomination for governor on his "End Poverty In California" program. Sinclair received nearly a million votes while losing to Republican Frank Merriam.

Both Senators in 1994 were women: Democrat Barbara Boxer, who won election in 1992; and Dianne Feinstein, elected in 1992 to replace Senator Pete Wilson, who was elected Governor in 1990. Both Feinstein and Wilson won re-election in 1994. In 1995 California's delegation of US Representatives consisted of 28 Democrats and 24 Republicans, a gain of 2 seats by the Republicans. In the same year, the Democrats kept control of the State Senate but split control of the House with the Republicans.

Minority groups of all types are represented in California politics. As of 1992, elected officials included 260 blacks and 682 Hispanics. In 1993 there were 30 women serving in the state legislature and in elective executive office. One of the most prominent black elected officials in the 1970s and 1980s was Los Angeles Mayor Thomas Bradley, who served from 1973–90. Organized groups of homosexuals became involved in San Francisco politics during the 1970s.

14 LOCAL GOVERNMENT

As of 1992, California had 57 counties, about 1,080 school districts, and 2,897 special districts. There were 460 municipal governments in 1992.

County government is administered by an elected board of supervisors. Government operations are administered by several elected officials, the number varying according to the population of the county. Most counties have a district attorney, assessor, treasurer-tax collector, superintendent of schools, sheriff, and coroner.

Municipalities are governed under the mayor-council, council-manager, or commission system. Most large cities are run by councils of from 5 to 15 members responsible for taxes, public improvements, and the budget. An elected mayor supervises city departments and appoints most city officials.

15 JUDICIAL SYSTEM

California has a complex judicial system and a very large correctional system. The state's highest court is the supreme court, which may review appeals court decisions and superior court cases involving the death penalty. The high court has a chief justice and six associate justices, all of whom serve 12-year terms.

Courts of appeal, organized in six districts, review decisions of superior courts and, in certain cases, of municipal and justice courts. As of 1994 there were 88 district appeals court judgeships.

Superior courts in each of the 58 county seats have original jurisdiction in felony, juvenile, probate, and domestic relations cases, as well as in civil cases involving more than $15,000. They also handle some tax and misdemeanor cases and appeals from lower courts. Municipal courts, located in judicial districts with populations of more than 40,000, hear misdemeanors (except those involving juveniles) and civil cases involving $15,000 or less. In districts with less than 40,000 population, justice courts have jurisdiction similar to that of municipal courts. All trial court judges are elected to six-year terms.

As of December 1993 there were 119,951 prisoners in state and federal prisons in California. The State Department of Corrections maintains 13 correctional institutions, 3 reception centers, 33 conservation camps, and more than 60

California Presidential Vote by Political Parties, 1948–92

Year	California Winner	Democrat	Republican	Progressive	Socialist	Prohibition
1948	*Truman (D)	1,913,134	1,895,269	190,381	3,459	16,926
					Soc. Labor	
1952	*Eisenhower (R)	2,197,548	2,897,310	24,692	273	16,117
1956	*Eisenhower (R)	2,420,135	3,027,668		300	11,119
1960	Nixon (R)	3,224,099	3,259,722		1,051	21,706
1964	*Johnson (D)	4,171,877	2,879,108		489	
					Peace/Freedom	
1968	*Nixon (R)	3,244,318	3,467,664		27,707	
				American	People's	Libertarian
1972	*Nixon (R)	3,475,847	4,602,096	232,554	55,167	980
				Communist		
1976	Ford (R)	3,742,284	3,882,244	12,766	41,731	56,388
				Citizens	Peace/Freedom	
1980	*Reagan (R)	3,039,532	4,444,044	9,687	60,059	17,797
1984	*Reagan (R)	3,922,519	5,467,009	New Alliance	26,297	49,951
1988	*Bush (R)	4,702,233	5,054,917	31,181		70,105
				Ind. (Perot)		
1992	*Clinton (D)	5,121,325	3,630,574	2,296,006	18,597	48,139

*Won US presidential election.

parole offices. According to the FBI, California's crime rate in 1994 was 6,173.8 crimes per 100,000 population. In that year, 1,940,497 crimes were reported to the police, including 318,395 violent crimes and 1,622,102 crimes against property.

16 MIGRATION

A majority of Californians today are migrants from other states. The first great wave of migration, the Gold Rush beginning in 1848, brought at least 85,000 prospectors by 1850. Many thousands of Chinese were brought in during the latter half of the 19th century to work on farms and railroads. When Chinese immigration was banned by the US Congress in 1882, Japanese migration provided farm labor. By 1940, about 94,000 Japanese lived in California.

During the depression of the 1930s, approximately 350,000 migrants came to California, most of them looking for work. Many thousands of people came there during World War II to take jobs in the growing war industries. After the war, some 300,000 discharged servicemen settled in the state. All told, between 1940 and 1990, California registered a net gain from migration of 12,426,000 people, representing well over half of its population growth during that period. As of 1992, nearly 22% of all foreign immigrants in the US were living in California, a higher proportion than in any other state.

Although the 1970s brought an influx of refugees from Indochina, and, somewhat later, from Central America, the bulk of postwar foreign immigration has come from neighboring Mexico. Hundreds of thousands—perhaps even millions—of illegal Mexican immigrants have crossed the border in search of jobs and then, unless they were caught and deported (forcibly returned), stayed on.

In 1991, California admitted 732,735 foreign immigrants (more than any other state and 40% of the US total that year), including 504,631 Mexicans. Counting these state residents for census purposes is extremely difficult, since many of them are unwilling to declare themselves for fear of being identified and deported. As of 1990, California's foreign-born population was reported at 6,458,825, or 22% of the state's total.

Intrastate (within California) migration has followed two general patterns: rural to urban until the mid-20th century, and urban to suburban after that. In particular, the percentage of blacks increased in Los Angeles, San Francisco, and San Diego between 1960 and 1970. This occurred as black people settled or remained in the cities while whites moved into the surrounding suburbs. By 1990, 46.4% of all state residents had been born in California.

17 ECONOMY

California leads the 50 states in economic output and total personal income. The state ranks first in the US in such important industries as food products, machinery, electric and electronic equipment, aerospace, dairy production, and beef cattle. California also leads the nation in retail sales, foreign trade, and corporate profits.

The Gold Rush of the mid-19th century made mining the principal economic activity and gave impetus to agriculture and manufacturing. Many unsuccessful miners took up farming or went to work for the big cattle ranches and wheat growers. In the 1870s, California became the most important cattle-raising state and the second-leading wheat producer. Manufacturing outstripped both mining and agriculture to produce goods valued at $258 million by 1900, and ten times that by 1925. Thanks to a rapidly growing work force, industrial output continued to expand during and after both world wars, while massive irrigation projects enabled farmers to make full use of the state's rich soil and favorable climate.

By the late 1970s, one of every four California workers was employed in high-technology industry. California has long ranked first among the states in defense-related manufacturing, and in 1992, contracts awarded to California firms surpassed the combined totals of New York and Texas.

From its beginnings in the late 18th century, California's wine industry has grown to encompass some 500 wineries. By the early 1980s, they accounted for about 90% of total US production. By 1985, California had surpassed Chicago to rank second in advertising among the states.

Its highly diversified economy makes California less sensitive to national recessions than most other states. During the first half of the 1980s, the state generally outperformed the national economy. The boom was short-lived, however. Cuts in the military budget in the late 1980s, a decline in Japanese investment, and the national recession in the early 1990s had a devastating impact on the state, particularly on southern California. Unemployment in 1992 rose to 9.1%, up from 5.1% in 1989.

18 INCOME

With a per capita (per person) income of $22,353 in 1994, California ranked 14th among the 50 states. Total personal income was $702.6 billion—more than 12% of the US total. Despite California's relatively high average personal income, however, over 5.8 million state residents (18.2%) were below the federal poverty level in 1993. At the other end of the spectrum, California is justly noted for its large number of wealthy residents, particularly in the Los Angeles, Sacramento, and San Francisco metropolitan areas.

19 INDUSTRY

California is the nation's leading industrial state, ranking first in almost every general manufacturing category: number of establishments, number of employees, total payroll, value of shipments, and new capital spending. California ranks among the leaders in machinery, fabricated metals, agricultural products, food processing, computers, aerospace technology, and many other industries.

Computers and aerospace manufacturers stand out among California's largest publicly owned corporations. Hewlett-Packard, Sun Microsystems, Tandem Computers, Varian Associates, and Silicon

Graphics are leading names of the Silicon Valley (Santa Clara County) area just south of San Francisco. Southern California's manufacturing leaders are Rockwell International, Lockheed, Northrop, and Computers Sciences.

California's motion-picture producing industry is based primarily in Los Angeles. A 1992 research report shows the film and TV production industry generating an annual payroll of $7.4 billion, paying $8.9 billion to suppliers, and providing jobs to 35,000 Californians.

20 LABOR

California has the largest work force in the nation and the greatest number of employed workers. In 1994, the state's civilian labor force totaled 15,471,000, of whom 8.6% were unemployed.

As of 1993, there were 47 national unions operating in California. As of 1994, 17.9% of all workers in California belonged to a labor union.

During the 1960s, a Mexican-American laborer named César Chávez established the National Farm Workers Association (now the United Farm Workers of America). After a long struggle, this union won bargaining rights from grape, lettuce, and berry growers in the San Joaquin Valley. Chávez's group was helped by a secondary boycott against these California farm products throughout the US.

21 AGRICULTURE

California leads the 50 states in agricultural production. Famous for its specialty crops, California produces practically all the almonds, apricots, avocados, broccoli, dates, figs, nectarines, olives, pomegranates, safflower, and walnuts grown commercially in the US.

Less than one-third of California's total land area was devoted to farming in 1993, when some 76,000 farms comprised about 30 million acres (12 million hectares). The leading cash crops are grapes (used for raisins, and especially for wine), cotton, hay, and lettuce. Grapes, along with greenhouse and nursery products, accounted for 8.3% and 9.8% of total agricultural receipts in 1994, respectively. California's total farm marketings amounted to $20.2 billion in 1994.

The following table shows harvested acreage and production (in pounds unless otherwise stated) for 15 of the leading California cash crops in 1994:

CROP	ACRES (1,000)	PRODUCTION (1,000,000)
Grapes	660.5	5.31 tons
Cotton	1,175.8	2.91 bales*
Hay	1,470.0	8.21 tons
Lettuce	128.5	4,369.00 pounds
Tomatoes†	347.5	20,786.00 pounds
Oranges	185.0	62.60 boxes†
Strawberries	23.3	1,304.80 pounds
Almonds (shelled)	410.0	69,500.00 pounds
Rice	485.0	4,122.40 pounds
Wheat	569.0	44.36 bushels
Potatoes	41.7	1,526.70 pounds
Broccoli	94.5	982.80 pounds
Celery	24.5	1,543.50 pounds

*One bale weighs about 480 pounds.
†One box weighs about 75 pounds.

Irrigation is essential for farming in California, and agriculture consumes 79% of the state's water supply. The major irrigation systems include the Colorado River Project, the Central Valley Project, the

Photo credit: Robert Holmes.

Vineyards in the Carneros District, Napa Valley.

Feather River Project, and, largest of all, the California Water Project.

22 DOMESTICATED ANIMALS

California is a leading producer of livestock and dairy products, which together accounted for 27% of the state's farm income in 1994. Beef cattle, raised principally in the Central Valley, were California's fourth most important farm product in 1994, when sales of cattle totaled 7% of agricultural receipts. At the end of 1994 there were an estimated 4,700,000 cattle, 1,060,000 sheep, and 255,000 hogs on California farms and ranches.

California is the second-leading milk producer (behind Wisconsin) among the 50 states. Dairy products accounted for 14.5% of the state's agricultural receipts in 1994, and 14.7% of the nation's dairy receipts that year. Milk cows, raised mainly in the southern interior, totaled 1,250,000 head in 1995. California ranks first among the 50 states in egg and honey production as well.

23 FISHING

The Pacific whaling industry, with its chief port at San Francisco, was important to the California economy in the 19th century, and commercial fishing is still central to the food-processing industry. In 1992, California ranked fourth in the US in commercial fishing, with a catch of 302.3 million pounds, valued at $136.3 million. In 1991, principal species caught included squid, 68,144,000 pounds; mackerel, 63,292,000 pounds; anchovies, 19,125,000 pounds; Pacific herring, 15,984,000 pounds; hake, 15,197,000 pounds; shrimp 12,522,000 pounds; and yellowfin tuna, 5,056,000 pounds.

Deep-sea fishing is a popular sport. As of 1991, world records for giant sea bass, California halibut, white catfish, and sturgeon had been set in California. The Coleman National Fish Hatchery distributed over 18.3 million coldwater fish and eggs (mostly Chinook salmon) within the state in 1991–92.

24 FORESTRY

California has more forests than any other state except Alaska. In 1994, forests covered 37,000,000 acres (15,000,000 hectares). Nearly 43% of the state's forested area is used to produce commercial timber. Forests are concentrated in the northwestern part of the state and in the eastern Sierra Nevada.

About half of the state's forests are protected as national forests and state parks or recreational areas. Although California's giant redwood trees have been preserved in national and state parks since the late 19th century, only about 15% remain of the original 2,000,000 acres (800,000 hectares) of redwoods between Monterey Bay and southern Oregon.

As of 1991, there were six national forests in California. Total area within their boundaries amounted to 2,091,412 acres (846,394 hectares). Reforestation of public lands is supervised by the National Forest Service and the California Department of Forestry. In 1992–93, 26,585 acres (10,759 hectares) were reforested.

25 MINING

According to data compiled by the US Bureau of Mines, California was the third leading state in the nation in the value of nonfuel minerals produced during 1994, accounting for over 7% of the US total. The value of the nonfuel mineral commodities produced in the state during the year was estimated to be $2.5 billion. The principal minerals produced are portland cement, sand and gravel, and gold. California leads all other states in the production of boron minerals (1.0 million metric tons, valued at $332.7 million) and portland cement (9.1 million short tons, worth $548.7 million).

26 ENERGY AND POWER

In 1991, petroleum supplied an estimated 53% of the state's energy needs; natural gas, 33%; hydroelectric power, 5%; nuclear power, 5%; coal, 1%; and other sources, about 3%. California ranks seventh among the 50 states in production of electric power, third in crude oil, and eighth in natural gas. Despite its ample energy resources, California is a net importer of electric power because of its heavy industrial, residential, and commercial requirements.

In 1993, electrical output totaled 125.8 billion kilowatt hours. About 25% was generated from hydroelectric plants, 42% from natural gas, less than 1% from oil, 25% from nuclear power plants, and about 8% from geothermal and other sources.

In 1991, sales of electric power in the state totaled 208.6 billion kilowatt hours, of which 38% went to commercial businesses, 31% to home consumers, 27% to industries, and 4% to other users. Largely because of the mild California climate, utility bills are lower than in many other states. In 1991, per capita (per person) energy consumption in California was 235.7 million Btu, or 44th among the states.

California's proved oil reserves as of 31 December 1991 were estimated at more than 4.2 billion barrels, nearly 11% of the US total and third behind Alaska and Texas. In 1993 petroleum production totaled 293 million barrels, representing more than 11% of the domestic output. Production of natural gas totaled 316 billion cubic feet, 1.6% of the US total, and proved reserves were nearly 3.1 trillion cubic feet (1.7%). Nearly all the coal consumed for electric power generation is shipped in from other states.

California has been a leader in developing solar and geothermal power as alternatives to fossil fuels. State tax credits encourage the installation of solar energy devices in commercial and residential property. Geothermal, wind, and solar energy capacity amounts to 1,692,000 kilowatts per year, or nearly 4% of the total electric capacity for the state. Over 98% of the geothermal, wind, and solar electric capacity nationally comes from California.

27 COMMERCE

The state's 1993 retail sales amounted to $233.7 billion. Of total 1993 sales in establishments with payrolls, food stores accounted for 18.3%; automobile dealers, 20.2%; general merchandise stores, 12.8%; eating and drinking places, 11%; gasoline service stations, 6.3% and other establishments, 31.4%. Wholesale trade sales were $432.9 billion, first in the nation, while service establishment receipts were $224.9 billion, also first in the nation.

Foreign trade is important to the California economy. Goods exported from California are valued at an estimated $81 billion, and goods imported at more than $111.4 billion. Leading exports include data-processing equipment, electrical tubes and transistors, scientific equipment, measuring instruments, optical equipment, aircraft parts, and spacecraft. California's leading agricultural export is cotton.

San Francisco and San Jose have been designated as federal foreign-trade zones, where imported goods may be stored duty-free for reshipment abroad, or customs duties avoided until the goods are actually marketed in the US.

28 PUBLIC FINANCE

California's general budget is the largest of all the states in both expenditures and revenues. The state's public finances became the focus of national attention when, on 6 June 1978, California voters approved Proposition 13, a constitutional amendment that reduced local property taxes by more than 50%. This new measure threatened to reduce the public services of county and municipal governments, whose funds came largely from property taxes, by cutting their total revenues by $6.8 billion. As a result of Proposition 13, government employment was reduced by 30,000 as of November 1978 and drastic cuts were made in the state's budget surplus for 1979/80 and future years.

The state budget is prepared by the Department of Finance and presented by the governor to the state legislature for approval. Consolidated state revenues for 1993 totaled $108 billion, and state expenditures were $104 billion.

California's total public debt exceeded $41.3 billion, or $1,323 per person as of 1993. The total debt amount is second only to New York State's.

29 TAXATION

In the mid-1970s, Californians were paying more in taxes than residents of any other state, but this heavy tax burden was reduced by the passage in 1978 of Proposition 13. The state ranked 12th in federal tax burden per capita (per person) in 1990. In the same year, California's revenues from state taxes and fees totaled more than $44.8 billion. An income tax credit is available for the cost of purchasing and installing solar energy systems in the home.

The state sales tax as of 1 January 1994 was 6% on retail sales (excepting food for home consumption, prescription medicines, gas, water, electricity, and certain other exempt products). Localities derive most of their revenue from property taxes,

which were limited in 1978 by Proposition 13 to 1% of market value, with annual increases in the tax not to exceed 2%. The drastic revision reduced property tax collections by about 57% to an estimated $4.9 billion in the 1978/79 fiscal year.

In 1992, California bore a heavier share of the federal tax burden than any other state, contributing $129 billion in federal taxation, or more than 11.5% of the US total. But California also received more federal expenditures than any other state—$139.6 billion, for a net benefit of $10.6 billion.

30 HEALTH

California ranked below the national death rate in 1991 for five of the six leading causes of death (the exception was suicide, which was equivalent to the US rate). Principal causes of deaths and their rates per 100,000 population during 1992 included: heart disease, 217.2; cancer, 162.5; cerebrovascular diseases, 49.1; pulmonary diseases, 32.6; accidents, 30.7; and human immunodeficiency virus (HIV) infection, 19.5. From 1981 to 1990, California recorded 27,653 AIDS cases, second only after New York.

In 1993, California's 429 community hospitals admitted 3,052,000 patients. The average expense per inpatient day amounted to $1,221—the highest average daily expenses in the nation. Medical personnel licensed to practice in California in 1993 included 74,165 nonfederal physicians. There were 173,973 active registered nurses in the state during 1992.

Medi-Cal is a statewide program that pays for the medical care of persons who otherwise could not afford it. California has also been a leader in developing new forms of health care, including the health maintenance organization (HMO), which provides preventive care, diagnosis, and treatment for which the patient pays a fixed annual premium. In 1993 over 19% of California's residents did not have health insurance.

31 HOUSING

California ranks first nationwide in the number of housing units (11,182,882 in 1990). Between 1960 and 1990, some 6.3 million houses and apartments were built in the state, comprising more than 56% of California housing stock. In 1993, 84,341 housing units were authorized, of which 82% were single family units and 18% were multi-dwelling structures. The value of housing construction in 1993 totaled $10.1 billion.

The earliest homes in southern California were Spanish colonial structures renowned for their simplicity and harmony with the landscape. The fusion of Spanish adobe structures and traditional American wooden construction appeared in the 1930s, and "California style" houses gained great popularity throughout the West. Adapted from the functional international style of Frank Lloyd Wright and other innovative architects, modern domestic designs emphasizing split-level surfaces and open interiors won enthusiastic acceptance in California. Wright's finest California homes include the Freeman house in Los Angeles and the Millard house in Pasadena.

In 1990, California had 856,165 condominiums, more than any other state except Florida. California also was second to Florida in 1990 in the number of mobile homes, or trailers, at 556,411. The median monthly cost for a mortgaged, owner-occupied housing unit in 1990 was $1,077; the median monthly rent for a housing unit was $620.

32 EDUCATION

California ranks first among the states in enrollment in public schools and in institutions of higher learning. California's expenditure on public schools in 1993 was estimated at $4,620 per pupil—39th in the US.

In 1990 almost 76% of the state's adult population had completed four years of high school. In addition, about 4,575,000 Californians had completed four or more years of college, representing 22% of the adult population. During the 1992/93 school year, California's 7,666 public schools enrolled 5,195,777 pupils. In fall 1993, enrollment was up to 5,267,277. Kindergarten through grade 8 had 3,837,849 pupils, and grades 9 through 12 had 1,429,428 pupils. There were 223,932 teachers and 32,809 other professionals in the public school system that year.

In 1993/94, the number of public high school graduates was 249,320; private, 23,481. That year, 4,005 private schools enrolled 574,243 pupils and had 34,350 full-time teachers. As of 1 January 1994, there were 586 Roman Catholic elementary schools with 176,189 pupils and 105 Roman Catholic high schools with 64,964 pupils. Some 500,000 students per year participate in special education programs, at a cost of about $2.1 billion.

As of fall 1992, the University of California, a state university, enrolled 165,804 students, 156,029 of them full-time. The California state college and university system—which should not be confused with the University of California—had an additional 313,900 students (199,800 full-time). Also, private colleges and universities that reported enrollments to the state had 165,520 students (119,933 full-time); public community colleges, 1,518,918 in 1991 (376,099 full-time); private two-year colleges, 1,354 (723 full-time); and other public institutions, 3,568 (3,546 full-time).

The University of California has its main campus at Berkeley and branches at Davis, Irvine, Los Angeles (UCLA), Riverside, San Diego, San Francisco, Santa Barbara, and Santa Cruz. California's 19 state universities include those at Los Angeles, Sacramento, San Diego, San Francisco, and San Jose; state colleges are located at Bakersfield, San Bernardino, and Stanislaus.

Privately endowed institutions with the largest student enrollments are the University of Southern California (USC), with 29,657 students in 1990, and Stanford University (13,758). California has 16 Roman Catholic colleges and universities, including Loyola Marymount University of Los Angeles.

33 ARTS

The arts have always thrived in California. They first appeared in the Franciscan chapels with their religious paintings and church music, later in the art galleries, gas-lit theaters, and opera houses of San Francisco and Los Angeles, and today in seaside artists' colonies, regional theaters, numerous concert halls, and, not least, in the motion-picture studios of Hollywood. The motion-picture industry did not begin in Hollywood—the first commercial films were made in New York City and New Jersey in the 1890s—but within a few decades this Los Angeles suburb had become synonymous with the new art form. In the 1960s, Hollywood replaced New York City as the main center for the production of television programs.

Many gifted composers—including Irving Berlin, George Gershwin, and Kurt Weill—came to Hollywood to write film music. In addition, a number of famed musicians fleeing Europe during the Nazi era, such as composers Igor Stravinsky and Arnold Schoenberg, were longtime residents of the state. Symphony orchestras include the renowned Los Angeles Philharmonic, the San Francisco Symphony, and professional orchestras in Oakland and San Jose. Resident opera companies perform regularly in San Francisco and San Diego. Annual musical events include the Monterey Jazz Festival and summer concerts at the Hollywood Bowl.

California has also played a major role in the evolution of popular music since the 1960s. The "surf sound" of the Beach Boys dominated California pop music in

Embarcadero Wharf in San Francisco.

the mid-1960s. By 1967, "acid rock" bands such as the Grateful Dead, the Jefferson Airplane (later Jefferson Starship, and then Starship), and the Doors began to gain national recognition. During the 1970s, California was strongly identified with a group of resident singer-songwriters, including Neil Young, Joni Mitchell, Randy Newman, and Jackson Browne. Los Angeles is a main center of the popular-music industry, with numerous recording studios and branch offices of the leading record companies.

California has nurtured generations of writers, many of whom moved there from other states. In 1864, Mark Twain, a Missourian, came to California as a newspaperman. The writer perhaps most strongly associated with California is Nobel Prize-winner John Steinbeck, a Salinas native. Hollywood's film industry has long been a magnet for writers. San Francisco in the 1950s was the gathering place for a group, later known as the Beats (or "Beat Generation"), that included Jack Kerouac and Allen Ginsberg. The City Lights Bookshop, owned by poet Lawrence Ferlinghetti, was the site of readings by Beat poets during this period.

A California law, effective 1 January 1977, was the first in the nation to provide living artists with royalties on the profitable resale of their work. From 1987 to

1991, aid to the arts amounted to $157,039,489. In this four-year period, arts programs in California reached audiences totaling 740,015,000 people. By 1991, arts associations in California numbered 1,400 with 230 local programs for the promotion of the arts.

[34] LIBRARIES AND MUSEUMS

As of 1990/91, California had 168 main public libraries and 284 academic libraries that held a total of 70.6 million volumes. In 1990/91, the book stock was nearly 50 million volumes. Circulation of all library materials in 1990/91 totaled 150,546,359.

California has three of the largest public library systems in the nation, along with some of the country's finest private collections. The Los Angeles Public Library System had 5,500,000 volumes in 1990/91; the San Francisco Public Library, 2,008,169; and the San Diego Public Library, 1,693,184. Outstanding among academic libraries is the University of California's library at Berkeley, with its Bancroft collection of western Americana.

California has nearly 500 museums and 50 public gardens. Outstanding museums include the California Museum of Science and Industry, Los Angeles County Museum of Art, and Natural History Museum, all in Los Angeles; San Francisco's Museum of Modern Art, Fine Arts Museum, and Asian Art Museum; the San Diego Museum of Man; the California State Indian Museum in Sacramento; the Norton Simon Museum in Pasadena; and the J. Paul Getty Museum at Malibu.

[35] COMMUNICATIONS

The state's first radio broadcasting station, KQW in San Jose, began broadcasting speech and music on an experimental basis in 1912. California stations pioneered in program development with the earliest audience-participation show (1922) and the first "soap opera," *One Man's Family* (1932).

California ranks first in the US in the number of commercial television stations. In 1993 there were 247 AM and 421 FM radio stations and 103 television stations (including 17 public stations). Los Angeles is the home of the Pacifica Foundation, which operated 6 listener-sponsored FM radio stations (2 in Berkeley, 1 in Los Angeles, and 3 outside the state). Affiliates of the Public Broadcasting System serve Los Angeles, San Francisco, and Sacramento. In 1993, 86 large systems provided cable television service. California has more telephones than any other state. In March 1993, 95.4% of the state's 11,187,000 occupied housing units had telephones.

[36] PRESS

California's newspapers rank first in number and second in circulation among the 50 states. Los Angeles publishes one of the nation's most influential dailies, the *Los Angeles Times,* and San Francisco has long been the heart of the influential Hearst newspaper chain.

In 1994 there were 64 morning dailies and 55 evening dailies, plus 69 Sunday newspapers. The *Los Angeles Times* is the only California paper whose daily circulation exceeds 1 million. California's leading newspapers, with 1994 daily circulation figures are the *Los Angeles Times* (1,164,388); the *San Francisco Chronicle* (570,304); the *San Diego Union Tribune* (406,860); and the *Sacramento Bee* (273,844).

California has more book publishers—about 225—than any state except New York. Among the many magazines published in the state are *Architectural Digest, Bon Appetit, Motor Trend, PC World, Runner's World,* and *Sierra.*

37 TOURISM, TRAVEL, AND RECREATION

California's scenic wonders attract millions of state residents, out-of-state visitors, and foreign tourists each year. Mexico provides about 23.8% of the state's international tourists, and Canada, 13%. California had $27 billion in receipts from tourism in 1990.

The San Francisco and Los Angeles metropolitan areas offer the most popular tourist attractions. San Francisco's Fisherman's Wharf, Chinatown, and Ghirardelli Square are popular for shopping and dining. Tourists also frequent the city's unique cable cars, splendid museums, Opera House, and Golden Gate Bridge. The Golden Gate National Recreation Area comprises 68 square miles (176 square kilometers) on both sides of the entrance to San Francisco Bay and includes the National Maritime Museum with seven historic ships, and the Muir Woods, located 17 miles (27 kilometers) north of the city.

The Los Angeles area has the state's principal tourist attractions. These include the Disneyland amusement center at Anaheim, and Hollywood, which features visits to motion-picture and television studios and sight-seeing tours of film stars' homes in Beverly Hills. One of Hollywood's most popular spots is Mann's (formerly Grauman's) Chinese Theater, where the impressions of famous movie stars' hands and feet (and sometimes paws or hooves) are embedded in concrete. Southwest of Hollywood, the Santa Monica Mountain National Recreation Area was created by Congress in 1978 as the country's largest urban park, covering 150,000 acres (61,000 hectares).

The rest of the state offers numerous tourist attractions. These include Redwood, Yosemite, and Sequoia national parks—some of the largest and most beautiful parks in the US—and Lake Tahoe, on the Nevada border.

38 SPORTS

There are sixteen major league professional sports teams in California, more than in any other state. The state's five baseball teams are the Los Angeles Dodgers, the San Francisco Giants, the San Diego Padres, the Oakland Athletics, and the California Angels. Football teams are the Oakland Raiders, the San Francisco 49ers, and the San Diego Chargers. Basketball teams are the Los Angeles Lakers, the Los Angeles Clippers, the Golden State Warriors, and the Sacramento Kings. In hockey, there are the Los Angeles Kings, the Anaheim Mighty Ducks, and the San Jose Sharks.

Another popular professional sport is horse racing at such well-known tracks as Santa Anita and Hollywood Park. Because of the moderate climate, there is racing practically year round.

California's collegiate teams have been very successful. The University of Southern California's baseball team won five consecutive national championships between 1970 and 1974. The UCLA basketball team won 10 NCAA titles.

39 FAMOUS CALIFORNIANS

Richard Milhous Nixon (1913–94) is the only native-born Californian ever elected to the presidency. Elected to his first term in 1968, he scored a resounding reelection victory four years later, but within a year his administration was beset by the Watergate scandal. On 9 August 1974, after the House Judiciary Committee had voted articles of impeachment, Nixon became the first president ever to resign the office.

The nation's 31st president, Herbert Hoover (b.Iowa, 1874–1964), moved to California as a young man. Former film actor Ronald Reagan (b.Illinois, 1911) served two terms as state governor (1967–75) before becoming president in 1981. He was elected to a second presidential term in 1984.

In 1953, Earl Warren (1891–1974) became the first Californian to serve as chief justice of the US Supreme Court (1953–69). Warren, a native of Los Angeles, was elected three times to the California governorship and served in that office (1943–53) longer than any other person.

Californians have won Nobel Prizes in several categories. Linus Pauling (b.Oregon, 1901–94) won the Nobel Prize for chemistry in 1954 and the Nobel Peace Prize in 1962. Members of the Berkeley faculty who have won the Nobel Prize for physics include Ernest Orlando Lawrence (b.South Dakota, 1901–58), in 1939; and Luis W. Alvarez (1911–88), in 1968. Stanford professor William Shockley (b.England, 1910–89) shared the physics prize with two others in 1956. The only native-born Californian to win the Nobel Prize for literature was novelist John Steinbeck (1902–68), in 1962.

Other prominent California scientists are world-famous horticulturist Luther Burbank (b.Massachusetts, 1849–1926) and nuclear physicist Edward Teller (b.Hungary, 1908). Naturalist John Muir (b.Scotland, 1838–1914) fought for the establishment of Yosemite National Park. The best-known contemporary labor leader in California is César Chávez (b.Arizona, 1927–93).

California's long-standing dominance in the aerospace industry is a product of the efforts of such native Californians as John Northrop (1895–1981) and self-taught aviator Allen Lockheed (1889–1969). Leaders of the state's world-famous wine and grape-growing industry include immigrant Paul Masson (b.France, 1859–1940), as well as two Modesto natives, Ernest (b.1910) and Julio (1911–93) Gallo. It was at the mill of John Sutter (b.Germany, 1803–80) that gold was discovered in 1848.

'Olympiad 1984' sculpture in front of Stuart Ketchum Hall in Los Angeles.

The leading figure among the state's newspaper editors and publishers was William Randolph Hearst (1863–1951), whose publishing empire began with the *San Francisco Examiner*. Pioneers of the state's electronics industry include David Packard (b.Colorado, 1912) and William R. Hewlett (b.Michigan, 1913). Stephen Wozniak (b.1950) and Steven Jobs (b.1955) were cofounders of Apple Computer. Other prominent business leaders include clothier Levi Strauss (b.Germany, 1830–1902) and cosmetics manufacturer Max Factor (b.Poland, 1877–1938).

California has been home to a great many creative artists. Native California writers include John Steinbeck, adventure writer Jack London (1876–1916), novelist and dramatist William Saroyan (1908–81), and novelist-essayist Joan Didion (b.1934). One California-born writer whose life and works were divorced from his place of birth was Robert Frost (1874–1963), a native of San Francisco.

Important composers who have lived and worked in California include native John Cage (1912–92), and immigrants Arnold Schoenberg (b.Austria, 1874–1951) and Igor Stravinsky (b.Russia, 1882–1971). Immigrant painters include landscape artist Albert Bierstadt (b.Germany, 1830–1902), as well as abstract painter Hans Hofmann (b.Germany, 1880–1966). Contemporary artists working in California include Berkeley-born Elmer Bischoff (b.1916) and Richard Diebenkorn (b.Oregon, 1922–93). San Francisco native Ansel Adams (1902–84) is the best known of a long line of California photographers.

Many of the world's finest performing artists have also been Californians: violinists Yehudi Menuhin (b.New York, 1916) and Isaac Stern (b.Russia, 1920) both grew up in the state. Another master violinist, Jascha Heifetz (b.Russia, 1901–84), made his home in Beverly Hills. California jazz musicians include Dave Brubeck (b.1920).

Native Californians on the screen include child actress Shirley Temple (Mrs. Charles A. Black, b.1928) and such greats as Marilyn Monroe (Norma Jean Baker, 1926–62). Other longtime residents of the state include John Wayne (Marion Michael Morrison, b.Iowa, 1907–79), Bette Davis (b.Massachusetts, 1908–89), and Clark Gable (b.Ohio, 1901–60). Contemporary actors born in California include Clint Eastwood (b.1930), Robert Duvall (b.1931), Robert Redford (b.1937), Kevin Costner (b.1955), and Dustin Hoffman (b. 1937).

Hollywood has also been the center for such pioneer film producers and directors as Cecil B. DeMille (b.Massachusetts, 1881–1959), Samuel Goldwyn (b.Poland, 1882–1974), and master animator Walt Disney (b.Illinois, 1901–66).

California-born athletes have excelled in every professional sport. A representative sampling includes Baseball Hall of Famer Joe DiMaggio (b.1914), along with Richard A. "Pancho" Gonzales (1928–95) and Billie Jean (Moffitt) King (b.1943) in tennis, Frank Gifford (b.1930) in football, and Mark Spitz (b.1950) in swimming. Robert B. "Bob" Mathias (b.1930) won the gold medal in the decathlon at the 1948 and 1952 Olympic Games.

40 BIBLIOGRAPHY

Caughey, John W. *California: A Remarkable State's Life-History. 4th ed.* Englewood Cliffs. N.J.: Prentice-Hall, 1982.

Davie, Michael. *California: The Vanishing Dream.* New York: Dodd Mead, 1972.

Jackson, Donald Dale. *Gold Dust.* New York Knopf, 1980.

Lavender, David. *California: A Bicentennial History.* New York: Norton, 1976.

Muir, John. *Mountains of California.* New York: Penguin, 1985.

Rawls, James J. *Indians of California: The Changing Image.* Norman: University of Oakland, 1984.

Robinson, W. W. *Los Angeles: From the Days of the Pueblo.* San Francisco: California Press, 1979.

Watkins, T. H. *California: An Illustrated History.* New York: Outlet, 1983.

COLORADO

State of Colorado

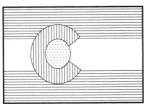

ORIGIN OF STATE NAME: From the Spanish word *colorado,* meaning red or reddish brown. The Colorado River often runs red during flood stages.

NICKNAME: The Centennial State.

CAPITAL: Denver.

ENTERED UNION: 1 August 1876 (38th).

SONG: "Where the Columbines Grow."

MOTTO: *Nil sine numine* (Nothing without providence).

COAT OF ARMS: The upper portion of a heraldic shield shows three snow-capped mountains surrounded by clouds; the lower portion has a miner's pick and shovel, crossed. Above the shield are an eye of God and a Roman fasces, symbolizing the republican form of government; the state motto is below.

FLAG: Superimposed on three equal horizontal bands of blue, white, and blue is a large red "C" encircling a golden disk.

OFFICIAL SEAL: The coat of arms surrounded by the words "State of Colorado 1876."

ANIMAL: Rocky Mountain bighorn sheep.

BIRD: Lark bunting.

FISH: Greenback cutthroat trout.

FLOWER: Rocky Mountain columbine.

TREE: Colorado blue spruce.

GEM: Aquamarine.

TIME: 5 AM MST = noon GMT.

1 LOCATION AND SIZE

Located in the Rocky Mountain region of the US, Colorado ranks eighth in size among the 50 states. The state's total area is 104,091 square miles (269,596 square kilometers). Shaped in an almost perfect rectangle, Colorado extends 387 miles (623 kilometers) east-west and 276 miles (444 kilometers) north-south. The total length of Colorado's boundaries is 1,307 miles (2,103 kilometers).

2 TOPOGRAPHY

With a mean average elevation of 6,800 feet (2,100 meters), Colorado is the nation's highest state. Dominating the state are the Rocky Mountains. Colorado has 54 peaks that are 14,000 feet (4,300 meters) or higher, including Pikes Peak, at 14,110 feet (4,301 meters). The eastern third of the state is part of the western Great Plains and contains Colorado's lowest point, 3,350 feet (1,021 meters). Slightly west of the state's geographic center is the Continental Divide, which separates the Rockies into the Eastern and Western slopes. South of the Front Range, crossing into New Mexico, is the Sangre de Cristo Range. Colorado's western region is mostly mesa country—broad, flat plateaus accented by deep ravines and gorges.

Blue Mesa Reservoir in Gunnison County is Colorado's largest lake. The Colorado River runs southwest from the Rockies to Utah. Five other major river systems originate in Colorado: the South Platte; the North Platte; the Rio Grande; the Arkansas; and the Republican. Eighteen hot springs are still active in Colorado; the largest is at Pagosa Springs.

3 CLIMATE

Colorado has a highland continental climate. Winters are generally cold and snowy; summers are characterized by warm, dry days and cool nights. The average annual temperature statewide ranges from 54°F (12°C) at Lamar and at John Martin Dam to about 32°F (0°C) at the top of the Continental Divide. Bennett recorded the highest temperature in Colorado, 118°F (48°C), on 11 July 1888; the record low was –61°F (–52°C), in Moffat County on 1 February 1985. Annual precipitation ranges from a low of 7 inches (18 centimeters) in Alamosa to a high of 25 inches (64 centimeters) in Crested Butte. The average annual precipitation statewide is 16.5 inches.

4 PLANTS AND ANIMALS

Colorado has a variety of vegetation, distributed among five zones: plains, foothills,

Colorado Population Profile

Estimated 1995 population:	
Population change, 1980–90:	14.0%
Leading ancestry group:	German
Second leading group:	English
Foreign born population:	4.3%
Hispanic origin†:	12.9%
Population by race:	
White:	88.2%
Black:	4.0%
Native American:	0.8%
Asian/Pacific Islander:	1.8%
Other:	5.2%

Population by Age Group

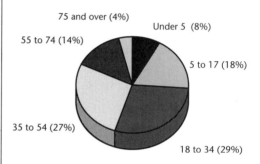

75 and over (4%)
Under 5 (8%)
55 to 74 (14%)
5 to 17 (18%)
35 to 54 (27%)
18 to 34 (29%)

Top Cities with Populations Over 25,000

City	Population	National rank	% change 1980–90
Denver	483,852	27	–5.0
Colorado Springs	295,815	53	30.7
Aurora	239,626	66	40.1
Lakewood	125,957	147	12.1
Pueblo	98,552	205	–3.0
Fort Collins	93,335	225	34.8
Arvada	93,330	226	5.5
Boulder	85,616	253	8.6
Westminster	80,721	280	48.7
Greeley	61,774	390	14.2

Notes: †A person of Hispanic origin may be of any race. NA indicates that data are not available.
Sources: Economic and Statistics Administration, Bureau of the Census. *Statistical Abstract of the United States, 1994–95.* Washington, DC: Government Printing Office, 1995; Courtenay M. Slater and George E. Hall. *1995 County and City Extra: Annual Metro, City and County Data Book.* Lanham, MD: Bernan Press, 1995.

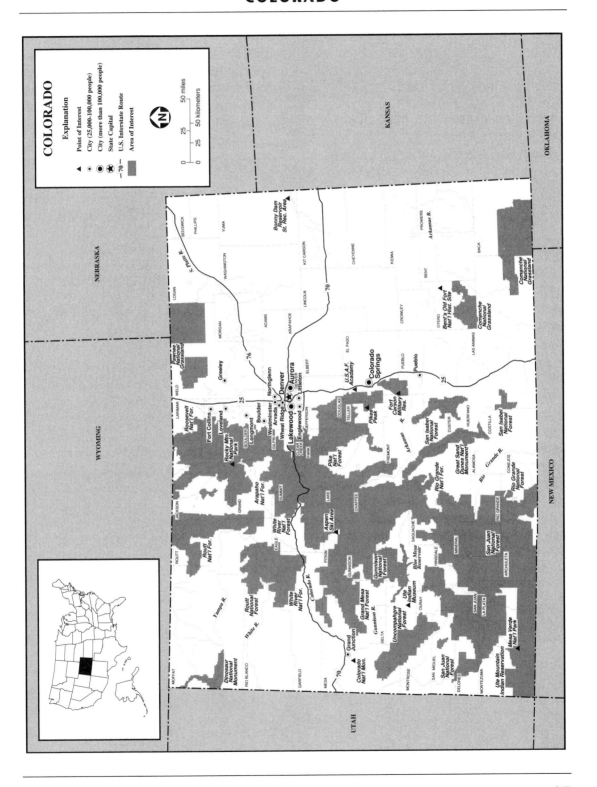

Denver skyline and the city park.

montane, subalpine, and alpine. The plains teem with grasses and as many as 500 types of wildflowers. Arid regions contain two dozen varieties of cacti. Aspen and Engelmann spruce are found up to the timberline.

Colorado has 747 nongame wildlife species and 113 sport-game species. Principal big-game species include the elk, mountain lion, and Rocky Mountain bighorn sheep (the state animal). The lark bunting is the state bird. Colorado has about 100 sport-fish species. The greater prairie chicken, Canada lynx, wolverine, river otter, and bonytail are among endangered species.

5 ENVIRONMENTAL PROTECTION

Air pollution, water supply problems, and hazardous wastes head the list of Colorado's current environmental concerns. A motor vehicle emissions inspection system was inaugurated in January 1982 for gasoline-powered vehicles and in January 1985 for diesel-powered vehicles. Cars must use oxygenated fuels and pass tough vehicle emissions controls, and driving is discouraged on high pollution days. The use of woodburning fireplaces is banned in some cities during high pollution days. Some 98% of Colorado's drinking water complies with federal and state standards.

There are 18 hazardous waste sites in the state.

6 POPULATION

Colorado was the 30th most populous state in 1990. The 1990 census population was 3,294,394; 81.5% of that population lived in metropolitan areas. The population density in 1990 was 31 persons per square mile (12 persons per square kilometer). The estimated median age in 1990 was 32.2 years. The population in the year 2000 is projected to be 3,424,000.

Denver is the state's largest city. Its 1992 population was 483,852, but its metropolitan area encompassed over 1,900,000. Other major cities, with their 1992 population figures, are Colorado Springs, 295,815; Aurora, 239,626; and Lakewood, 125,957.

7 ETHNIC GROUPS

Native Americans in 1990 numbered 28,000, including 303 Eskimos and 67 Aleuts. The black population is also small, 4% (the figure for Denver, however, was 12.8%). Hispanic residents numbered 424,000, comprising nearly 13% of the population. Of over 60,000 Asians and Pacific Islanders, 15,198 were Japanese; 12,490, Korean; 6,679, Vietnamese; 9,117, Chinese; and 7,270, Filipino.

8 LANGUAGES

Colorado English is a mixture of the Northern and Midland dialects. In the southern half of the state, the large Hispanic population has introduced many Spanish words, such as *penco* (pet lamb), into the language. About 2.7 million Coloradans—89% of the residents five years old and older—speak only English at home.

9 RELIGIONS

Roman Catholics comprise the single largest religious group in the state, with over 483,000 adherents. The largest Protestant denomination is the United Methodist Church, with 91,310 members. Other major denominations include Southern Baptist, 81,627; Presbyterian, 50,831; Church of Jesus Christ of Latter-day Saints (Mormon), 70,313; Lutheran Church–Missouri Synod, 47,262; and Episcopal, 36,119. According to recent estimates, there are 48,550 Jews in Colorado, nearly all in the Denver area.

10 TRANSPORTATION

As the hub of the Rocky Mountain states, Colorado maintains extensive road and rail systems. As of 1992 there were 3,079 rail miles (4,954 kilometers) of track in the state. Amtrak trains in Colorado had 302,362 riders in 1992. Colorado's extensive network of roads includes 29 mountain passes. As of 1993 there were 12,903 miles (20,761 kilometers) of municipal roads and 65,818 miles (105,901 kilometers) of rural roads. Of the 3,032,088 motor vehicles registered in 1993, 2,253,697 were automobiles; 772,825, trucks; and 5,566, buses.

A total of 209 public and private airfields served the state in 1991. Stapleton International Airport in Denver was the state's busiest. In 1991, it handled 12,313,733 departing passengers and 110,974 tons of cargo. As of 1994, Denver

Cliff Palace, Mesa Verde.

International Airport replaced Stapleton as the state's main passenger airport. Passenger travel at the new airport, located about 15 miles northeast of Stapleton, has decreased due mainly to the closing of several airlines.

11 HISTORY

By AD 800 there were tribes of Pueblos in present-day Colorado, who practiced advanced forms of agriculture and pottery making. From the 11th through the 13th centuries, the Pueblos constructed elaborate apartment-like dwellings in the cliffs of the Colorado canyons and planted their crops both on the mesa tops and in the surrounding valleys.

The explorer Juan de Onate is believed to have traveled into the southeastern area in 1601. In 1706, Juan de Uribarri claimed southeastern Colorado for Spain, joining it with New Mexico. Meanwhile, the French had claimed most of the area east of the Rocky Mountains. In 1763, France formally ceded the Louisiana Territory to Spain, which returned it to the French in 1801. Two years later, as part of the Louisiana Purchase, Colorado east of the Rockies became US land; the rest of Colorado still belonged to Spain.

Eastern Colorado remained a wilderness for the next few decades, although traders and scouts like Kit Carson did venture into the largely uncharted land, establishing friendly relations with the Indians. Between 1842 and 1853, John C. Frémont led five expeditions into the region, the first three for the US government. Western and southern Colorado came into US possession after the Mexican War (1846–48).

The magnet that drew many Americans to Colorado was the greatly exaggerated report of a gold strike in Cherry Creek (present-day Denver) in July 1858. The subsequent boom led to the founding of such mining towns as Boulder, Colorado City, Central City, and Gold Hill. By 1860, the population exceeded 30,000. A bill to organize the Territory of Colorado was passed by the US Congress on 28 February 1861. Colorado sided with the Union during the Civil War, though some settlers fought for the Confederacy.

The 1860s also saw the most serious conflict between Indians and white settlers in Colorado history. After ceding most of their tribal holdings to the US government, the Cheyenne and Arapaho, unsuccessful at farming, resumed a nomadic lifestyle. They hunted buffalo, raided towns, and attacked travelers along the Overland and Sante Fe trails. On 29 November, US military forces under the command of Colonel John Chivington brutally massacred as many as 200 Native Americans near their reservation in the Arkansas Valley.

Statehood

Colorado entered the Union as the 38th state on 1 August 1876, during the presidency of Ulysses S. Grant. In the early years of statehood, silver strikes at Leadville and Aspen brought settlers and money into Colorado. Rail lines, smelters, and refineries were built, and large coalfields were opened up. The High Plains attracted new farmers, and another new industry—tourism—emerged. As early as the 1860s, resorts had opened near some of the state's mineral springs.

Colorado's boom years ended with a depression during the early 1890s, when the silver market declined. By the dawn of the 20th century, farmers were returning to the land. The development of the automobile and the advent of good roads opened up more of the mountain areas, bringing a big boom in tourism by the 1920s.

From 1920 to 1940, statewide employment declined, and population growth lagged behind that of the US as a whole. World War II brought military training camps, airfields, and jobs to the state. After the war, the placement of both the North American Air Defense Command and the US Air Force Academy in Colorado Springs helped stimulate the growth of defense, federal research, and aerospace-related industries in the state.

As these and other industries grew, so too did Colorado's population and income. Between 1960 and 1983, the state's population growth rate was more than twice that of the nation as a whole; and between 1970 and 1983, Colorado moved from 18th to 9th rank among the states in income per capita (per person). In the 1970s and early 1980s, Colorado experienced a boom in its oil, mining, and electronics industries. The economy began to shrink, however, in the mid-1980s with the drop in oil prices and the closing of mines. Business starts declined by 23% between 1987 and 1988.

12 STATE GOVERNMENT

Colorado's general assembly, which meets annually, consists of a 35-member senate and 65-member house of representatives. There is no constitutional limit to the length of a session, and the legislature may call special sessions by request of two-thirds of the members of each house.

The executive branch is headed by the governor, who submits the budget and legislative programs to the general assembly, and appoints judges, department heads, boards, and commissions. Elected with the governor is the lieutenant governor, who assumes the governor's duties in the governor's absence.

Bills may originate in either house of the general assembly and become law when passed by majority vote of each house and signed by the governor. A bill may also become law if the governor fails to act on it within 10 days after receiving it. A two-thirds vote in each house is needed to override a gubernatorial veto.

13 POLITICAL PARTIES

The Republicans controlled most statewide offices prior to 1900. Since then, the parties have been more evenly balanced. Of the 2,003,379 registered voters in 1994, 680,777 (34%) were Democrats; 668,051 (33%) were Republicans; and 654,551 (33%) were unaffiliated. Following the

Colorado Presidential Vote by Political Parties, 1948–92

YEAR	COLORADO WINNER	DEMOCRAT	REPUBLICAN	PROGRESSIVE	SOCIALIST	SOC. LABOR
1948	*Truman (D)	267,288	239,714	6,115	1,678	—
					CONSTITUTION	
1952	*Eisenhower (R)	245,504	379,782	1,919	2,181	—
1956	*Eisenhower (R)	263,997	394,479	—	759	3,308
					SOC. WORKERS	
1960	Nixon (R)	330,629	402,242	—	563	2,803
1964	*Johnson (D)	476,024	296,767	—	2,537	—
				AMERICAN IND.		
1968	*Nixon (R)	335,174	409,345	60,813	235	3,016
				AMERICAN		
1972	*Nixon (R)	329,980	597,189	17,269	666	4,361
						LIBERTARIAN
1976	Ford (R)	460,801	584,278	397	1,122	5,338
				STATESMAN	CITIZENS	
1980	*Reagan (R)	368,009	652,264	1,180	5,614	25,744
1984	Reagan (R)	454,975	821,817	NEW ALLIANCE	—	11,257
1988	*Bush (R)	621,453	728,177	2,491	—	15,482
				IND. (Perot)		
1992	*Clinton (D)	629,681	562,850	366,010	1,608	—

* Won US presidential election.

November 1994 election, the state had one Democratic and one Republican US senator, and four Republican and two Democratic US representatives.

The Republicans control the state senate (19 Republicans to 16 Democrats). The state house is split, with 31 representatives from each party. Colorado's governor, Democrat Roy Romer, was elected to a four-year term in 1990 and was re-elected in 1994. In 1992, 40% of all Coloradan voters cast their ballots for Democrat Bill Clinton; Republican George Bush won 36% of the vote; Independent Ross Perot received 23% of the vote. Republican Hank Brown was elected Senator in 1990, and Ben Nighthorse Campbell, a Native American, was elected Senator in 1992.

14 LOCAL GOVERNMENT

As of 1992 there were 62 counties (63, including the consolidated city/county of Denver), 266 municipal governments, cities, towns, and designated places, and 180 school districts. The administrative and policymaking body in each county is the board of county commissioners. Other county officials include the county clerk, treasurer, assessor, sheriff, coroner, superintendent of schools, surveyor, and attorney.

Statutory cities are those whose structure is defined by the state constitution. Power is delegated by the general assembly to either a council-manager or mayor-council form of government. Towns, which generally have fewer than 2,000 residents, are governed by a mayor and a six-member board of trustees.

Denver, the only city in Colorado that is also a county, exercises the powers of both levels of government. It is run by a mayor and city council. A city auditor, independently elected, serves as a check on the mayor.

15 JUDICIAL SYSTEM

The supreme court, the highest court in Colorado, consists of seven justices elected on a nonpartisan ballot. The next highest court, the court of appeals, consists of ten judges and is confined to civil matters. The 22 district courts have original jurisdiction in civil, criminal, juvenile, mental health, domestic relations, and probate cases, except in Denver. There, probate and mental health matters are heard by the probate court and all juvenile matters by the juvenile court.

County courts hear minor civil disputes and misdemeanors. Appeals from the Denver county courts are heard in Denver's superior court. Municipal courts throughout the state handle violations of municipal ordinances. Colorado's FBI Crime Index crime rate in 1994 was 5,318.4 per 100,000 people.

16 MIGRATION

Since the end of World War II, net migration into the state has been substantial, amounting to over 880,000 between 1950 and 1990. The largest increase has been in the Denver metropolitan area. A number of migrant workers, mostly Mexican Americans, work seasonally in the western orchards and fields. In the 1980s, migration accounted for 27% of the net population increase, with some 117,000 persons.

In 1990, native Coloradans made up 43.3% of the population.

17 ECONOMY

With its abundant reserves of coal, natural gas, and other minerals—and the economic potential of its vast oil-shale deposits—Colorado is a major mining state, although the mineral industry's share of the state economy has declined throughout this century. Trade is the leading source of employment, while manufacturing (fourth in employment) is the principal contributor to the gross state product. The US government employed 105,000 civilian and military personnel in the state in 1993.

18 INCOME

In 1994, Colorado ranked 15th among the 50 states in per capita (per person) income, with $22,320. Total personal income in 1994 reached $81.59 billion. About 9.9% of all Coloradans were below the federal poverty level in 1993.

19 INDUSTRY

Accounting for an estimated 11% of all nonagricultural employment in 1993, manufacturing is a major segment of the economy. Colorado is the main manufacturing center of the Rocky Mountain states. The major industries are food and food products; printing and publishing; nonelectric machinery; instruments and related products; electric and electronic equipment; fabricated metal products; transportation equipment; and chemicals and petroleum.

High-technology research and manufacturing grew notably in Colorado during the 1980s and early 1990s. Storage Technology in Louisville is the largest high-tech company with headquarters in the state, but many large out-of-state companies—including Apple Computer, IBM, Hewlett-Packard, Eastman Kodak, Digital Equipment, and MCI Telecommunications—have divisions there.

20 LABOR

In 1994, an average of 1,996,000 Coloradans were employed in the civilian labor force; some 10.9% were union members. Colorado's leading areas of employment in 1992 were services (27.7%); wholesale and retail trade (24%); government jobs (18%); and manufacturing (11.6%).

21 AGRICULTURE

Colorado ranked 17th among the 50 states in agricultural income in 1994, at over $4 billion. Estimated total crop marketings for 1994 exceeded $1.2 billion. As of 1994, there were about 25,300 farms and ranches covering about 32.8 million acres (13 million hectares). Colorado's 1994 agricultural output (and national rankings) included potatoes, 2,872 million pounds (3d); onions, 612.5 million pounds (5th); sunflowers, 96.3 million pounds (5th); pears, 4,000 tons (7th); and wheat, 79,734,000 bushels (8th). Weld County accounted for about 28.7% of the state's agricultural receipts in 1992.

22 DOMESTICATED ANIMALS

A leading sheep-producing state, Colorado is also a major area for cattle and other livestock. Receipts for livestock and products amounted to over $2.7 billion in 1994. Cattle production accounted for 55.4% of Colorado's agricultural receipts in 1994, or 6.1% of the national total. Dairy products contributed 5.3% to the state's agricultural receipts that year. Colorado had 2,950,000 cattle and 545,000 sheep at the beginning of 1995.

23 FISHING

There is practically no commercial fishing in Colorado. Warm-water lakes lure the state's sport anglers with perch, black bass, and trout, while walleyes are abundant in mountain streams. In 1992, federal hatcheries distributed 2.2 million cold water and 1.2 million warm water species of fish and roe (fish eggs) within the state.

24 FORESTRY

Although approximately 22,271,000 acres (9,013,000 hectares) of forested lands are located in Colorado, commercial forestry is not a major element of the state's economy.

25 MINING

According to the US Bureau of Mines estimates, the value of 1994 nonfuel mineral production was about $440 million. In 1992, Colorado mined 40,000,000 short tons of sand and gravel; 11,500,000 short tons of crushed stone; 2,073 kilograms of gold; and 251,674 metric tons of clay. Production of construction sand and gravel constitutes nearly 35% of the total value of nonfuel mineral production in Colorado.

26 ENERGY AND POWER

An abundant supply of coal, oil, and natural gas makes Colorado a major energy-producing state. During 1993, 32.7 billion kilowatt hours of electricity were generated in Colorado, about 93% of that in coal-fired plants; installed capacity was 6.6 million kilowatts. Petroleum production in 1993 was 30.6 million barrels; natural gas production in 1993 was 360 billion cubic feet.

Colorado's coal output was 20.4 million short tons in 1993. Colorado holds the major portion of the nation's proved oil shale reserves. Because of its ample sunshine, Colorado is also well suited to solar energy development.

27 COMMERCE

Colorado is the leading wholesale and retail distribution center for the Rocky Mountain states. Sales from wholesale trade totaled $46.9 billion in 1992; retail sales totaled $33.3 billion in 1993, a 9.9% increase over 1992. Service establishment receipts totaled $21 billion in 1992.

28 PUBLIC FINANCE

In 1992 Colorado's citizens passed a constitutional amendment, entitled the Taxpayer's Bill of Rights (TABOR), that restricts state expenditures, based on population growth and inflation. The amendment also requires a vote of the people for any new or increased taxes. Revenues for the 1993/94 general fund budget were $3,570.8 million, and expenditures were $3,559.6 million. Colorado's outstanding debt totaled $3.1 billion or $875 per capita.

29 TAXATION

As of 1994, Colorado's state income tax had a flat rate of 5.0%. The state also imposed a 3% sales and use tax, along with taxes on cigarettes, alcoholic beverages, racing, fossil fuel production, motor fuel sales, and insurance premiums. Colorado municipalities are also allowed to levy sales and use taxes. In 1990, Colorado ranked 22d in federal income taxes paid, with almost $6.3 billion. In 1994 Colorado received $19 billion in federal funds or over $5,000 per capita (per person).

30 HEALTH

Death rates for heart disease, cancer, and cerebrovascular diseases are far below the US norm, while those for accidents are about the same. The suicide rate of 16.7 per 100,000 is considerably higher than the US rate of 12.2. In 1993, Colorado had 72 accredited hospitals, with 10,300 beds. In 1993, the average cost per inpatient day in hospitals providing services in Colorado was $961. The state had 7,830 nonfederal physicians in 1993 and 26,697 nurses. Over 12% of Colorado's population does not have health insurance.

31 HOUSING

In July 1993, there were an estimated 1,522,000 year-round housing units, an increase of nearly 30% from 1980. In 1993, 29,913 new privately-owned housing units were authorized. The Denver-Boulder area is Colorado's primary region of housing growth, with some 23,000 housing units completed from 1990 to 1992. In 1990, the median home value was $82,700.

32 EDUCATION

Colorado residents are better educated than the average American. According to the 1990 census, 27.0% of the adult population of Colorado had completed four years of college, ranking first among the 50 states. Almost 84.5% of all adult Coloradans were high school graduates (third in the US). Colorado spends an average of $5,050 per pupil on primary and secondary education.

In fall 1993, Colorado's public elementary and secondary schools had 626,000 pupils. There were 33,093 elementary and secondary school teachers that year, with an average salary of $31,819. More than 214,000 students were enrolled in 35 colleges and universities. These include the Colorado School of Mines; the University of Colorado (Boulder), the largest university in the state; Colorado State University; and the University of Denver. The US Air Force Academy is located in Colorado Springs.

33 ARTS

Arts organizations include the Colorado Springs Symphony and Colorado Opera Festival of Colorado Springs; the Central City Opera House Association; and the Four Corners Opera Association in Durango. Aspen is an internationally renowned center for classical music performance and education. From 1987 to 1991, Colorado generated $14,591,462 in federal and state funds for the development of the arts.

34 LIBRARIES AND MUSEUMS

Public libraries in the state hold nearly 9.2 million volumes and circulate more than 24 million. The largest system is the Denver Public Library with 2,253,096 million volumes in 21 branches. The leading academic library is at the University of Colorado at Boulder, with nearly 2.5 million volumes.

Colorado has more than 150 museums and historic sites. One of the most prominent museums in the West is the Denver Art Museum, with its large collection of Native American, South Seas, and Oriental art. Another major art museum is the Colorado Springs Fine Arts Center, specializing in southwestern and western American art.

35 COMMUNICATIONS

Over 96% of the state's 1,363,000 occupied housing units had telephones as of March 1993. Of the 182 radio stations in operation in 1993, 76 were AM and 106 were FM. There were 24 commercial and 4 educational television stations. Nine large cable television systems also were in operation that year.

36 PRESS

As of 1994, there were 10 morning dailies, 19 afternoon dailies, and 12 Sunday papers. The leading newspapers were the *Rocky Mountain News,* with a circulation of 374,009 in the mornings and 432,502 on Sundays; and the *Denver Post,* 252,624 mornings and 417,779 Sundays.

Photo credit: Denver Metro Convention & Visitors Bureau.

Tyrannosaurus rex in the Denver Museum of Natural History.

37 TOURISM, TRAVEL, AND RECREATION

Scenery, history, and skiing combine to make Colorado a prime tourist mecca. Annually, travel and tourism generate over $6 billion in expenditures in the state. Vail and Aspen are popular ski resort centers. Colorado has over 25 ski areas. Skiing is in season from mid-November through late March. The US Air Force Academy near Colorado Springs is a popular tourist attraction, as is nearby Pikes Peak. Besides its many museums, parks, and rebuilt Larimer Square district, Denver's main attraction is the US Mint. All nine national forests in Colorado are open for camping, as are the state's two national parks: Rocky Mountain and Mesa Verde. These two parks attracted 3.1 million visitors in 1994.

38 SPORTS

There are four major league professional sports teams in Colorado, all in Denver: the Broncos of the National Football League, the Nuggets of the National Basketball Association, and the Colorado Rockies of Major League Baseball, an expansion team which began play in the 1993 season. In 1995, the Québec Nordiques of the National Hockey League moved to Colorado and became the Denver Avalanche. The Buffaloes of the University of Colorado produced some excellent football teams in the late 1980s and early 1990s and were named national Champions in 1990 (with Georgia Tech).

39 FAMOUS COLORADANS

Fort Collins was the birthplace of Byron R. White (b.1917), an associate justice of the US Supreme Court since 1962. Gary Hart (b.Kansas, 1937) was a senator and a presidential candidate in 1984 and 1988. Early explorers of the Colorado region include Zebulon Pike (b.New Jersey, 1779–1813). Silver tycoon Horace Austin Warner Tabor (b.Vermont, 1830–99) served as mayor of Leadville and spent money on lavish buildings in Leadville and Denver. Willard F. Libby (1909–80), won the Nobel Prize for chemistry in 1960.

Among the performers born in the state were actor Lon Chaney (1883–1930) and band leader Paul Whiteman (1891–1967). Singer John Denver (Henry John Deutschendorf, Jr., b.New Mexico, 1943) lives in Aspen. Colorado's most famous sports personality is Jack Dempsey (1895–1983), who held the world heavyweight boxing crown from 1919 to 1926.

40 BIBLIOGRAPHY

Athearn, Robert G. *The Coloradans*. Albuquerque: University of New Mexico Press, 1982.

Sprague, Marshall. *Colorado: A Bicentennial History*. New York: Norton, 1976.

Ubbelohde, Carol, Maxine Benson, and Duane A. Smith. *A Colorado History*. 5th ed. Boulder: Pruett, 1982.

CONNECTICUT

State of Connecticut

ORIGIN OF STATE NAME: From the Mahican word *quinnehtukqut,* meaning "beside the long tidal river."

NICKNAME: The Constitution State (also: the Nutmeg State).

CAPITAL: Hartford.

ENTERED UNION: 9 January 1788 (5th).

SONG: "Yankee Doodle."

MOTTO: *Qui transtulit sustinet* (He who transplanted still sustains).

COAT OF ARMS: On a rococo shield, three grape vines, supported and bearing fruit, stand against a white field. Beneath the shield is a streamer bearing the state motto.

FLAG: The coat of arms appears on a blue field.

OFFICIAL SEAL: The three grape vines and motto of the arms surrounded by the words *Sigillum reipublicæ Connecticutensis* (Seal of the State of Connecticut).

ANIMAL: Sperm whale.

BIRD: American robin.

FLOWER: Mountain laurel.

TREE: White oak.

MINERAL: Garnet.

INSECT: European praying mantis.

SHIP: *USS Nautilus.*

TIME: 7 AM EST = noon GMT.

1 LOCATION AND SIZE

Located in New England in the northeastern US, Connecticut ranks 48th in size among the 50 states. The state's area is 5,018 square miles (12,997 square kilometers). Connecticut has an average length of 90 miles (145 kilometers) east-west, and an average width of 55 miles (89 kilometers) north-south. It has a boundary length of 328 miles (528 kilometers) and a shoreline of 253 miles (407 kilometers).

2 TOPOGRAPHY

Connecticut is divided into four main geographic regions: the Central Lowlands, formed by the Connecticut and Quinnipiac river valleys; the Eastern Highlands; the Western Highlands, an extension of the Green Mountains in the northwest; and the Coastal Lowlands, with good harbors at Bridgeport, New Haven, New London, Mystic, and Stonington. Mt. Frissell, near the Massachusetts border, is the highest point in the state at 2,380 feet (725 meters).

Connecticut has more than 6,000 lakes and ponds. The main river is the Connecticut, New England's longest river at 407 miles (655 kilometers). This waterway divides the state roughly in half before emptying into Long Island Sound. Other principal rivers include the Thames, Housatonic, and Naugatuck.

③ CLIMATE

Connecticut has a generally temperate climate, with mild winters and warm summers. The January mean temperature is 27°F (–3°C) and the July mean is 70°F (21°C). Coastal areas have warmer winters and cooler summers than the interior. The highest recorded temperature in Connecticut was 105°F (41°C) in Waterbury on 22 July 1926; the lowest, –32°F (–36°C) in Falls Village on 16 February 1943. The annual rainfall is about 44 to 48 inches (112 to 122 centimeters) and is evenly distributed throughout the year. The state receives some 25 to 60 inches (64 to 150 centimeters) of snow each year.

④ PLANTS AND ANIMALS

Connecticut has an impressive variety of vegetation zones. Along the shore of Long Island Sound are tidal marshes with salt grasses. On slopes fringing the marshes are black grass, switch grass, and march elder. Vegetation in the swamp areas includes various ferns, abundant cattails, and skunk cabbage. The state's hillsides and uplands support a variety of flowers and plants, including mountain laurel (the state flower), pink azalea, and Queen Anne's lace. Endangered species in the state include showy lady's slipper, ginseng, showy aster, nodding pogonia, goldenseal, climbing fern, and chaffseed.

The impact of human settlement on Connecticut wildlife has been profound, however. Only the smaller mammals—the

Connecticut Population Profile

Estimated 1995 population:	3,274,000
Population change, 1980–90:	5.8%
Leading ancestry group:	Italian
Second leading group:	Irish
Foreign born population:	8.5%
Hispanic origin†:	6.5%
Population by race:	
White:	87.1%
Black:	8.3%
Native American:	0.2%
Asian/Pacific Islander:	1.5%
Other:	2.9%

Population by Age Group

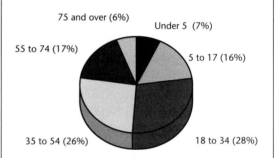

75 and over (6%)
Under 5 (7%)
55 to 74 (17%)
5 to 17 (16%)
35 to 54 (26%)
18 to 34 (28%)

Top Cities with Populations Over 25,000

City	Population	National rank	% change 1980–90
Bridgeport	137,020	137	–0.6
Hartford	131,995	143	2.5
New Haven	123,966	149	3.5
Stamford	107,590	180	5.5
Waterbury	106,904	184	5.5
Norwalk	78,528	291	0.7
New Britain	72,919	313	2.2
Danbury	65,297	367	8.5
Bristol	61,146	393	5.7
Meriden	58,585	418	4.1

Notes: †A person of Hispanic origin may be of any race. NA indicates that data are not available.
Sources: Economic and Statistics Administration, Bureau of the Census. *Statistical Abstract of the United States, 1994–95.* Washington, DC: Government Printing Office, 1995; Courtenay M. Slater and George E. Hall. *1995 County and City Extra: Annual Metro, City and County Data Book.* Lanham, MD: Bernan Press, 1995.

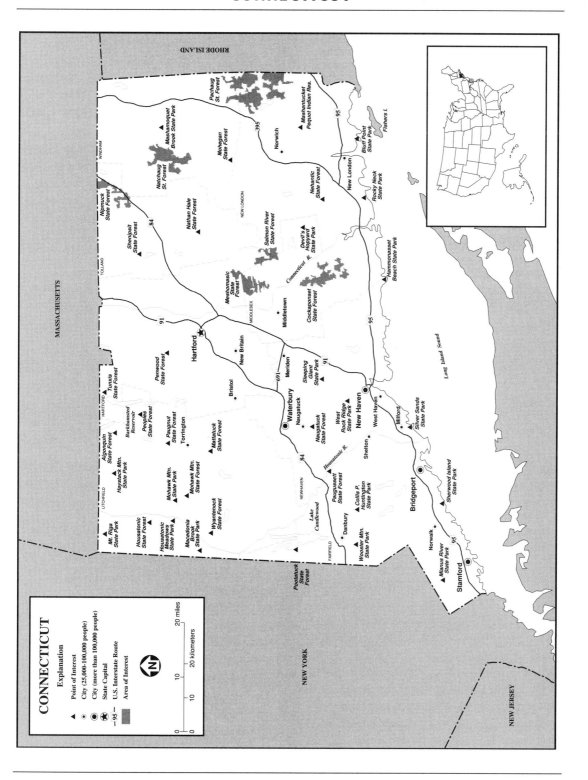

RHODE ISLAND

MASSACHUSETTS

Pachaug
St. Forest

Mashamoquet
Brook State Park

Mohegan
State Forest

Mashantucket
Pequot Indian Res.

Natchaug
St. Forest

Norwich

Nipmuck
State Forest

Nathan Hale
State Forest

New London

Bluff Point
State Park

Fishers I.

Shenipsit
State Forest

WINDHAM

Nehantic
State Forest

Rocky Neck
State Park

TOLLAND

NEW LONDON

Salmon River
State Forest

Devil's
Hopyard
State Park

91

Meshomasic
State
Forest

Cockaponset
State Forest

Hammonasset
Beach State Park

Connecticut R.

MIDDLESEX

Middletown

84

Hartford

New Britain

Penwood
State Forest

Tunxis
State Forest

91

691

Meriden

Sleeping
Giant
State Park

91

Long Island Sound

Algonquin
State Forest

HARTFORD

Barkhamsted
Reservoir

Peoples
State Forest

Paugnut
State Forest

Torrington

Bristol

Waterbury

Naugatuck

West
Rock Ridge
State Park

New Haven

West Haven

Milford

Silver Sands
State Park

Haystack Mtn.
State Park

Mohawk Mtn.
State Park

Mohawk Mtn.
State Forest

Mattatuck
State Forest

Naugatuck
State Forest

LITCHFIELD

Housatonic R.

Shelton

Mt. Riga
State Park

Housatonic
State Forest

Housatonic
State Park

Macedonia
Brook
State Park

Wyantenock
State Forest

84

NEWHAVEN

Paugussett
State Forest

Collis P.
Huntington
State Park

Bridgeport

Sherwood Island
State Park

Lake
Candlewood

Danbury

Wooster Mtn.
State Park

FAIRFIELD

Norwalk

Mianus River
State Park

95

Stamford

Pootatuck
State
Forest

NEW YORK

NEW JERSEY

CONNECTICUT

Explanation

▲ Point of Interest

⊙ City (25,000–100,000 people)

◉ City (more than 100,000 people)

★ State Capital

—95— U.S. Interstate Route

▨ Area of Interest

N

20 miles

0 10 20

20 kilometers

0 10 20

woodchuck, gray squirrel, cottontail, eastern chipmunk, porcupine, raccoon, and striped skunk—remain common. Freshwater fish are abundant, and aquatic life in Long Island Sound even more so. Common birds include the robin (the state bird), blue jay, song sparrow, wood thrush, and many species of waterfowl.

Threatened or endangered wildlife listed by the US Department of the Interior include Atlantic and shortnose sturgeon, American peregrine falcon, Indiana bat, bald eagle, and eastern cougar.

5 ENVIRONMENTAL PROTECTION

The Department of Environmental Protection spends about $19 per capita (per person) annually on environmental programs. However, only a portion of the state's major rivers met the federal government's "swimmable-fishable" standards, and millions of gallons of sewage continued to be poured into Long Island Sound.

In the early 1980s, ozone levels were among the highest in the US. Automobiles produce 90% of the carbon monoxide and 50% of the hydrocarbons in the Connecticut environment. The vehicles emission program established by the state in January 1983 reduced carbon monoxide and hydrocarbon pollution. Connecticut's other major air pollution problem is "acid rain," much of which originates in New York and New Jersey.

In 1994, the state had 16 hazardous waste sites. Some 2.9 million tons of solid waste are generated in Connecticut each year, and the state has only 60 landfill sites. The state has 150 curbside recycling programs and 5 municipal incinerators.

6 POPULATION

The 1990 census total for Connecticut was 3,287,116. The estimated population for 1995 was 3,274,000. The state had a population gain of 5.8% (about 180,000 residents) for the entire decade of the 1980s, compared with a US population growth of 9.7%. One sign of the population lag is that in 1990 Connecticut had the 11th lowest birthrate in the US, 14.5 live births per 1,000 population.

The 2000 population is projected at 3,422,000. Connecticut ranked fourth among the 50 states in population density in 1990 with 678.4 persons per square mile (260.7 persons per square kilometer). About 79.1% of all Connecticut residents lived in urban areas and 20.9% in rural areas. Major cities with 1992 populations are Bridgeport, 137,020; Hartford, 131,995; New Haven, 123,966; Stamford, 107,590 and Waterbury, 106,904.

7 ETHNIC GROUPS

Connecticut has large populations of second-generation European descent. The biggest groups came from Italy, Ireland, Poland, and Quebec, Canada. Most of these immigrants clustered in the cities of New Haven, Hartford, Bridgeport, and New London.

In 1990, the black population numbered 274,000, about 8.3% of the state total. According to the 1990 federal census, there were also about 213,000 residents of Hispanic origin, of whom 93,608 were Puerto Ricans. In addition Connecticut had 7,000 Native Americans and 51,000 Asians and Pacific Islanders.

8 LANGUAGES

Connecticut English is basically that of the Northern dialect, but features of the eastern New England subdialect occur east of the Connecticut River. Almost 2.6 million Connecticuters (85% of the population five years old and older) speak only English at home. Other languages spoken at home, and the number of people who speak them, include Spanish, 167,007; Italian, 71,309; French, 53,586; Polish, 40,306; and Portuguese, 24,936.

9 RELIGIONS

Since World War I, Roman Catholics have been the most numerous religious group in the state. As of 1990, there were 1,374,747 Roman Catholics and 557,439 known members of Protestant denominations. Leading groups included Congregationalists (United Church of Christ), 135,231; Episcopalians, 78,804; and United Methodists, 56,372. In 1990, the state's estimated Jewish population was 115,460.

10 TRANSPORTATION

As of 1991/92, Amtrak operated about 18 trains through the state, serving 13 stations with a total of 1,060,776 riders. Local bus systems provide intracity transportation. Intercity bus service (not subsidized by the state or the federal government) is provided in 31 municipalities by 23 companies.

Connecticut has an extensive system of expressways, state highways, and local roads, totaling 20,357 miles (32,754 kilometers) in 1993. Over 99% of the roads are either paved or hard-surfaced. As of 1993 there were 2,455,811 automobiles, 130,348 trucks, 37,156 motorcycles, and 8,210 buses registered in the state.

Most of Connecticut's waterborne traffic is handled through the three major ports of New Haven, New London, and Bridgeport, which collectively handled 12.4 million tons of cargo in 1991, and at the shallow-draft terminals in Norwalk and Stamford. The latter two cities together handled 1.3 million tons of goods that year.

In 1991 Connecticut had 57 airports. The principal air terminal is Bradley International Airport at Windsor Locks, 14 miles (23 kilometers) north of Hartford. Served by seven major airlines and nine commuter lines, Bradley handled 2.1 million passengers during 1991.

11 HISTORY

By the early 17th century, Connecticut had between 6,000 and 7,000 Native Americans organized into 16 tribes. Because of their fear of the warlike Pequot along the shore and of the Mohawk to the west, most of Connecticut's other Native Americans sought the friendship of English newcomers in the 1630s. The impact of English settlers on Connecticut's friendly tribesmen was devastating, however. The Native Americans lost their land, were made dependents in their own territory, and were ravaged by such European diseases as smallpox and measles. By

Mystic Seaport, whaling museum.

the 1770s, Connecticut's Native American population was less than 1,500.

The early English settlers were part of a great migration of some 20,000 English Puritans between 1630 and 1642. In 1639, the Puritan settlements at Windsor, Wethersfield, and Hartford joined together to form the Connecticut Colony. A separate Puritan colony established at New Haven in 1638 joined them in 1665. Connecticut functioned throughout the colonial period much like an independent republic. It was the only American colony that generally did not follow English legal and legislative practices.

With its Puritan roots and historic autonomy, Connecticut was a patriot stronghold during the American Revolution. The state's most famous Revolutionary War figure was Nathan Hale, executed as a spy by the British in New York City in 1776. On 9 January 1788, Connecticut became the fifth state to ratify the Constitution. Connecticut strongly disagreed with the foreign policy of Presidents Thomas Jefferson and James Madison and opposed the War of 1812, even refusing to allow its militia to leave the state.

Long before the Civil War, Connecticut was stoutly antislavery. Connecticut had a number of antislavery societies whose members routed escaped slaves to Canada via the Underground Railroad. Some 55,000 Connecticut men served in the Civil War, suffering more than 20,000 casualties. The contributions by Connecticut industries to the war effort signaled the state's emergence as a manufacturing giant. Its industrial development was helped by abundant waterpower, an elaborate transportation network, and, most important, the technological and marketing expertise of the people.

1900–1945

The state's textile industry ranked sixth in the nation in 1900, with an annual output of $50 million. By 1904, Connecticut's firearms industry was producing more than one-fourth of the total value of all firearms manufactured by nongovernment factories in the US. These great strides in manufacturing transformed Connecticut from a rural, agrarian society in the early 1800s to an increasingly urban state.

The state's contribution to the Allied forces in World War I more than equaled its Civil War effort. About 66,000 Connecticuters served in the armed forces, and by 1917–18, four-fifths of Connecticut's industry was involved in defense production. During the 1920s, the state became a national leader in the production of specialty parts for the aviation, automotive, and electric power industries.

The stock market crash of 1929 and the subsequent depression of the 1930s hit highly industrialized Connecticut hard. By the spring of 1932, the state's unemployed totaled 150,000 and cities such as Bridgeport fell deeply in debt. Connecticut was pulled out of the unemployment doldrums in 1939, when the state's factories were once again stimulated by defense contracts. During World War II, Connecticut's factories turned out submarines, Navy Corsair fighter aircraft, helicopters, 80% of all ball bearings manufactured in the US, and many thousands of small arms. Approximately 220,000 Connecticut men and women served in the US armed forces.

Post-World War II

Since 1945, Connecticut has seen substantial population growth, economic diversification with a greater proportion of service industries, the expansion of middle-class suburbs, and an influx of black and Hispanic migrants to the major cities. Urban renewal projects in Hartford and New Haven have resulted in expanded office and recreational facilities, but not much desperately needed new housing. A major challenge facing Connecticut in the 1980s was once again how to handle the social and economic integration of this incoming wave of people and industries.

Connecticut became the nation's wealthiest state during the 1980s, achieving the highest per capita (per person) income in 1986. The state's prosperity came in part from the expansion of the military budget, as 70% of Connecticut's manufacturing sector was defense-related. The end of the Cold War, however, brought cuts in military spending which reduced the value of defense-related contracts in Connecticut from $6 billion in 1989 to $4.2 billion in 1990. Department of Defense spending per capita fell from $1,800 in the 1980s to $1,289 in 1992. By 1992, manufacturing jobs had declined by 25% while jobs in such service industries as retail, finance, insurance, and real estate increased by 23%. The total number of jobs, however, dropped by 10%.

In the 1980s and early 1990s, Connecticut witnessed an increasing contrast between the standard of living enjoyed by urban and suburban residents, blacks and whites, and the wealthy and the poor. In 1992, the median family income in many of the state's suburbs was nearly twice that of families living in urban areas.

12 STATE GOVERNMENT

The state legislature is called the general assembly, consisting of a 36-member senate and 151-member house of representatives. Legislators are elected to both houses for two-year terms. Elected members of the executive branch are the governor and lieutenant governor (who run jointly and must each be at least 30 years of age), secretary of state, treasurer, comptroller, and attorney general. All are elected for four-year terms and may be reelected.

A bill becomes law when approved by both houses of the general assembly and signed by the governor. If the governor fails to sign it within 5 days when the legislature is in session, or within 15 days when it has adjourned, the measure also becomes law. A bill vetoed by the governor may be overridden by a two-thirds vote of the members of each house.

Photo credit: Connecticut Department of Economic Development.

State capitol building, Hartford.

13 POLITICAL PARTIES

Connecticut's Democrats have held power in most years since the mid-1950s. As of 1994, Democratic Party registration in Connecticut was 736,914 (38%); Republican, 506,115 (26%); and Independent, 721,239 (37%). In the November 1992 elections, Democrat Bill Clinton carried the state with 42% of the popular vote; Republican George Bush won 36%, and Independent Ross Perot received 22%. That same year, the Democrats controlled the state senate and state house. Connecticut's delegation of US Representatives consisted of three Democrats and three Republicans.

In 1994, Republican John G. Rowland was elected governor on a platform that included a promise to repeal the State income tax. The Republicans also gained one seat in the State Senate which gave them a majority. However, the Democrats increased their substantial majority in the State House of Representatives. US Representative Gary Franks, the first black member of the US House of Representatives from Connecticut and the first black House Republican in 55 years, won re-election.

14 LOCAL GOVERNMENT

As of 1992, Connecticut had 8 counties and 30 municipal governments. Counties in Connecticut have been geographical subdivisions without governmental functions since county government was abolished in 1960.

Connecticut's cities generally use the council-manager or mayor-council forms of government. The council-manager system provides for an elected council that determines policy, enacts local legislation, and appoints the city manager. The mayor-council system employs an elected chief executive with extensive appointment power and control over administrative agencies.

In most towns, an elected, three-member board of selectmen heads the administrative branch. The town meeting, in which all registered voters may participate,

Connecticut Presidential Vote by Political Parties, 1948–92

YEAR	CONNECTICUT WINNER	DEMOCRAT	REPUBLICAN	PROGRESSIVE	SOCIALIST
1948	Dewey (R)	423,297	437,754	13,713	6,964
1952	*Eisenhower (R)	481,649	611,012	1,466	2,244
1956	*Eisenhower (R)	405,079	711,837	—	—
1960	*Kennedy (D)	657,055	565,813	—	—
1964	*Johnson (D)	826,269	390,996	—	—
				AMERICAN IND.	
1968	Humphrey (D)	621,561	556,721	76,660	—
					AMERICAN
1972	*Nixon (R)	555,498	810,763	—	17,239
					US LABOR
1976	Ford (R)	647,895	719,261	7,101	1,789
				LIBERTARIAN	CITIZENS
1980	*Reagan (R)	541,732	677,210	8,570	6,130
				CONN-ALLIANCE	COMMUNIST
1984	*Reagan (R)	569,597	890,877	1,274	4,826
				LIBERTARIAN	NEW ALLIANCE
1988	*Bush (R)	676,584	750,241	14,071	2,491
					IND. (Perot)
1992	*Clinton (D)	682,318	578,313	5,391	348,771

* Won US presidential election.

is the legislative body. Boroughs are generally governed by an elected warden, and borough meetings exercise major legislative functions.

15 JUDICIAL SYSTEM

Connecticut's judicial system has undergone significant streamlining in recent years, with the abolition of municipal, circuit, and juvenile courts. Currently, the Connecticut judicial system consists of the supreme court, appeals court, superior court, and probate courts.

The supreme court comprises the chief justice, five associate justices, and two senior associate justices. The high court hears cases on appeal, primarily from the appeals court but also from the superior court in certain special instances, such as the review of a death sentence, reapportionment, election disputes, invalidation of a state statute, or censure of a probate judge.

The superior court, the sole general trial court, has the authority to hear all legal controversies except those over which the probate courts have exclusive jurisdiction. The superior court sits in 12 state judicial districts and is divided into trial divisions for civil, criminal, and family cases. Connecticut had an inmate population of 13,691 at the end of 1993. The total crime rate in 1994 was 4,548 per 100,000.

16 MIGRATION

After World War II, the rush of middle-class whites (many from neighboring states) to Connecticut suburbs, fueled in part by the "baby boom" that followed the war, was accompanied by the flow of minority groups to the cities. All told, Connecticut had a net increase from migration of 561,000 between 1940 and 1970, followed by a net loss of 113,000 from 1970 to 1990.

17 ECONOMY

Connecticut's most important economic pursuit is manufacturing. In the 1980s, Connecticut became a leader in the manufacture of aircraft engines and parts, bearings, hardware, submarines, helicopters, typewriters, electronic instrumentation, electrical equipment, guns and ammunition, and optical instruments.

Because defense production has traditionally been important to the state, the economy has fluctuated with the rise and fall of international tensions. Connecticut has lessened its dependence on the defense sector somewhat by attracting nonmilitary domestic and international firms to the state. Between 1984 and 1991, manufacturing employment declined 22.4%, while nonmanufacturing jobs rose by 11.6%.

However, the state was hit hard by cuts in military spending in the late 1980s and early 1990s. In 1992, 70% of manufacturing was still defense-related. Pratt and Whitney, the jet engine maker, and General Dynamics Electric Boat Division, manufacturer of submarines, announced in 1992 that they would lay off a total of 16,400 workers over the next six years. Unemployment in 1993 was 7.3%. However, even during the recession in 1991 and 1992, Connecticut retained its status as the state with the highest per capita (per person) income, a ranking which it first achieved in 1986.

18 INCOME

On a per capita (per person) basis, the average Connecticuter received $29,044 in 1994, the highest among the states. Only 8.5% of all state residents were below the federal poverty level in 1993.

19 INDUSTRY

Six main groups of industries drive the state's economy: aerospace and advanced manufacturing; communications, information and education; financial services; health and biomedical; business services; and tourism and entertainment.

The state's value of shipments of manufactured goods totaled $40 billion in 1991. Leading industrial and service corporations with headquarters in Connecticut include, in order of 1993 sales, General Electric, United Technologies, GTE, Xerox, and American Brands. In 1992, 27 Connecticut-based firms appeared on *Fortune* magazine's list of the 500 biggest industrial companies in the US.

20 LABOR

The state's civilian labor force in 1994 was approximately 1,726,000, of whom 5.6% were unemployed. Some 20% of all workers were union members.

21 AGRICULTURE

Agriculture is no longer of much economic importance in Connecticut. The number of farms declined from 22,241 in 1945 to 3,800 in 1994. In 1994, cash receipts from all agricultural sales totaled $472.7 million, of which $221.8 million was from crop sales. Connecticut ranked 15th in tobacco production in 1994 at 2,625,000 pounds. Other principal crops are hay, greenhouse and nursery products, potatoes, sweet corn, tomatoes, apples, pears, and peaches.

22 DOMESTICATED ANIMALS

Cash farm income from the sale of livestock and livestock products totaled $250.9 million in 1994. In 1994 there were 75,000 cattle on Connecticut farms. Receipts of eggs and dairy products accounted for 17% and 15.8% of agricultural receipts, respectively, in 1994.

23 FISHING

Commercial fishing does not play a major role in the economy. In 1992, the value of commercial landings was $62.6 million for a catch of 19,634,000 pounds of edible finfish and shellfish.

24 FORESTRY

By the early 20th century, the forests that covered 95% of Connecticut in the 1630s were mostly destroyed. Woodland recovery has been stimulated since the 1930s by an energetic reforestation program. In 1991, 747 acres of trees were planted. State woodlands include 91 state parks and 30 state forests covering some 168,000 acres (69,055 hectares).

25 MINING

The value of nonfuel mineral production in Connecticut in 1994 was estimated by the US Bureau of Mines to be nearly $97 million. Crushed stone and construction sand and gravel are the state's two leading mineral commodities produced. Other commodities include clays, industrial sand, and dimension stone.

26 ENERGY AND POWER

In 1992, Connecticut's fuel bill was $6.5 billion, of which 57% was for petroleum products, 15% for natural gas, and 25% for electricity. In 1991, prices were 71% higher than the national average for natural gas, 41% higher for electricity, and about 4% higher for petroleum products.

Production of electricity was 28.7 billion kilowatt hours in 1993. The use of coal to generate electric power declined from 85% of the total fuel used in 1965 to 6.6% in 1993, as a result of the increased utilization of nuclear energy and oil. As of 1994, Connecticut had four nuclear reactors. Having no petroleum or gas resources of its own, Connecticut must rely primarily on imported oil.

27 COMMERCE

Considering its small size, Connecticut is a busy commercial state. In 1992, sales from wholesale trade totaled $78.3 billion, and retail trade sales amounted to $29 billion in 1993. Service establishment receipts totaled $21.6 billion. The estimated value of Connecticut's goods exported abroad was $5.01 billion. Tobacco is the major agricultural export.

28 PUBLIC FINANCE

In 1991, the state of Connecticut underwent a major reorganization of its finances, including the enactment of a personal income tax at a rate of 4.5%. Also included in the revenue restructuring was a 25% drop in the sales tax rate (from 8% to 6%) and a reduction in the corporate tax rate from 13.8% to 11.5%.

Revenues for 1993/94 were $7,895.4 million; expenditures were $7,958.8 million. In 1993 Connecticut's outstanding debt totaled $12.8 billion or $3,920 per capita (per person).

29 TAXATION

Connecticut ranked 21st in state tax revenues in 1991, with receipts of $4.9 billion, or $1,514.2 per capita (per person). Principal taxes are a 7.5% sales and use tax, a corporation business tax, a tax on dividends and interest at a rate of 1–13%, and a motor fuels tax of 23 cents per gallon. Other state taxes are levied on cigarettes, alcoholic beverages, and theater admissions. Property taxes are the main source of local revenue.

30 HEALTH

Connecticut is one of the healthiest states in the US. The two leading causes of death are heart disease and cancer. Death rates for cerebrovascular diseases, accidents and adverse effects, motor vehicle accidents, and suicide were below their respective national rates in 1992. In 1993, Connecticut had 35 community hospitals, with 9,200 beds and 44,800 personnel. Hospital expenses in 1993 averaged $1,058 per day and $7,478 per stay, well above the US average. Connecticut had 10,482 nonfederal physicians in 1993, 31,000 nurses, and 2,370 dentists. In 1993 10% of the state's population did not have health insurance.

31 HOUSING

A July 1993 estimate based on the 1990 Census of Population and Housing reported that there were 1,345,000 housing units in Connecticut, an increase of about 18% over the 1980 census total. Virtually every town increased its housing stock during that period; the smallest increases were in the big cities, however. As of 1990, year-round housing units in Connecticut had a median monthly mortgage and owner cost of $1,096 and a median monthly rent of $598.

32 EDUCATION

As of 1990, 81.9% of adult state residents were high school graduates, and 29.4% had completed four or more years of college. As of fall 1993, Connecticut's public schools had about 34,400 teachers and 500,000 students. The state's private preparatory schools include Choate Rosemary Hall, Taft, Westminster, Loomis Chaffee, and Miss Porter's. In 1993 the state spent an average of $8,170 per pupil on primary and secondary education (4th in the nation).

Public institutions of higher education include the University of Connecticut at Storrs, with 25,000 students; four divisions of the Connecticut State University; 12 regional community colleges; and 5 state technical colleges. Connecticut's 23 private four-year colleges and universities have 43,000 students. Among the oldest institutions is Yale University in New Haven, founded in 1701.

33 ARTS

Art museums in Connecticut include the Wadsworth Atheneum in Hartford, the oldest (1842) free public art museum in the US; the Yale University Art Gallery and the Yale Center for British Art in New Haven; the New Britain Museum of American Art; and the Lyman Allyn Museum of Connecticut College in New London. Professional theaters include the American Shakespeare Festival Theater in Stratford, the Long Wharf Theater and the Yale Repertory Theater in New Haven, the Hartford Stage Company, and the Eugene O'Neill Memorial Theater Center in Waterford.

The state's foremost metropolitan orchestras are the Hartford and New Haven symphonies. Professional opera is presented by the Stamford State Opera and by the Connecticut Opera in Hartford. Prominent dance groups include the Connecticut Dance Company in New Haven, the Hartford Ballet Company, and the Pilobolus Dance Theater in the town of Washington. From 1987 to 1991, Connecticut generated $26,864,986 in federal and state funds to develop the arts.

34 LIBRARIES AND MUSEUMS

As of 1991/92, Connecticut had 194 public libraries. The leading public library is the Connecticut State Library (Hartford), which houses about 715,000 bound volumes and over 2,100 periodicals, and which also serves as the official state historical museum. Connecticut's most distinguished academic collection is the Yale University library system (9 million volumes) in New Haven, headed by the

Sterling Memorial Library and the Beinecke Rare Book and Manuscript Library. In all, Connecticut libraries held 12.5 million volumes in 1991/92 and had a combined circulation of 27.4 million.

Connecticut has more than 150 museums, in addition to its historic sites. The Peabody Museum of Natural History at Yale in New Haven includes an impressive dinosaur hall. Connecticut's historical sites include the Henry Whitfield House in Guilford (1639), said to be the oldest stone house in the US.

35 COMMUNICATIONS

As of March 1993, 97.4% of the state's 1,236,000 occupied housing units had telephones. In the same year, Connecticut had 41 AM and 55 FM radio stations, and 13 television stations. There were educational television stations in Bridgeport, Hartford, and Norwich. In addition, in 1993, 17 large cable television systems served the state.

36 PRESS

The *Hartford Courant,* founded in 1764, is generally considered to be the oldest US newspaper in continuous publication. The leading Connecticut dailies in 1994 were the *Courant,* with an average morning circulation of 221,177 (Sundays, 323,084), and the *New Haven Register,* with an average evening circulation of 101,427 (Sundays, 133,784). Statewide, in 1994 there were 10 morning newspapers, 12 evening newspapers, and 10 Sunday newspapers. In 1994, Connecticut also had 88 newspapers that appeared weekly or up to three times a week. Leading periodicals

are *American Scientist, Connecticut Magazine, Fine Woodworking, Golf Digest,* and *Tennis.*

37 TOURISM, TRAVEL, AND RECREATION

Tourism has become an increasingly important part of the state economy in recent decades, with tourist expenditures climbing to more than $3.2 billion in 1990. Popular tourist attractions include the Mystic Seaport restoration and its aquarium, the Mark Twain House and state capitol in Hartford, and the Yale campus in New Haven. Outstanding events include the Harvard-Yale regatta held each June on the Thames River in New London.

38 SPORTS

Connecticut's only major league professional team is the Hartford Whalers of the National Hockey League. New Haven has a minor league hockey franchise, the Red Sox. Auto racing takes place at Lime Rock Race Track, in Salisbury. Connecticut schools, colleges, and universities provide amateur athletic competitions, highlighted by Ivy League football games on autumn Saturdays at the Yale Bowl in New Haven.

39 FAMOUS CONNECTICUTERS

Connecticut cannot claim any US president or vice-president as a native son. Two Connecticut natives have served as chief justice of the US: Oliver Ellsworth (1745–1807) and Morrison R. Waite (1816–88). Other prominent federal officeholders were Dean Acheson (1893–1971), secretary of state;

Photo credit: Connecticut Department of Economic Development.

Mark Twain's house, Nook Farm Museum.

and Abraham A. Ribicoff (b.1910), secretary of health, education, and welfare. Connecticut senator Lowell P. Weicker, Jr. (b.France, 1931) was brought to national attention by his work during the Watergate hearings in 1973. Ella Tambussi Grasso (1919–81), elected in 1974 and reelected in 1978, was the first woman governor in the US who did not succeed her husband in the post.

Shapers of US history include Jonathan Edwards (1703–58), a Congregationalist minister who sparked the 18th-century religious revival known as the Great Awakening; Connecticut's most revered Revolutionary War figure, Nathan Hale (1755–76), who was executed for spying behind British lines; radical abolitionist John Brown (1800–1859); and Henry Ward Beecher (1813–87), a religious leader and abolitionist.

Connecticuters prominent in US cultural development include painter John Trumbull (1756–1843); Noah Webster (1758–1843), who compiled the *American Dictionary of the English Language* (1828); and Harriet Beecher Stowe (1811–96), who wrote one of the most widely read books in history, *Uncle Tom's Cabin* (1852). Mark Twain (Samuel L. Clemens, b.Missouri, 1835–1910) was living in Hartford when he wrote *The Adventures of Huckleberry Finn* (1885). Charles Ives (1874–1954) was one of the nation's most distinguished composers. A renowned voice in modern poetry, Wallace Stevens (b.Pennsylvania, 1879–1955), wrote most of his work while employed as a Hartford insurance executive. James Merrill (b.New York, 1926), a poet whose works have won the National Book Award (1967) and many other honors, lived in Stonington.

Among the premier inventors born in Connecticut were Eli Whitney (1765–1825), inventor of the cotton gin; Samuel Colt (1814–62), inventor of the six-shooter; and Edwin H. Land (1909–91), inventor of the Polaroid Land Camera.

Other prominent Americans born in Connecticut include circus promoter Phineas Taylor "P. T." Barnum (1810–91), pediatrician Benjamin Spock (b.1903), actress Katharine Hepburn (b.1909), soprano Eileen Farrell (b.1920), and consumer-advocate Ralph Nader (b.1934).

40 BIBLIOGRAPHY

Bachman, Ben. *Upstream: A Voyage on the Connecticut River*. Boston: Houghton Mifflin, 1985.

Bixby, William. *Connecticut: A New Guide*. New York: Scribner, 1974.

Janick, Herbert F. *A Diverse People: Connecticut, 1914 to the Present*. Chester, Conn.: Pequot Press, 1975.

DELAWARE

State of Delaware

ORIGIN OF STATE NAME: Named for Thomas West, Baron De La Warr, colonial governor of Virginia; the name was first applied to the bay.

NICKNAMES: The First State; the Diamond State.

CAPITAL: Dover.

ENTERED UNION: 7 December 1787 (1st).

SONG: "Our Delaware."

COLORS: Colonial blue and buff.

MOTTO: Liberty and Independence.

COAT OF ARMS: A farmer and a rifleman flank a shield that bears symbols of the state's agricultural resources—a sheaf of wheat, an ear of corn, and a cow. Above is a ship in full sail; below, a banner with the state motto.

FLAG: Colonial blue with the coat of arms on a buff-colored diamond; below the diamond is the date of statehood.

OFFICIAL SEAL: The coat of arms surrounded by the words "Great Seal of the State of Delaware 1793, 1847, 1907." The three dates represent the years in which the seal was revised.

BIRD: Blue hen's chicken.

FISH: Weakfish.

FLOWER: Peach blossom.

TREE: American holly.

ROCK: Sillimanite.

INSECT: Ladybug.

TIME: 7 AM EST = noon GMT.

1 LOCATION AND SIZE

Located on the eastern seaboard of the US, Delaware ranks 49th in size among the 50 states. The state's total area is 2,044 square miles (5,295 square kilometers). Delaware extends 35 miles (56 kilometers) east-west at its widest; its maximum north-south extension is 96 miles (154 kilometers). Delaware's boundary length is 200 miles (322 kilometers).

2 TOPOGRAPHY

Delaware lies entirely within the Atlantic Coastal Plain except for its northern tip, which is part of the Piedmont Plateau. The state's highest elevation is 442 feet (135 meters). The rolling hills and pastures of the north give way to marshy regions in the south, with sandy beaches along the coast. Delaware's mean elevation, 60 feet (18 meters), is the lowest in the US. The Nanticoke, Choptank, and Pocomoke rivers flow westward into Chesapeake Bay. Other rivers flow into Delaware Bay.

3 CLIMATE

Delaware's climate is temperate and humid. The average annual temperature in Wilmington ranges from 31°F (–1°C) in January to 76°F (24°C) in July. Both the record low and high temperatures for the state were established at Millsboro: –17°F (–27°C) on 17 January 1893, and 110°F (43°C) on 21 July 1930. The average annual precipitation is 41 inches (104 centimeters).

4 PLANTS AND ANIMALS

Common trees include black walnut, hickory, and sweetgum. Shadbush and sassafras are found chiefly in southern Delaware. Mammals native to the state include the white-tailed deer, muskrat, and common cottontail. The quail, robin, and cardinal are native birds. The southern bald eagle and the Delmarva Peninsula fox squirrel are endangered.

5 ENVIRONMENTAL PROTECTION

The traffic of oil tankers into the Delaware Bay represents an environmental hazard. The Coastal Zone Act has restricted industrial development, oil drilling, and tanker movement along Delaware's coastline since the early 1970s. The state's municipal governments have constructed three municipal landfills to handle the 750 tons of solid waste produced yearly by the state's 680,000 residents. There were 19 hazardous waste sites as of 1994.

6 POPULATION

Delaware ranked 46th among the 50 states in January 1990, with a population of 666,168; the population density was 340.8 persons per square mile (131 persons per square kilometer). The estimated

Delaware Population Profile

Estimated 1995 population:	739,000
Population change, 1980–90:	12.1%
Leading ancestry group:	Irish
Second leading group:	German
Foreign born population:	3.3%
Hispanic origin†:	2.4%
Population by race:	
White:	80.3%
Black:	16.9%
Native American:	0.3%
Asian/Pacific Islander:	1.4%
Other:	1.1%

Population by Age Group

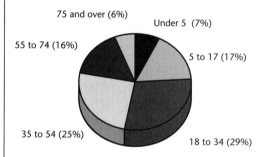

75 and over (6%)
Under 5 (7%)
55 to 74 (16%)
5 to 17 (17%)
35 to 54 (25%)
18 to 34 (29%)

Top Cities with Populations Over 25,000

City	Population	National rank	% change 1980–90
Wilmington	72,411	319	1.9
Dover	28,227	982	17.6
Newark	25,492	1,059	–0.6

Notes: †A person of Hispanic origin may be of any race. NA indicates that data are not available.
Sources: Economic and Statistics Administration, Bureau of the Census. *Statistical Abstract of the United States, 1994–95.* Washington, DC: Government Printing Office, 1995; Courtenay M. Slater and George E. Hall. *1995 County and City Extra: Annual Metro, City and County Data Book.* Lanham, MD: Bernan Press, 1995.

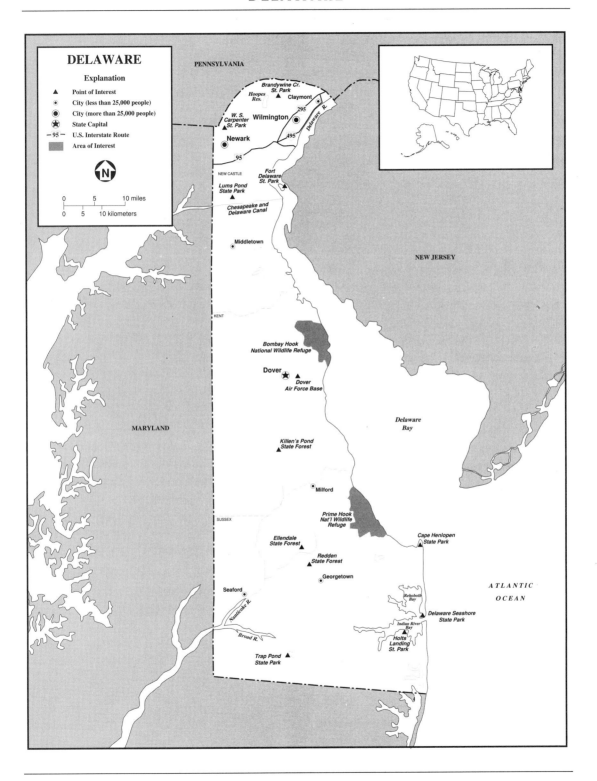

DELAWARE

Explanation

▲ Point of Interest
⊙ City (less than 25,000 people)
◉ City (more than 25,000 people)
★ State Capital
—95— U.S. Interstate Route
▓ Area of Interest

0   5   10 miles
0   5   10 kilometers

PENNSYLVANIA

Brandywine Cr. St. Park ▲
Hoopes Res.
Claymont ⊙
W. S. Carpenter St. Park ▲
Wilmington ◉
295
Delaware R.
Newark ◉
495
95
NEW CASTLE
Fort Delaware St. Park ▲
Lums Pond State Park ▲
Chesapeake and Delaware Canal
Middletown ⊙
NEW JERSEY
KENT
Bombay Hook National Wildlife Refuge
Dover ★
Dover Air Force Base ▲
Delaware Bay
MARYLAND
Killen's Pond State Forest ▲
Milford ⊙
Prime Hook Nat'l Wildlife Refuge
SUSSEX
Ellendale State Forest ▲
Redden State Forest ▲
Cape Henlopen State Park ▲
Georgetown ◉
ATLANTIC OCEAN
Seaford ⊙
Nanticoke R.
Rehoboth Bay
Delaware Seashore State Park ▲
Indian River Bay
Broad R.
Holts Landing St. Park ▲
Trap Pond State Park ▲

population for 1995 is 739,000. The largest cities in 1992 were Wilmington, with 72,411; and Dover, the capital, with 28,227.

7 ETHNIC GROUPS

Black Americans constitute Delaware's largest racial minority, numbering 112,000 in 1990 and comprising about 17% of the population. Approximately 16,000, or 2.4% of the total population, is of Hispanic origin.

8 LANGUAGES

English in Delaware is basically North Midland, with Philadelphia features in Wilmington and the northern portion. Over 575,000 Delawareans speak only English at home. Other languages spoken at home (and number of speakers) include Spanish (15,302), and German (4,206).

9 RELIGIONS

There are about 116,000 Catholics and an estimated 9,500 Jews in Delaware. The leading Protestant groups are the United Methodist Church, 61,091; the Episcopal Church, 13,307; and the Presbyterian Church, 15,401. The first Methodist services conducted in America were held in Delaware in the late 18th century. The African Methodist Episcopal Church was also founded by slaves and ex-slaves from Delaware.

10 TRANSPORTATION

As of 1992 there were 272 rail miles (438 kilometers) of track. Amtrak operated approximately 30 trains through Delaware, and the state had 5,524 miles (8,888

Photo credit: Delaware Tourism Office.

Liberty bell in front of Legislative Hall in Dover, Delaware's state capital.

kilometers) of public highways, roads, and streets. The Lewes–Cape May Ferry provides auto and passenger service between southern Delaware and New Jersey. Wilmington is Delaware's chief port. Greater Wilmington Airport is the largest and busiest civilian airport.

11 HISTORY

At the time of the first European contact, the Leni-Lenape people occupied northern Delaware, while several tribes, including the Nanticoke and Assateague, inhabited southern Delaware. Permanent

Photo credit: Delaware Tourism Office.

The courthouse in New Castle, site of the first Dutch settlement in 1651.

settlements were made by the Swedes in 1638 at Wilmington and by the Dutch in 1651 at New Castle. The Dutch conquered the Swedes in 1655, and were in turn conquered in 1664 by the English, who placed Delaware under the control of William Penn.

In the War for Independence, Delaware troops fought so well that they gained the nickname "Blue Hen's Chicken," after a famous breed of now-extinct fighting gamecocks. On 7 December 1787, Delaware became the first state to ratify the federal Constitution. Although Delaware had not abolished slavery, it remained loyal to the Union during the Civil War. However, white Delawareans manipulated

registration laws to deny blacks voting rights until 1890. Delaware refused ratification of the three "Civil War" constitutional amendments (abolition of slavery, equal protection, voting rights for black men) until 1901.

The key event in the state's early economic history was the completion of a railroad between Philadelphia and Baltimore through Wilmington in 1838. Foreign immigration contributed to the state's growth, largely from the British Isles and Germany in the mid-19th century and from Italy, Poland, and Russia in the early 20th century. In the early 1900's, E. I. du Pont de Nemours and Co., founded near Wilmington in 1802 as a gunpowder manufacturer, made the city famous as a center for the chemical industry.

During the 1950s, Delaware's population grew by an unprecedented 40%. Although many neighborhood schools became racially integrated during the 1950s, massive busing was instituted by court order in 1978 to achieve a racial balance in schools throughout northern Delaware. This court order was lifted in 1995.

The 1980s ushered in a period of dramatic economic improvement. Some of Delaware's prosperity came from a 1981 state law that raised interest rate limits and lowered taxes for large financial institutions. More than thirty banks established themselves in Delaware, and the state also succeeded in attracting foreign companies. Two industrial parks were built in Sussex, Delaware's southernmost county, and a third complex in the center of the state.

Although business has grown in Delaware, urban and rural poverty are still present. Delaware's teenage pregnancy rate is one of the highest in the country, while its welfare benefits are lower than any other mid-Atlantic state with the exception of West Virginia. Delaware's unemployment rate, however, has consistently been lower than the national average since the early 1980s.

12 STATE GOVERNMENT

Delaware's legislative branch is the general assembly, consisting of a 21-member senate and a 41-member house of representatives. Delaware's major elected executives include the governor and lieutenant governor (elected separately), treasurers, and attorney general.

13 POLITICAL PARTIES

Since the 1930s, the two major parties have been relatively evenly matched. As of 1994, 142,542 voters were registered as members of the Democratic party, comprising 43% of the total number of registered voters, while 125,829, or 37%, were registered as Republicans. There were 67,717 voters registered as independents or with minor parties.

In November 1992, Delaware gave the Democratic nominee, Bill Clinton, a narrow victory with 43.5% of the vote. Incumbent President George Bush received 35.3%, and Independent Ross Perot collected 20.4%. Democrat Thomas R. Carper was elected Governor in 1992, Republican William Roth was re-elected Senator in 1994, and Democrat Joseph Biden won reelection to the Senate in 1990. Republican Michael Castle won reelection in 1994 to remain Delaware's sole US Representative.

Delaware Presidential Vote by Major Political Parties, 1948–92

YEAR	DELAWARE WINNER	DEMOCRAT	REPUBLICAN
1948	Dewey (R)	67,813	69,588
1952	*Eisenhower (R)	83,315	90,059
1956	*Eisenhower (R)	79,421	98,057
1960	*Kennedy (D)	99,590	96,373
1964	*Johnson (D)	122,704	78,078
1968	*Nixon (R)	89,194	96,714
1972	*Nixon (R)	92,283	140,357
1976	*Carter (D)	122,596	109,831
1980	*Reagan (R)	105,700	111,185
1984	*Reagan (R)	101,656	152,190
1988	*Bush	108,647	139,639
1992**	*Clinton	126,054	102,313

* Won US presidential election.

**Independent Ross Perot received 59,213 votes.

14 LOCAL GOVERNMENT

Delaware is divided into three counties. In New Castle, voters elect a county executive and a county council; in Sussex, the members of the elective county council choose a county administrator. Kent operates under an elected levy court. Most of Delaware's 57 municipalities elect a mayor and council.

15 JUDICIAL SYSTEM

Delaware's highest court is the supreme court, composed of a chief justice and four associate justices. Other state courts include the court of chancery and the superior court. The court of chancery handles all corporate cases and is one of the busiest of such courts in the US due to Delaware's high concentration of incorporated businesses. In 1994, Delaware had a total crime rate of 4,147.6 per 100,000.

16 MIGRATION

Delaware enjoyed a net gain from migration of 122,000 persons between 1940 and 1970. Between 1970 and 1990, however, there was a net migration of only about 25,000. Half of all residents in 1990 were born within the state.

17 ECONOMY

Since the 1930s, and particularly since the mid-1970s, Delaware has been one of the nation's most prosperous states. Although manufacturing—primarily the chemical and automotive industries—is the major contributor to the state's economy, it is only the third largest employer after services and trade. The banking industry is an important part of the economy.

Tourism also plays a major role in the state's economy.

18 INCOME

Average personal income per capita (per person) in Delaware was $23,015 in 1994, eleventh highest among the 50 states. In 1993, some 10.2% of the state's residents were living below the federal poverty level.

19 INDUSTRY

Wilmington is called the "Chemical Capital of the World," largely because of E. I. du Pont de Nemours and Co., the chemical industry giant. Important manufactured products, in addition to chemicals and transportation equipment, include apparel, processed meats and vegetables, paper, printing and publishing, scientific instruments, and plastic products.

20 LABOR

The civilian labor force totaled 384,000 in 1994. Some 19,000 Delawareans were unemployed, for an unemployment rate of 4.9%. Some 15.3% of all workers were union members in 1994. As of 1993, about 23,000 people commuted to jobs in Delaware from other states.

21 AGRICULTURE

Though small by national standards, Delaware's agriculture is efficient and productive. About 47% of the state's land area was used for farms and ranches in 1992. In 1994, Delaware's farm industry income was $660 million (40th in the US) with crops accounting for 23% of the total. The major field crops are corn, soybeans, barley, wheat, melons, potatoes, mushrooms, lima beans, and green peas. Production in 1994 included corn for grain, 18,750,000 bushels; soybeans, 8,140,000 bushels; wheat, 3,780,000 bushels; and barley, 1,890,000 bushels.

22 DOMESTICATED ANIMALS

Livestock and livestock products accounted for about 77% of Delaware's farm income in 1994. Sales of chickens and broilers in 1994 made up 69.4% of agricultural receipts. Delaware had 33,000 hogs and 29,000 cattle at the end of 1994.

23 FISHING

Fishing, once an important industry in Delaware, has declined in recent decades. The total commercial landings in 1992 were 6,554,000 pounds, worth $4,207,000.

24 FORESTRY

Delaware had 400,000 acres (164,000 hectares) of forestland in 1994. Sussex County has large areas of southern yellow pine, nearly all of it privately owned.

25 MINING

The value of nonfuel mineral production in Delaware in 1994 was about $16 million. An estimated 5.0 million short tons of construction sand and gravel are produced annually. Delaware also produces magnesium compounds for use in chemical and pharmaceutical production.

26 ENERGY AND POWER

In 1993, production of electric power reached 8.3 billion kilowatt hours. Most power is supplied by coal- and oil-fired plants.

27 COMMERCE

In 1993, sales from wholesale trade in Delaware totaled over $12.3 billion, while retail establishments had sales exceeding $6.8 billion. Service establishment receipts totaled $3.1 billion.

28 PUBLIC FINANCE

Delaware's annual state budget is prepared by the Office of the Budget and submitted by the governor to the general assembly for amendment and approval. State general revenues for 1993/94 (budgeted) were $1,317.4 million; expenditures were $1,260.3 million.

At the close of fiscal 1994, the outstanding debt of Delaware state and local governments was more than $4.1 billion, or $5,936 per capita.

29 TAXATION

Delaware's state tax revenues come primarily from taxes on personal and corporate income, inheritance and estates, motor fuels, cigarettes, betting, and alcoholic beverages. There is no state sales tax. Delaware paid $22.8 billion in federal taxes in 1992.

30 HEALTH

Delaware has lower death rates than the nation as a whole for heart diseases, cerebrovascular diseases, accidents and adverse effects, motor vehicle accidents, and suicide, but higher for cancer. Delaware's eight community hospitals had

The skyline of Wilmington, the largest city in Delaware.

2,200 beds in 1993. The average expense of a community hospital for care was $1,028 per inpatient day. Delaware had 1,453 physicians and 6,137 nurses in 1993. Over 10% of the population does not have health insurance.

31 HOUSING

A July 1993 estimate put the number of housing units at 306,000. In 1990, the median value of a home in Delaware was $100,100, and the median rent for a housing unit was $495 per month.

32 EDUCATION

Nearly 80.1% of adult Delawareans were high school graduates in 1992. The state spends a per pupil average of $6,420 on primary and secondary education. In 1993, 106,000 students were enrolled in public schools, and 23,600 students were enrolled in public higher education. Delaware has two public four-year institutions: the University of Delaware (Newark), and Delaware State College (Dover).

33 ARTS

The restored Grand Opera House in Wilmington, Delaware's Center for the Performing Arts, is the home of the Delaware Symphony and the Delaware Opera Guild. From 1987 to 1991, Delaware received $7,386,980 in federal and state funds for the development of the arts.

34 LIBRARIES AND MUSEUMS

Delaware had 29 public libraries in 1992, with 1,205,427 books and a circulation of 2,922,543. The University of Delaware's Hugh M. Morris Library (Newark) is the largest academic library in the state. Notable among the state's 23 museums are the Delaware History Museum, Winterthur Museum, the Hagley Museum and Delaware Art Museum, all in Wilmington.

35 COMMUNICATIONS

In March 1993, about 269,000 (96.9%) of Delaware's housing units had telephones. The state had 9 AM and 17 FM radio stations and 3 educational television stations in 1993.

36 PRESS

The *Wilmington Morning News* and the *Wilmington Evening Journal* merged to form the *News Journal* in 1989. The paper's daily circulation is 119,043 (139,272 on Sunday).

37 TOURISM, TRAVEL, AND RECREATION

Rehoboth Beach on the Atlantic Coast bills itself as the "Nation's Summer Capital" because of the many federal officials and foreign diplomats who summer there. Fishing, clamming, crabbing, boating, and swimming are the main recreational attractions.

38 SPORTS

Delaware has two major horse-racing tracks: Harrington and Dover Downs, which also has a track for auto racing. The Dover 500 is an annual NASCAR event.

39 FAMOUS DELAWAREANS

John Dickinson (b.Maryland, 1732–1808) was known as the "Penman of the Revolution." Three Delawareans have served as US secretary of state: Louis McLane (1786–1857), John M. Clayton (1796–1856), and Thomas F. Bayard (1828–98). Eleuthère I. du Pont (b.France, 1771–1834) founded the company that bears his name. Delaware authors include Henry Seidel Canby (1878–1961), critic; and novelist Anne Parrish (b.Colorado, 1888–1957). Dr. Henry J. Heimlich (b.1920), developer of the anti-choking "Heimlich maneuver," is also from Delaware. Famous actors include Judge Reinhold (b.1958) and Valerie Bertinelli (b. 1960).

40 BIBLIOGRAPHY

Hoffecker. Carol E. *Delaware: A Bicentennial History*. New York: Norton, 1977.
Vessels, Jane. *Delaware: Small Wonder*. New York: Abrams, 1984.

FLORIDA

State of Florida

ORIGIN OF STATE NAME: Named in 1513 by Juan Ponce de León, who landed during *Pascua Florida,* the Easter festival of flowers.

NICKNAME: The Sunshine State.

CAPITAL: Tallahassee.

ENTERED UNION: 3 March 1845 (27th).

SONG: "Old Folks at Home" (also known as "Swanee River").

POET LAUREATE: Dr. Edmund Skellings.

MOTTO: In God We Trust.

FLAG: The state seal appears in the center of a white field, with four red bars extending from the seal to each corner; the flag is fringed on three sides.

OFFICIAL SEAL: In the background, the sun's rays shine over a distant highland; in the foreground are a sabal palmetto palm, a steamboat, and an Indian woman scattering flowers on the ground. The words "Great Seal of the State of Florida" and the state motto surround the whole.

ANIMAL: Florida panther.

MARINE MAMMALS: Manatee, dolphin.

BIRD: Mockingbird.

FISH: Largemouth bass (freshwater), Atlantic sailfish (saltwater).

FLOWER: Orange blossom.

TREE: Sabal palmetto palm.

GEM: Moonstone.

STONE: Agatized coral.

SHELL: Horse conch.

BEVERAGE: Orange juice.

TIME: 7 AM EST = noon GMT; 6 AM CST = noon GMT.

1 LOCATION AND SIZE

Located in the extreme southeastern US, Florida is the second-largest state east of the Mississippi River and ranks 22d in size among the 50 states. The total area of Florida is approximately 58,664 square miles (151,939 square kilometers). Florida extends 361 miles (581 kilometers) east-west; its maximum north-south extension is 447 miles (719 kilometers). The state comprises a peninsula surrounded by ocean on three sides, with a panhandle of land in the northwest.

Offshore islands include the Florida Keys, extending form the state's southern tip into the Gulf of Mexico. The total boundary length of Florida is 1,799 miles (2,895 kilometers).

2 TOPOGRAPHY

Florida is a huge plateau, much of it barely above sea level. No point in the state is more than 70 miles (113 kilometers) from salt water. Most of the panhandle region is gently rolling country, much like that of southern Georgia and Alabama, with large swampy areas cutting in from the Gulf coast. Peninsular Florida, which contains extensive swampland, has a relatively elevated central section of rolling country, dotted with lakes and springs. Its east coast is shielded from the Atlantic by a string of sandbars. The west coast is cut by numerous bays and inlets, and near its southern tip are the Ten Thousand Islands, a mass of mangrove-covered islets. Southwest of the peninsula lies Key West, the southernmost point of the US mainland.

Almost all the southeastern peninsula and the entire southern end are covered by the Everglades, the world's largest sawgrass swamp, with an area of approximately 4,000 square miles (10,400 square kilometers). To the west and north of the everglades is Big Cypress Swamp, covering about 2,100 square miles (5,400 square kilometers).

Lake Okeechobee, in south-central Florida, is the largest of the state's approximately 30,000 lakes, ponds, and sinks. Although quite shallow, it has a surface area of about 700 square miles (1,800 square kilometers), making it the fourth-largest natural lake located entirely within the US. Crystal River, in Citrus County, has the largest average flow of all inland springs, 878 cubic feet (24.8 cubic meters) per second.

Florida has more than 1,700 rivers, streams, and creeks; the longest river is the

Florida Population Profile

Estimated 1995 population:	14,210,000
Population change, 1980–90:	32.7%
Leading ancestry group:	German
Second leading group:	Irish
Foreign born population:	12.9%
Hispanic origin†:	12.2%
Population by race:	
White:	83.1%
Black:	13.6%
Native American:	0.3%
Asian/Pacific Islander:	1.2%
Other:	1.8%

Population by Age Group

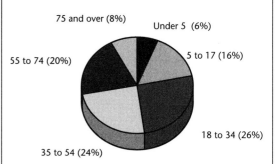

75 and over (8%)
Under 5 (6%)
55 to 74 (20%)
5 to 17 (16%)
18 to 34 (26%)
35 to 54 (24%)

Top Cities with Populations Over 25,000

City	Population	National rank	% change 1980–90
Jacksonville	700,852	15	NA
Miami	367,016	44	3.4
Tampa	284,737	56	3.1
St. Petersburg	235,306	68	0.0
Hialeah	191,702	84	29.4
Orlando	174,215	100	28.4
Fort Lauderdale	148,524	116	–2.5
Tallahassee	130,357	144	53.0
Hollywood	121,732	150	0.3
Miami Beach	90,896	232	–3.8

Notes: †A person of Hispanic origin may be of any race. NA indicates that data are not available.
Sources: Economic and Statistics Administration, Bureau of the Census. *Statistical Abstract of the United States, 1994–95.* Washington, DC: Government Printing Office, 1995; Courtenay M. Slater and George E. Hall. *1995 County and City Extra: Annual Metro, City and County Data Book.* Lanham, MD: Bernan Press, 1995.

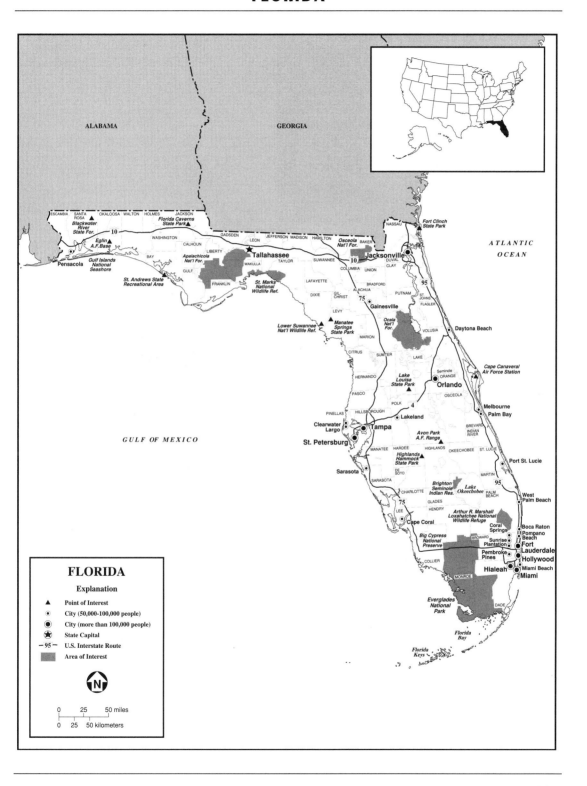

ALABAMA

GEORGIA

ATLANTIC OCEAN

ESCAMBIA SANTA ROSA OKALOOSA WALTON HOLMES JACKSON

Blackwater River State For.

Florida Caverns State Park ▲

GADSDEN

JEFFERSON MADISON HAMILTON

NASSAU

Fort Clinch State Park

Eglin A.F. Base

WASHINGTON

CALHOUN

LEON

LIBERTY

★ **Tallahassee**

WAKULLA

Apalachicola Nat'l For.

BAY

Gulf Islands National Seashore

Pensacola

St. Andrews State Recreational Area

GULF

FRANKLIN

TAYLOR

SUWANNEE

Osceola Nat'l For.

BAKER

Jacksonville

DUVAL

CLAY

COLUMBIA

UNION

10

St. Marks National Wildlife Ref.

LAFAYETTE

DIXIE

GIL-CHRIST

BRADFORD

ALACHUA

PUTNAM

ST. JOHNS

FLAGLER

95

Lower Suwannee Nat'l Wildlife Ref.

Manatee Springs State Park ▲

LEVY

Gainesville

75

MARION

Ocala Nat'l For.

VOLUSIA

Daytona Beach

CITRUS

SUMTER

LAKE

Cape Canaveral Air Force Station ▲

HERNANDO

Lake Louisa State Park ▲

Seminole

ORANGE

Orlando

OSCEOLA

PASCO

4

PINELLAS

HILLSBOROUGH

POLK

Lakeland

Melbourne

Palm Bay

Clearwater

Largo

Tampa

BREVARD

INDIAN RIVER

Avon Park A.F. Range ▲

St. Petersburg

MANATEE

HARDEE

HIGHLANDS

OKEECHOBEE

ST. LUCIE

Highlands Hammock State Park ▲

Sarasota

SARASOTA

DE SOTO

Port St. Lucie

MARTIN

95

Brighton Seminole Indian Res.

Lake Okeechobee

PALM BEACH

CHARLOTTE

GLADES

West Palm Beach

LEE

HENDRY

75

Cape Coral

Arthur R. Marshall Loxahatchee National Wildlife Refuge

Coral Springs

Boca Raton

Pompano Beach

Big Cypress National Preserve

BROWARD

Sunrise

Plantation

Fort Lauderdale

GULF OF MEXICO

COLLIER

Pembroke Pines

Hollywood

Hialeah

Miami Beach

Miami

MONROE

DADE

Everglades National Park

Florida Bay

Florida Keys

FLORIDA

Explanation

▲ Point of Interest

⊙ City (50,000-100,000 people)

◉ City (more than 100,000 people)

★ State Capital

—95— U.S. Interstate Route

▨ Area of Interest

N

| 0 | 25 | 50 miles |

| 0 | 25 | 50 kilometers |

St. Johns, which empties into the Atlantic. Other major rivers are the Suwannee and the Apalachicola. Jim Woodruff Lock and Dam, built on the Apalachicola in 1957, created Lake Seminole, most of which is in Georgia. More than 4,500 islands ring the mainland. Best known are the Florida Keys, of which Key Largo—about 29 miles (47 kilometers) long and less than 2 miles (3 kilometers) wide—is the largest.

3 CLIMATE

A mild, sunny climate is one of Florida's most important natural resources, making it a major tourist center and a retirement home for millions of transplanted northerners. Average annual temperatures range from 65°F to 70°F (18°C to 21°C) in the north, and from 74°F to 77°F (23°C to 25°C) in the southern peninsula and on the Keys. The record high temperature 109°F (43°C), was registered at Monticello on 29 June 1931; the record low, –2°F (–19°C), at Tallahassee on 13 February 1899.

At Jacksonville, the average annual precipitation is 53 inches (135 centimeters), with an average of 116 days of precipitation a year. More than half the annual rainfall generally occurs between June and September; periods of extremely heavy rainfall are common. Florida's long coastline makes it highly vulnerable to hurricanes and tropical storms, which may approach from either the Atlantic or the Gulf coast, bringing winds of up to 150 miles per hour (240 kilometers per hour).

4 PLANTS AND ANIMALS

Generally, Florida has seven floral zones: flatwoods, scrublands, grassy swamps, savannas, salt marshes, hardwood forests (hammocks), and pinelands. North Florida's native plants include longleaf and other pines, oaks, and cypresses. One giant cypress, called "the Senator," is thought to be 3,500 years old. The state is known for its wide variety of palms. Dense mangrove thickets grow along the lower coastal regions, and northern hardwood forests include varieties of rattan, magnolia, and oak. All species of cacti and orchids are regarded as threatened, as are most types of ferns and palms. Endangered species include the prickly apple, key tree cactus, cowhorn orchid, and Harper's beauty.

Florida once claimed more than 80 land mammals. Today the white-tailed deer, wild hog, and gray fox can still be found in the wild. Such small mammals as the raccoon, squirrel, and cottontail and marsh rabbits remain common. The mockingbird was named the state bird in 1927. Among game birds are the bobwhite quail, wild turkey, and at least 30 duck species. The Arctic tern stops in Florida during its remarkable annual migration between the North and South poles.

Common Florida reptiles are the diamondback rattler and various water snakes. Turtle species include mud, green, and loggerhead, and various lizards abound. More than 300 native butterflies have been identified. The peninsula is famous for its marine life: scores of freshwater and saltwater fish, rays, shrimps, live coral reefs, and marine worms.

The state's unusually long list of threatened and endangered wildlife includes the

Photo credit: Orlando/Orange County Convention & Visitors Bureau, Inc.

Citrus fruit ripening under the Florida sun. Citrus groves are scattered throughout Central Florida.

American crocodile, American alligator, shortnose sturgeon, West Indian manatee, Key Largo woodrat, Everglade kite, Bahama swallowtail butterfly, and a number of other species.

5 ENVIRONMENTAL PROTECTION

Throughout the 20th century, a rapidly growing population, the expansion of agriculture, and the exploitation of such resources as timber and minerals have put severe pressure on Florida's natural environment.

The state agency principally responsible for safeguarding the environment is the Department of Environmental Protection (DEP), created in 1993 by the merger of the Departments of Natural Resources and Environmental Protection. State spending for environmental protection in 1993/94 was more than $1 billion.

Contamination of groundwater and control of storm water are the state's most serious environmental problems. Groundwater, surface water, and soil contamination have been found across the state. Major contaminants include the pesticide ethylene dibromide (EDB). Florida has one of the nation's largest programs to clean groundwater contaminated by leaking underground storage tanks.

Contamination of groundwater is not the state's only water problem. Salt water from the Atlantic and the Gulf of Mexico has begun seeping into the layers of porous limestone that hold Florida's reserves of fresh water, as increased demand for water has reduced the subterranean runoff of fresh water into these bodies.

In 1960, the only undersea park in the US, the John Pennekamp Coral Reef State Park, was established in a 75-square mile (194-square-kilometer) sector off the Atlantic coast of Key Largo. This is an effort to protect a portion of the beautiful reefs, rich in tropical fish and other marine life, that adjoin the Keys.

6 POPULATION

Florida, the most populous state in the southeastern US, is also one of the fastest-growing of the 50 states. In 1960, it was the tenth most populous state; by 1980, it ranked seventh; and by 1990, it ranked fourth, with a population of 12,937,926. The estimated population for 1995 was 14,210,000. US Census Bureau projections indicate that Florida will have a population of 16,315,000 by the year 2000.

Of the 1990 population, 90.8% lived in metropolitan areas; the average population density in 1990 was 240 persons per square mile (about 93 persons per square kilometer). Some 28% of the population was 55 years of age or over, the highest such percentage of all the states and nearly 50% above the US average.

The most populous city in Florida is Jacksonville, the 15th largest city in the US in 1990. Its population in 1992 was 700,852. Miami is Florida's second-largest city, with a 1992 population of 367,016. The Miami-Fort Lauderdale metropolitan area, the state's largest metropolitan region, had an estimated 3,193,000 residents (11th in the US) in 1990. Fort Lauderdale had a city population of 148,524 in 1992. Tallahassee, the state capital, had a population of 130,357.

7 ETHNIC GROUPS

Florida's population consists mainly of whites of northern European heritage, blacks, and Hispanics. The largest group of first- and second-generation residents are Cubans, who represented 4% of Florida's population in 1990. The state also has the highest number of foreign-born Nicaraguans, and is second behind New York as a residence of individuals from Jamaica, Colombia, Haiti, and Trinidad & Tobago. There were 1,574,000 individuals

of Hispanic origin in 1990, including 541,011 Cubans, 174,445 Puerto Ricans, and 134,161 Mexicans. The black population, as reported in 1990, was 1,759,534, or almost 13.6%.

The 1990 census reported a population of 42,619 Native Americans from 34 tribes. Florida has the ninth largest population of Asian and Pacific Islanders of the 50 states. In 1990 there were 37,531 Filipinos, 28,787 Chinese, 22,240 Asian Indians, 14,586 Vietnamese, 15,401 Japanese, 14,722 Koreans, and 3,075 Hawaiians.

8 LANGUAGES

Massive migration from the North Central and North Atlantic areas, including a large number of speakers of Yiddish, has affected the previously rather uniform Southern speech of much of the state. Borrowing from the Spanish of the expanding number of Cubans and Puerto Ricans in the Miami area has had a further effect. Indian place-names in Florida include Okeechobee, Apalachicola, Kissimmee, Sarasota, Pensacola, and Hialeah.

About 10 million Floridians (83%) speak only English at home. Other languages spoken at home included Spanish (1,447,000); French (194,000); German (81,000); Italian (70,000); and Yiddish (27,000).

9 RELIGIONS

Protestant denominations claim the majority of church members in Florida. The largest Protestant denominations are the Southern Baptist Convention, with 786,000 members; United Methodist

Church, 462,000; Presbyterian Church (USA), 202,000; Episcopal Church, 120,000; Assembly of God, 134,000; and Lutheran Church–Missouri Synod, 68,000. The Roman Catholic population of Florida numbers 1,598,000. The state also has a sizable Jewish population. A Greek Orthodox community is centered in Tarpon Springs.

10 TRANSPORTATION

As of 1992, there were a total of 2,874 rail miles (4,624 kilometers) of track in Florida, operated by 14 railroads. As of 1992, Amtrak provided passenger service to 29 Florida stations; 1,076,510 Florida passengers rode the Amtrak system that year. As of 1992, Florida had 110,640 miles (178,020 kilometers) of public roads. Of this total, 11,870 miles (19,098 kilometers) constituted the state highway system. Florida had 10,169,556 registered motor vehicles in 1993 including 8,072,492 automobiles and 38,761 buses.

Inland waterways in Florida include the southernmost section of the Atlantic Intracoastal Waterway and the easternmost section of the Gulf Intracoastal Waterway. Both are navigable, federally maintained coastal channels for commercial vessels and pleasure craft. Florida has several commercially important ports. By far the largest port is Tampa, which handled 49,548,191 tons of cargo in 1991, making it the 11th busiest port in the US. Other major ports include Jacksonville, Port Everglades Pensacola, and Miami.

Florida is the third-ranking state in terms of aircraft, pilots, and airline passengers. During 1993, more than 43,187,000 passengers took off from Florida's 22 commercial service airports. Florida's busiest airport is Miami International, which boarded 14,030,586 passengers in 1993.

11 HISTORY

By about 2000 BC, Native Americans in north Florida had an agricultural and hunting economy organized around village life. The southern groups did not practice agriculture until about 450 BC, when they began to plant corn in villages around Lake Okeechobee. As they spread over Florida and adjusted to widely different local conditions, the various tribes fell into six main divisions, with numerous subgroups and distinctive cultural traits. When Europeans arrived in the early 16th century, they found nearly 100,000 Native Americans, including the Apalachee, Timucua, Tocobaga, Calusa, and Tequesta tribes.

The Spaniards sought to Christianize the Native Americans and settle them around missions to grow food, supply labor, and help defend the province. The impact of the Europeans on the native population was, on the whole, disastrous. They died of European-introduced diseases, were killed in wars with whites or with other Indians, or moved away. When the Spanish departed Florida in 1763, the remaining 300 of the original 100,000 Native Americans left with them.

As early as 1750, small groups of Creek tribes from Georgia and Alabama began to move into the north Florida area vacated by the previous tribes. Called Seminole, the Creek word for runaway or refugee, these groups numbered only

5,000 when Florida became part of the US. However, pressures on the US president and Congress to remove the Seminole intensified after runaway black slaves began seeking refuge with them. When the Seminole resisted being removed to present-day Oklahoma (after first being confined to reservations) the result was the longest and most costly of Indian wars, the Seminole War of 1835–42. The warfare and the succeeding forced migration left fewer than 300 Seminole in Florida.

European Settlement

The history of the twice-repeated annihilation of Florida Indians is, at the same time, the history of white settlers' rise to power in Florida. Sailing from Puerto Rico in search of the fabled island of Bimini, Juan Ponce de León sighted Florida on 27 March 1513. Ponce de León claimed the land for Spain and named it La Florida, for *Pascua Florida,* the Easter festival of flowers.

In 1562, Jean Ribault, with a small expedition of French Huguenots, arrived at the St. Johns River, east of present-day Jacksonville, and claimed Florida for France. Another group of French Huguenot settlers built nearby Fort Caroline two years later. In the summer of 1565, the Spaniard Pedro Menéndez de Avilés marched overland to take Fort Caroline by surprise, killing most of the occupants. St. Augustine was the first permanent European settlement in the US. It served primarily, under Spanish rule, as a military outpost, maintained to protect the wealth of New Spain. In 1763, when Spain ceded Florida to England in exchange for Cuba,

about 3,000 Spaniards departed from St. Augustine and 800 from Pensacola, leaving Florida to the Seminole.

British Florida reached from the Atlantic to the Mississippi River and became two colonies, East and West Florida. There, settlers established farms and plantations and moved steadily toward economic and political self-sufficiency (although these settlers did not join the American Revolution). In 1781, Spain attacked and captured Pensacola. Two years later, Britain ceded both Floridas back to Spain. During the second Spanish era, English influence remained strong. Florida west of the Perdido River was taken over by the US in 1810, as part of the Louisiana Purchase (1803).

Statehood

Present-day Florida was ceded to the US in 1821, in settlement of $5 million in claims by US citizens against the Spanish government. At this time, General Andrew Jackson, who three years earlier had led a punitive expedition against the Seminole, came back to Florida as military governor. In 1824 Tallahassee, in the wilderness of north-central Florida, was selected as Florida's capital. Middle Florida, as the Tallahassee region was then called, rapidly became an area of slave-owning cotton plantations and was for several decades the fastest-growing part of the territory. Floridians drew up a state constitution in 1838–39. But, being proslavery, Florida had to wait until 1845 to enter the Union, when it was paired with the free state of Iowa under the Missouri Compromise.

In 1861, Florida seceded from the Union and joined the Confederacy. Some 15,000 whites (one-third of whom died) served in the Confederate army, and 1,200 whites and almost as many blacks joined the Union army. Bitterness and some violence accompanied Republican Reconstruction government in 1868–76. The conservative Bourbon Democrats then governed for the rest of the century. The Spanish-American War in 1898, during which Tampa became the port of embarkation for an expedition to Cuba, stimulated the economy and advertised the state nationwide.

Twentieth Century

Feverish land speculation brought hundreds of thousands of people to Florida in the first half of the 1920s. Cresting in 1925, the real estate boom was already over in 1926, when a devastating hurricane struck Miami, burying all hope of recovery. The Florida depression that began in 1926 was compounded by the national depression that hit late in 1929. The state joined the federal government in assuming responsibility for relief and recovery. The state's first paper mill opened in the same year, revolutionizing the forest industry.

The 1940s opened with recovery and optimism, arising from the stimulus of production for World War II. New army and navy installations and training programs brought business growth. The number of army and navy airfield flying schools increased from 5 to 45. Families of thousands of trainees visited the state. Florida was on the eve of another boom.

Between 1940 and 1990, migration would bring Florida's population ranking from 27th in the nation up to 4th, with more than 12.8 million people.

In 1986, Florida absorbed 1,000 arrivals a day. Until the early 1980s, many of those migrants were 65 years of age or over. In the mid-1980s, however, the majority of newcomers were younger—25 to 44 years old. They came in search of the opportunities provided by Florida's growing and diversifying economy. The management of growth in Florida has dominated state politics in the postwar era, centering on conflicts between developers and those who seek to preserve the natural beauty of the state.

Racial and ethnic relations have become another central issue. There have been efforts to reapportion (reorganize) Florida's 23 Congressional districts and the Legislature's 40 Senate and 120 House seats. The reorganization has been complicated by battles between blacks and Hispanics over the number and character of minority districts. Tensions between the two groups led to violence in 1989 when a Hispanic police officer shot and killed a black motorcyclist. Riots broke out in the mostly black Overton section of Miami and continued for three days. Six people died and 27 stores were set on fire.

In August 1992, Hurricane Andrew caused over $10 billion in damages in south Florida, primarily in and around Homestead.

[12] STATE GOVERNMENT

Florida's legislature consists of a 40-member senate and a 120-member house of representatives. Senators serve four-year terms, with half the senate being elected every two years. Representatives serve two-year terms. The maximum length of a regular session is 60 calendar days, unless it is extended by a three-fifths vote of each house.

The governor is elected for a four-year term; a two-term limit is in effect. The lieutenant governor is elected on the same ticket as the governor. A six-member cabinet—consisting of the secretary of state, attorney general, comptroller, insurance commissioner and treasurer, commissioner of agriculture, and commissioner of education—is independently elected.

Each cabinet member heads an executive department. The governor appoints the heads of ten departments and shares supervision of seven additional departments with the cabinet. The governor and cabinet also share management of or membership in several other state agencies. These provisions make Florida's elected cabinet one of the strongest such bodies in any of the 50 states.

Passage of legislation requires a majority vote of those present and voting in both houses. A bill passed by the legislature becomes law if it is signed by the governor. The governor may veto legislation and, in general appropriations bills, may veto individual items. The governor's vetoes may be overridden by a two-thirds vote of the legislators present in each house.

[13] POLITICAL PARTIES

Aided from 1889 to 1937 by a poll tax, which effectively prevented the majority of the state's mostly Republican blacks from voting, the Democrats won every governor's election but one from 1876 through 1962. By the time Republican Claude R. Kirk, Jr. won the governorship in 1966, Florida had already become, for national elections, a two-party state, although Democrats retained a sizable advantage in party registration.

As of 1994, the state had 3,318,565 registered Democrats, comprising 51% of the total number of registered voters, and 2,672,968 registered Republicans, or 41%. Eight percent of the registered voters, numbering 523,292, are unaffiliated. In addition to the Democratic and Republican parties, organized groups include the Citizens and Libertarian parties.

Democrat Lawton Chiles, former senator, was elected governor in 1990 and was narrowly reelected in 1994. Connie Mack, a Republican, won the Senatorial race in 1988, and Democrat Robert Graham was re-elected to the Senate in 1992. Florida's US House delegation in 1994 had thirteen Republicans and ten Democrats. The state senate in 1994 contained 20 Democrats and 20 Republicans, and the state house of representatives had 71 Democrats and 49 Republicans. In the 1992 presidential election, Floridians gave 41% of the vote to Republican George Bush; 39% to Democrat Bill Clinton; and 20% to Independent Ross Perot.

14 LOCAL GOVERNMENT

In 1992, Florida had 66 counties, 390 municipalities, 95 school districts, and 489 special districts. Generally, legislative authority within each county is vested in a five-member elected board of county commissioners. Counties may generally enact any law not inconsistent with state law. Municipalities are normally incorporated and chartered by an act of the state legislature. Except where a county charter specifies otherwise, municipal ordinances override county laws. Municipal governments may provide a full range of local services. Consolidated city/county governments are found in Miami (Dade County) and Jacksonville (Duval County).

15 JUDICIAL SYSTEM

The state's highest court is the supreme court, a panel of seven justices that sits in Tallahassee. The supreme court has appeals jurisdiction only. Below the supreme court are five district courts of appeal. District courts hear appeals of lower court decisions and may review the actions of executive agencies.

The state's principal trial courts are its 20 circuit courts, which have original jurisdiction in many types of cases, including civil suits involving more than $15,000, felony cases, and all cases involving juveniles. Circuit courts may also hear appeals from county courts if no constitutional question is involved.

Each of Florida's 67 counties has a county court with original jurisdiction in misdemeanor cases, civil disputes involving $15,000 or less, and traffic-violation cases. Florida has one of the highest crime rates in the US. In 1994, the total crime rate was 8,250 per 100,000. As of 1993, a total of 53,048 persons were serving prison sentences in institutions run by

Florida Presidential Vote by Political Parties, 1948–92

Year	Florida Winner	Democrat	Republican	States' Rights Democrat	Progressive
1948	*Truman (D)	281,988	194,280	89,755	11,620
1952	*Eisenhower (R)	444,950	544,036		
1956	*Eisenhower (R)	480,371	643,849		
1960	Nixon (R)	748,700	795,476		
1964	*Johnson (D)	948,540	905,941		
				American Ind.	
1968	*Nixon (R)	676,794	886,804	624,207	
1972	*Nixon (R)	718,117	1,857,759		
				American	
1976	*Carter (D)	1,636,000	1,469,531	21,325	
					Libertarian
1980	*Reagan (R)	1,417,637	2,043,006	Ind. (Anderson)	30,457
1984	*Reagan (R)	1,448,816	2,730,350	189,099	744
				New Alliance	
1988	*Bush (R)	1,656,701	2,618,885	6,665	19,796
				Ind. (Perot)	
1992	Bush (R)	2,072,798	2,173,310	1,053,067	15,079

* Won US presidential election.

state and federal correctional authorities in Florida.

including 42,928 Mexicans, 30,375 Haitians, and 2,190 Dominicans.

16 MIGRATION

Florida is populated mostly by migrants from elsewhere. In 1990, only 30.5% of all state residents were Florida-born, compared with 61.8% for the US as a whole. Only Nevada had a lower proportion of native residents. Migration from other states accounted for more than 85% of Florida's population increase in the 1970s. From 1985 to 1990, net migration gains added another 1,461,550 new residents.

In the 20th century, US immigrants to Florida have come, for the most part, from the Northeast and Midwest, often to escape harsh northern winters, and a large proportion of the migrants have been retirees and other senior citizens. Although the state has had a significant Cuban population since the second half of the 19th century, the number of immigrants surged after the Cuban revolution of 1959. From December 1965 to April 1973, an airlift agreed to by the Cuban and US governments landed a quarter of a million Cubans in Miami. By 1990, a reported 541,011 ethnic Cubans were living in southern Florida.

Haitian "boat people" have arrived in Florida in significant numbers—often reaching the southern peninsula in packed, barely seaworthy small craft. The number of ethnic Haitians in Florida was reported at 105,495 in 1990. As of 1990, a reported 1,662,601 Floridians (13%) were foreign-born. In 1991, 141,068 foreign immigrants were admitted into Florida,

17 ECONOMY

Tourists and winter residents with second homes in Florida contribute billions of dollars annually to the state economy and make retailing and construction particularly important economic areas. However, this dependence on spending by visitors and part-time dwellers also makes the economy—and especially the housing industry—highly sensitive to recession. The economic downturn of the early 1980s hit Florida harder than the US generally. New housing starts, for example, which fell by about 2% in the US from 1981 to 1982, dropped by more than 20% in Florida during the same period.

An extremely low level of unionization among Florida workers encouraged growth in manufacturing in the 1970s and early 1980s—but may also help explain Floridians' below-average income levels. The arms build-up during the Reagan administration helped to expand Florida's aerospace and electronics industries. Even in 1991, after reduction of the military budget, Florida ranked seventh nationally in the value of Department of Defense contracts awarded. Miami is said to have one of the largest "underground economies" in the US, a reference both to the sizable inflow of cash from illicit drug trafficking and to the large numbers of Latin American immigrants working for low, unreported cash wages.

18 INCOME

In 1994, Florida's per capita (per person) income was $21,651, 20th among the 50 states. Total personal income rose to $302 billion in 1994. In 1993, 17.8% of all Floridians lived below the federal poverty level. In 1990, the West Palm Beach area ranked second highest in per capita personal income (at $28,097) of all metropolitan areas in the nation.

19 INDUSTRY

Florida ranked 14th in number of manufacturing employees in 1993 with 484,200. The state is not a center of heavy industry, and many of its manufacturing activities are related to agriculture and exploitation of natural resources. Leading industries include food processing, electric and electronic equipment, transportation equipment, and chemicals.

Florida ranks second only to California in both employment and number of firms engaged in the manufacture of guided missiles and space vehicles. Some 10% of all US aircraft engines and engine parts are manufactured in Florida. Nearly 20% of the nation's boat manufacturers are located in the state. Since the perfection of the laser by Martin–Marietta in Orlando in the 1950s, the greater Orlando area has grown to have the third-highest concentration of electro-optics and laser manufacturers in the US.

20 LABOR

Florida's civilian labor force averaged 6,824,000 in 1994. There was an unemployment rate of 6.6%. As in the US generally, unemployment was higher among nonwhites and teenagers than among white adults—and highest among black teenagers.

Reflecting the importance of tourism to Florida's economy, a higher proportion of the state's workers are employed in the trade and service industries than for the US as a whole. The proportion of workers in manufacturing is a little over half the US average.

Some 8.2% of all workers were union members in 1994. The state has a right-to-work law, and workers are not required to join a union.

21 AGRICULTURE

Florida's most important agricultural products, and the ones for which it is most famous, are its citrus fruits. Florida continues to supply the vast majority of orange juice consumed in the US. Florida produced 67.1% of the nation's oranges and 76.7% of its grapefruits in 1991/92. The state is also an important producer of other fruits, vegetables, sugarcane, and soybeans.

The total value of Florida's crops in 1994 exceeded $4.7 billion, fourth highest among the 50 states. Total farm marketings, including livestock marketings and products, totaled almost $6.0 billion in 1994 (9th in the US). There were about 39,000 farms covering some 10 million acres (4 million hectares) in 1993. This total represented more than 30% of the state's entire land area.

The orange crop totaled 174,200,000 90-pound boxes in 1994. The grapefruit crop was 51,050,000 85-pound boxes;

Kennedy Space Center–Spaceport USA is NASA's site for shuttle and other launches.

tangerines, 4,100,000 95-pound boxes; and tangelos and temple oranges, 3,350,000 and 2,250,000 90-pound boxes, respectively. There are 50 factories in Florida where citrus fruits are processed into canned or chilled juice, frozen or pasteurized concentrate, or canned fruit sections. Production of frozen orange juice concentrate totaled 151,396,000 gallons in the 1990/91 season. Citrus by-products include citrus molasses, alcohol, wines, preserves, and citrus seed oil.

Florida is one of the country's leading producers of vegetables. In 1994, Florida farmers harvested 1,604.7 million pounds of tomatoes; they sold 999.2 million pounds of potatoes. Florida's tomato and vegetable growers, who had at one time enjoyed a near monopoly of the US winter vegetable market, began in the late 1970s to face increasing competition from Mexican growers. Lower-priced Mexican produce had captured about half the market by 1980. Other important fresh fruits and vegetables produced in the state include strawberries, watermelons, sweet corn, bell peppers, and cucumbers.

Florida's major field crop is sugarcane, which enjoyed a sizable production increase in the 1960s and 1970s, following the cutoff of imports from Cuba. In 1994, Florida's sugarcane production was 15,120,000 tons. Florida's second-largest field crop is soybeans (1,302,000 bushels in 1994.) Hay, peanuts, cotton, and tobacco are other important field crops.

22 DOMESTICATED ANIMALS

Florida is an important cattle-raising state, ranked 15th in the US in number of cattle in 1994. Most of the beef cattle are sold to out-of-state feedlots; cash receipts from livestock marketings totaled $1,191.6 million in 1994. Other types of livestock raised commercially are hogs, sheep, rabbits, and poultry. At the end of 1994, Florida had 2,020,000 cattle and 100,000 hogs.

The raising of thoroughbred horses and the production of eggs and honey are also major industries. Florida ranks third in the US in number of thoroughbreds, surpassed only by Kentucky and California. Dairy products contributed 6.8% to total agricultural receipts in 1994.

23 FISHING

Florida's extensive shoreline and numerous inland waterways make sport fishing a major recreational activity. Commercial fishing is also economically important. In 1992, Florida's commercial fish catch was 152,169,000 pounds, with a value of $154,889,000. The most important commercial species of shellfish in 1991 were shrimp, spiny lobster, and crabs. Valuable finfish species included grouper, swordfish, and snappers. In 1992, Florida had 149 Atlantic and 333 Gulf coast processing and wholesale plants.

Both freshwater and saltwater fishing are important sports. Tarpon, sailfish, and redfish are some of the major saltwater sport species. Largemouth bass, panfish, sunfish, catfish, and perch are leading freshwater sport fish. In 1992, federal hatcheries distributed over 3.5 million (2,841 pounds) warmwater fish and roe (fish eggs) within the state.

24 FORESTRY

Over half of Florida's land area—16,549,012 acres (6,697,385 hectares)—was forested in 1992. The most common tree is the pine, which occurs throughout the state but is most abundant in the north. Florida's forestry industry shipped $4.3 billion worth of lumber and wood products in 1992. The most important forestry product is pulpwood for paper manufacturing. Lumber production that year was 900 million board feet, 877 million board feet of softwoods, and 23 million board feet of hardwoods.

Practically all of Florida's natural forest had been cleared by the mid-20th century. The forests existing today are thus almost entirely the result of reforestation. Since 1928, more than 5.1 billion seedlings have been planted in the state. Four national forests—Apalachicola, Ocala, Osceola, and Choctawatchee—are located in Florida.

25 MINING

Florida's estimated nonfuel mineral production in 1994 was valued at $1.5 billion. The state ranks sixth in US mineral production. Florida continued to lead the nation in phosphate rock, mineral sands, and peat output, and ranked among the top three states in crushed stone and masonry cement production.

Photo credit: Orlando/Orange County Convention & Visitors Bureau, Inc.

Canoeing in Orange County, Florida.

The state is a world leader in phosphate rock production and leads the nation in heavy-mineral output. Phosphate rock was the leading mineral commodity, in terms of value, accounting for over 50% of the estimated value. Crushed stone, sales of which were estimated at $268 million, was the second leading mineral commodity. Portland and masonry cement ranked third; sand and gravel and clays rounded out the top five commodities in terms of reportable value.

26 ENERGY AND POWER

In 1992, a total of 3,066 trillion Btu of energy was consumed in Florida. Per capita (per person) energy use in 1992 was 227.4 million Btu; per capita expenditure in 1992 was $1,510, lower than any other state. Florida's mild climate and abundant sunshine offer great potential for solar energy development, but this potential has not been extensively exploited. In 1993, electric energy production was 140.1 billion kilowatt hours. In 1993, 23% of electricity produced came from residual fuel oil, 44% from coal, 18.5% from nuclear power, and 14% from natural gas. Hydroelectricity and distillate fuels totaled less than 1%. There are five nuclear power plants in the state.

Florida ranked 20th in oil production in 1993. In 1993, the state produced 6 million barrels of crude oil. Proven reserves are 37 million barrels. Natural gas production in 1993 was 7 billion cubic feet. Proven natural gas reserves are 38 billion cubic feet.

27 COMMERCE

According to the 1992 US Census of Retail Trade, the state ranked fourth in number of retail establishments. The fashionable shops lining Palm Beach's Worth Avenue make it one of the nation's most famous shopping streets. Personal income earned in retail sales in 1992 exceeded $19 billion. At least 15.8% of retail trade employees worked in the 10,502 restaurants, cafeterias, bars, and similar establishments—a reflection, in part, of the importance of the travel business in Florida's economy.

The value of all imports into Florida through Tampa and Miami was $15.4 billion in 1992. Florida's exports of goods totaled $14.4 billion in 1992. Duty-free goods for reshipment abroad pass through Port Everglades, Miami, Orlando, Jacksonville, Tampa, and Panama City—free-trade zones established to bring international commerce to the state. Florida is a popular entry point for marijuana, cocaine, and other illicit drugs being smuggled into the US from Latin America.

28 PUBLIC FINANCE

The largest expenditure items are education, health and social concerns, general government, and transportation. By prohibiting borrowing to finance operating expenses, Florida's constitution requires a balanced budget. The general revenues for 1993 were $33.2 billion; expenditures were $30.1 billion.

The total indebtedness of Florida state and local governments in 1993 exceeded $13 billion. The state debt outstanding at the end of 1993 was $993 per capita (per person).

29 TAXATION

Florida ranked 39th among the 50 states in per capita (per person) state taxation in 1991 with a tax burden of $1,036.7 per capita. The 6% sales and use tax is the largest single source of state revenue, but property taxes make up the bulk of local receipts. The state constitution prohibits a personal income tax. For 1991, school districts levied $430 million in property taxes; property taxes thus represented nearly one-third of Florida public school moneys.

The state sales tax applies to most retail items, as well as to car and hotel room rentals and theater admissions. The use tax is levied on wholesale items brought into Florida for sale. Other taxes include those on gasoline and other motor fuels, cigarettes, alcoholic beverages, drivers' licenses and motor vehicles, and parimutuel betting. In 1990, Floridians paid nearly $25.6 billion in federal income taxes.

30 HEALTH

Florida exceeds the national rate in deaths from heart disease, cancer, cerebrovascular disease, accidents, and suicide. The leading causes of death are cardiovascular disease and cancer. The former accounted for 34% of all deaths in the state. Cancer claimed just over 25% of the total. Florida has the lowest rate of mortality due to congestive heart failure of all the states.

In 1993 there were 223 hospitals in Florida. The total number of beds available was 51,300; admissions totaled 1,705,600. As of 1 January 1993, the total number of licensed nonfederal physicians in the state was 29,209. There were 215 physicians per 100,000 population. The average expense for a hospital stay was $6,169; per inpatient day, $940. Over 19% of Floridians do not have health insurance.

31 HOUSING

In July 1993, there were an estimated 6,474,000 housing units in Florida. Multi-family housing ranges from beachfront luxury high-rises along the Gold Coast to dilapidated residential hotels in the South Beach section of Miami Beach. In 1990, the median monthly cost for an owner-occupied housing unit with a mortgage was $718; for a unit without a mortgage, it was $186. That year, the median rent for a housing unit was $481.

In 1990, 15.5% of all housing units were condominiums, a higher proportion than any other state except Hawaii. In numbers of condominiums, however, Florida led the nation in 1990, at 944,590. Large retirement communities, often containing thousands of condominium units, are commonplace in Dade, Broward, and Palm Beach counties. Florida also led the nation in number of mobile homes or trailers in 1990, at 762,855, which represented nearly 12.5% of all housing units.

In 1993, 115,103 new housing units were authorized, more than any other state. Of that total, over 20% were multi-unit dwellings. The total value of new housing authorized in 1993 was over $9.6 billion, second only to California.

32 EDUCATION

Over 78% of Floridians 25 years of age or older are high school graduates; 19.4% have four or more years of college. There were 1,518,000 students in grades K–8 and 524,000 in grades 9–12. Student achievement in reading, writing, and mathematics is measured by the State Student Assessment Test (SSAT), given annually to all 3d, 5th, 8th, and 11th graders. In 1993, the state spent a per pupil average of $5,314 on primary and secondary education. This amount ranks 27th among the 50 states.

Florida has nine state universities, with a total fall 1992 enrollment of 176,762. The largest is the University of South Florida (Tampa), followed by the University of Florida (Gainesville). Also part of the state university system are special university centers, such as the University of Florida's Institute of Food and Agricultural Science. The state's 28 community colleges have an enrollment of more than 263,000. Almost two-thirds of the community college students attended on a part-time basis. Of Florida's 48 private institutions of higher education, by far the largest is the University of Miami (Coral Gables).

33 ARTS

The Asolo Theater, which is located in Sarasota and is the site of an annual theater festival, was designated the state theater of Florida by the 1965 legislature. Regional and metropolitan symphony orchestras include the Florida Philharmonic (Miami),

Photo credit: Florida Department of Commerce, Division of Tourism.

St. Petersburg, Florida.

Florida Symphony (Orlando), and Jacksonville Symphony. Opera companies include the Asolo Opera Company, Florida Opera West, and Greater Miami Opera Association. From 1987 to 1991, the State of Florida generated $111,267,208 from federal and state sources to develop its arts programs.

34 LIBRARIES AND MUSEUMS

Florida had 8 multi-county library systems and 43 county systems in 1994. The book stock was 21.7 million, and circulation totaled 65.8 million. The State Library in Tallahassee housed 553,044 volumes and 334,351 microforms in 1994. The largest university library in the state is that of the University of Florida (Gainesville), with holdings of more than 2.3 million volumes in 1991.

Florida has about 230 museums, galleries, and historical sites, as well as numerous public gardens. The estates and homes of a number of prominent former Florida residents are now open as museums, including the homes of Ernest Hemingway and John James Audubon in Key West and Thomas Edison's house in Fort Myers.

The largest historic restoration in Florida is in St. Augustine, where several blocks of the downtown area have been restored to their 18th-century likeness under the auspices of the Historic St.

Augustine Preservation Board. The Metrozoo-Miami has an average annual attendance of 840,000.

35 COMMUNICATIONS

As of March 1993, 93.7% of Florida's 5,578,000 occupied housing units had telephones. In 1993, the state had 210 AM stations and 240 FM. There were 90 TV stations in Florida in 1993. Miami, with 11 stations, had more than any other Florida city. In 1993, Florida had 50 large cable television systems.

36 PRESS

The oldest newspaper still publishing is the *Jacksonville Times-Union* (now *Florida Times-Union*), which first appeared in February 1883. In 1994, the state had 39 daily newspapers. There were 27 morning papers, 11 evening papers, 1 all-day paper, and 33 Sunday papers. The leading English-language dailies and their daily circulations in 1994 were the *Miami Herald* (444,581); the *St. Petersburg Times* (352,135); the *Tampa Tribune* (321,626); and the *Orlando Sentinel* (287,270).

There were 210 weekly newspapers in 1994. Fifteen black newspapers and 4 Spanish-language newspapers were also published in Florida. There were 32 book publishers in Florida in 1994, including Academic Press and University Presses of Florida.

37 TOURISM, TRAVEL, AND RECREATION

Tourism is a mainstay of the state's economy. In 1992, Florida had almost 40.6 million visitors—who collectively spent nearly $23 billion there. Almost 21.1 million visitors entered the state by car in 1992; another 19.5 million visitors arrived by air. Most of Florida's tourists are from elsewhere in the US. But in the 1990s, Miami was attracting large numbers of affluent Latin American travelers, lured at least partly by the Latin flavor the large Cuban community has given the city.

In March 1993, the state had 772 licensed hotels, with a total of 128,265 units. In addition, Florida had 3,951 licensed motels with 205,220 units as of March 1993. Florida's biggest tourist attractions are its sun, sand, and surf. A major tourist attraction is Walt Disney World, a huge amusement park near Orlando. In 1982, EPCOT Center, a futuristic exhibition and amusement park, was opened at Walt Disney World. Both Busch Gardens (Tampa) and Sea World of Florida (Orlando) report average annual attendances of 3,000,000. Other major attractions are the Kennedy Space Center at Cape Canaveral and the St. Augustine historic district.

Nine parks and other facilities in Florida operated by the National Park Service draw millions of visitors annually. The most popular destination is the Gulf Islands National Seashore, located near Pensacola (5.4 million visitors), followed by the Canaveral National Seashore. Fishing and boating are major recreational activities. Off-track betting, horse-racing, dog-racing, jai alai, and bingo are all legalized forms of gaming.

The 72,000-seat Florida Citrus Bowl in Orlando.

38 SPORTS

Florida has eight major league professional sports teams: the Miami Dolphins, Tampa Bay Buccaneers, and Jacksonville Jaguars (a 1995 expansion team) of the National Football League; the Miami Heat and the Orlando Magic of the National Basketball Association; the Tampa Bay Lightning and Florida Panthers of the National Hockey League; and added in 1994, the Florida Marlins of Major League Baseball. Baseball's Tampa Bay Devil Rays will begin play in 1997. Several professional baseball teams also have spring training facilities in Florida.

Several tournaments on both the men's and women's professional golf tours are played in Florida. In auto racing, the Daytona 500 is a top race on the NASCAR circuit. Three of the major collegiate football bowl games are played in the state: the Orange Bowl in Miami, the Gator Bowl in Jacksonville, and the Florida Citrus Bowl in Orlando. In collegiate sports, football dominates. The University of Florida, Florida State, and the University of Miami all emerged as nationally ranked powerhouses in the 1980s and 1990s.

39 FAMOUS FLORIDIANS

Florida produced one of the major US military figures of World War II, General Joseph Warren Stilwell (1883–1946), dubbed "Vinegar Joe" for his strongly stated opinions. General Daniel James, Jr.

(1920–78), known as "Chappie," was the first black four-star general in the US. Janet Reno (b.1938), Attorney General of the United States in the Clinton presidency, was born in Miami. David Levy Yulee (b.St. Thomas, 1810–86) was appointed one of the state's first two US senators in 1845, thereby becoming the first Jew to sit in the Senate. He resigned in 1861 to serve in the Confederate Congress. Ruth Bryan Owen Rohde (b.Illinois, 1885–1954) became the first woman to head a US diplomatic office abroad when she was named minister to Denmark.

Military figures who have played a major role in Florida's history include the Spanish conquistadors Juan Ponce de León (c.1460–1521), the European discoverer of Florida, and Pedro Menéndez de Avilés (1519–74), founder of the first permanent settlement, St. Augustine.

In the 1880s, Henry Morrison Flagler (b.New York, 1830–1913) began to acquire and build railroads down the length of Florida's east coast and to develop tourist hotels, helping to create one of the state's major present-day industries. Among Floridians prominent in science was Dr. John F. Gorrie (b.South Carolina, 1802–55), who specialized in the treatment of fevers and developed an early version of air-conditioning.

The noted labor and civil rights leader A. Philip Randolph (1889–1979) was a native of Crescent City. Mary McLeod Bethune (b.South Carolina, 1875–1955) was an advisor to President Franklin D. Roosevelt on minority affairs and a prominent black educator.

Well-known Florida authors include James Weldon Johnson (1871–1938), perhaps best known for his 1912 novel *Autobiography of an Ex-Colored Man*. Marjorie Kinnan Rawlings (b.Washington, D.C., 1895–1953) wrote the Pulitzer Prize-winning *The Yearling* (1938), the poignant story of a 12-year-old boy on the Florida frontier in the 1870s. Zora Neale Hurston (1901–60), born in poverty in the all-Negro town of Eatonville, graduated from Barnard College and became an anthropologist and novelist, whose works include the novel *Their Eyes Were Watching God*.

Among the entertainers born in Florida are Sidney Poitier (b.1927), Charles Eugene "Pat" Boone (b.1934), Faye Dunaway (b.1941), Jim Morrison (1943–71), Ben Vereen (b.1946), and Delta Burke (b.1956). Florida's most famous sports figure is Chris Evert (Christine Marie Evert, b.1953), who became a dominant force in women's tennis in the mid-1970s.

40 BIBLIOGRAPHY

Douglas, Marjory Stoneman. *The Everglades: River of Grass*. Rev. ed. Miami: Banyan, 1978.

Hurston, Zora Neale. *Their Eyes Were Watching God*. New York: J.B. Lippincott, 1937.

Morris, Allen, comp. *The Florida Handbook 1985-86*. Tallahassee: Peninsular Publishing, 1985.

Rawlings, Marjorie Kinnan. *The Yearling*. New York: Scribner, 1938.

Tebeau, Charlton. *A History of Florida*. Coral Gables: University of Miami Press, 1981 (orig. 1971).

GEORGIA

State of Georgia

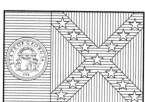

ORIGIN OF STATE NAME: Named for King George II of England in 1732.

NICKNAME: The Empire State of the South (also Peach State).

CAPITAL: Atlanta.

ENTERED UNION: 2 January 1788 (4th).

SONG: "Georgia."

MOTTO: Wisdom, Justice, Moderation.

COAT OF ARMS: Three columns support an arch inscribed with the word "Constitution;" intertwined among the columns is a banner bearing the state motto. Right of center stands a soldier with a drawn sword, representing the aid of the military in defending the Constitution. Surrounding the whole are the words "State of Georgia 1776."

FLAG: At the hoist, on a blue bar, is the coat of arms. The remainder comprises the battle flag of the Confederacy.

OFFICIAL SEAL: OBVERSE: same as the coat of arms. REVERSE: a sailing vessel and a smaller boat are offshore; on land, a man and horse plow a field, and sheep graze in the background. The scene is surrounded by the words "Agriculture and Commerce 1776."

BIRD: Brown thrasher.

FISH: Largemouth bass.

FLOWER: Cherokee rose.

WILDFLOWER: Azalea.

TREE: Live oak.

GEM: Quartz.

INSECT: Honeybee.

FOSSIL: Shark tooth.

TIME: 7 AM EST = noon GMT.

1 LOCATION AND SIZE

Located in the southeastern US, Georgia is the largest state east of the Mississippi River, and ranks 21st in size among the 50 states. The total area of Georgia is 58,910 square miles (152,576 square kilometers). Georgia extends 254 miles (409 kilometers) east-west; the maximum north-south extension is 320 miles (515 kilometers). The Sea Islands extend the length of the Georgia coast. The state's total boundary length is 1,039 miles (1,672 kilometers).

2 TOPOGRAPHY

The Blue Ridge Mountains end in northern Georgia, where Brasstown Bald, at 4,784 feet (1,458 meters), is the highest point in the state. The central region is characterized by the rolling hills of the Piedmont Plateau. The piedmont area ends in a ridge of sand hills running across the state from Augusta to Columbus. The coastal plain of southern Georgia, thinly populated except for towns at the mouths of inland rivers, ends in marshlands along the Atlantic Ocean. Lying offshore are the Sea Islands.

Two great rivers rise in the northeast: the Savannah and the Chattahoochee. The two largest rivers of central Georgia are the Ocmulgee and Oconee. Clark Hill Reservoir and Hartwell Reservoir are huge lakes created by dams on the Savannah River. Artificial lakes on the Chattahoochee River include Lake Seminole, Walter F. George Reservoir, and Lake Harding.

3 CLIMATE

The Chattahoochee River divides Georgia into separate climatic regions. The mountain region to the northwest is colder than the rest of Georgia, averaging 39°F (4°C) in January and 78°F (26°C) in July. The state experiences mild winters, ranging from a January average of 44°F (7°C) in the piedmont to 54°F (12°C) on the coast. Summers are hot in the piedmont and on the coast, with July temperatures averaging 80°F (27°C) or above. The record high is 113°F (45°C) at Greenville on 27 May 1978; the record low is –17°F (–27°C), registered in Floyd County on 27 January 1940.

Rainfall averages 50 inches (127 centimeters) annually in the lowlands, increasing to 75 inches (191 centimeters) in the mountains; snow falls occasionally in the interior. Tornadoes are an annual threat in mountain areas, and Georgia beaches are exposed to hurricane tides.

Georgia Population Profile

Estimated 1995 population:	7,102,000
Population change, 1980–90:	18.6%
Leading ancestry group:	African American
Second leading group:	Irish
Foreign born population:	2.7%
Hispanic origin†:	1.7%
Population by race:	
White:	71.0%
Black:	27.0%
Native American:	0.2%
Asian/Pacific Islander:	1.2%
Other:	0.6%

Population by Age Group

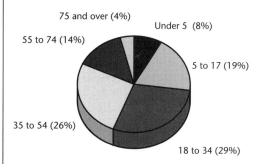

75 and over (4%)
Under 5 (8%)
55 to 74 (14%)
5 to 17 (19%)
35 to 54 (26%)
18 to 34 (29%)

Top Cities with Populations Over 25,000

City	Population	National rank	% change 1980–90
Atlanta	394,848	37	–7.3
Columbus	186,369	91	NA
Savannah	138,908	134	–2.7
Macon	107,257	182	–8.8
Albany	79,635	284	5.5
Roswell	50,667	515	105.4
Marietta	47,070	563	43.1
Athens	45,793	577	7.5
Warner Robins	45,661	579	9.6
Augusta	44,467	598	–6.1

Notes: †A person of Hispanic origin may be of any race. NA indicates that data are not available.
Sources: Economic and Statistics Administration, Bureau of the Census. *Statistical Abstract of the United States, 1994–95.* Washington, DC: Government Printing Office, 1995; Courtenay M. Slater and George E. Hall. *1995 County and City Extra: Annual Metro, City and County Data Book.* Lanham, MD: Bernan Press, 1995.

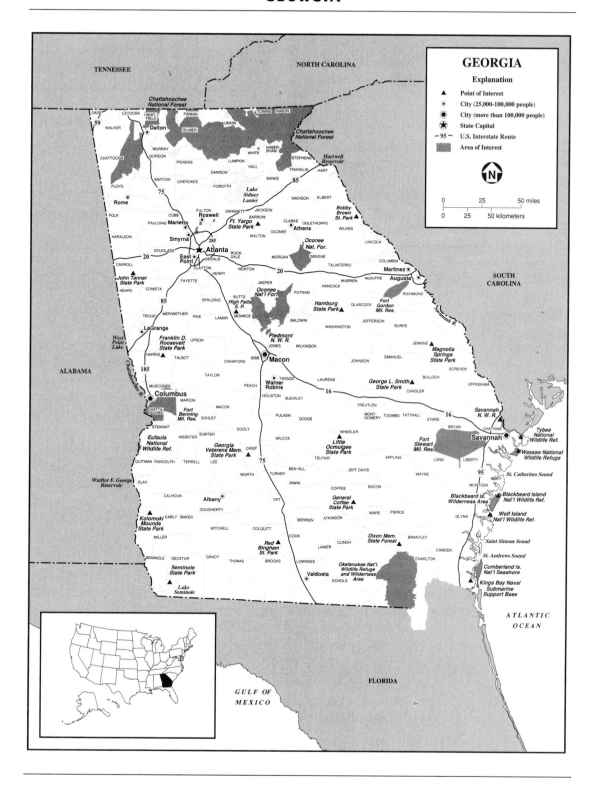

GEORGIA

Explanation

▲ Point of Interest
⊙ City (25,000-100,000 people)
◉ City (more than 100,000 people)
★ State Capital
—95— U.S. Interstate Route
▨ Area of Interest

0   25   50 miles
0   25   50 kilometers

TENNESSEE

NORTH CAROLINA

SOUTH CAROLINA

ALABAMA

FLORIDA

GULF OF
MEXICO

ATLANTIC
OCEAN

Chattahoochee
National Forest

Chattahoochee
National Forest

Hartwell
Reservoir

Lake
Sidney
Lanier

Bobby
Brown
St. Park

Ft. Yargo
State Park

Oconee
Nat. For.

Oconee
Nat'l For.

High Falls
S. P.

Hamburg
State Park

Fort
Gordon
Mil. Res.

Magnolia
Springs
State Park

Piedmont
N. W. R.

John Tanner
State Park

Franklin D.
Roosevelt
State Park

West
Point
Lake

George L. Smith
State Park

Fort Benning
Mil. Res.

Fort
Stewart
Mil. Res.

Savannah
N. W. R.

Tybee
National
Wildlife Ref.

Wassaw National
Wildlife Refuge

Eufaula
National
Wildlife Ref.

Georgia
Veterens Mem.
State Park

Little
Ocmulgee
State Park

St. Catherines Sound

Blackbeard Is.
Wilderness Area

Blackbeard Island
Nat'l Wildlife Ref.

Wolf Island
Nat'l Wildlife Ref.

Watlier F. George
Reservoir

Kolomoki
Mounds
State Park

General
Coffee ▲
State Park

Saint Simons Sound

St. Andrews Sound

Red
Bingham
St. Park

Dixon Mem.
State Forest

Cumberland Is.
Nat'l Seashore

Kings Bay Naval
Submarine
Support Base

Seminole
State Park

Lake
Seminole

Okefenokee Nat'l.
Wildlife Refuge
and Wilderness
Area

Cities and counties on map:
DADE, CATOOSA, WHITFIELD, FANNIN, TOWNS, RABUN, WALKER, Dalton, GILMER, UNION, CHATTOOGA, MURRAY, GORDON, WHITE, HABERSHAM, STEPHENS, FLOYD, PICKENS, LUMPKIN, HALL, FRANKLIN, HART, Rome, BARTOW, CHEROKEE, DAWSON, BANKS, POLK, FORSYTH, MADISON, ELBERT, GWINNETT, JACKSON, CLARKE, OGLETHORPE, WILKES, HARALSON, PAULDING, COBB, Roswell, FULTON, BARROW, Athens, OCONEE, LINCOLN, Marietta, Smyrna, WALTON, Atlanta, DEKALB, ROCKDALE, MORGAN, GREENE, TALIAFERRO, COLUMBIA, Martinez, Augusta, DOUGLAS, East Point, CLAYTON, HENRY, NEWTON, JASPER, PUTNAM, WARREN, McDUFFIE, RICHMOND, CARROLL, FAYETTE, BUTTS, HANCOCK, GLASCOCK, COWETA, SPALDING, LAMAR, MONROE, BALDWIN, WASHINGTON, JEFFERSON, BURKE, HEARD, TROUP, MERIWETHER, PIKE, JONES, WILKINSON, JENKINS, SCREVEN, LaGrange, UPSON, CRAWFORD, BIBB, Macon, JOHNSON, EMANUEL, HARRIS, TALBOT, TAYLOR, TWIGGS, Warner Robins, LAURENS, BULLOCH, EFFINGHAM, MUSCOGEE, PEACH, HOUSTON, BLECKLEY, TREUTLEN, CANDLER, Columbia, MARION, MACON, DOOLY, PULASKI, DODGE, MONTGOMERY, TOOMBS, TATTNALL, EVANS, BRYAN, CHATHAM, STEWART, WEBSTER, SCHLEY, WILCOX, WHEELER, LONG, Savannah, QUITMAN, RANDOLPH, TERRELL, LEE, CRISP, TELFAIR, APPLING, WAYNE, LIBERTY, CLAY, WORTH, TURNER, BEN HILL, JEFF DAVIS, McINTOSH, CALHOUN, Albany, DOUGHERTY, IRWIN, COFFEE, BACON, GLYNN, EARLY, BAKER, MITCHELL, TIFT, BERRIEN, ATKINSON, WARE, PIERCE, MILLER, COLQUITT, COOK, LANIER, CLINCH, BRANTLEY, CAMDEN, SEMINOLE, DECATUR, GRADY, THOMAS, BROOKS, Valdosta, LOWNDES, ECHOLS, CHARLTON

Interstate routes: 59, 75, 85, 20, 285, 185, 16, 95

Chattahoochee R., Savannah R.

Photo credit: Georgia Department of Industry, Trade, and Tourism.

An inhabitant of Okefenokee Swamp.

4 PLANTS AND ANIMALS

Georgia has some 250 species of trees. White and scrub pines, chestnut, and northern red oak cover the mountain zone, while loblolly and shortleaf (yellow) pines and whiteback maple are found throughout the piedmont. Pecan trees grow densely in southern Georgia, and white oak and cypress are plentiful in the eastern part of the state. Trees found throughout the state include scaly-bark and white hickories, sassafras, and various dogwoods and magnolias. Common flowering shrubs include yellow jasmine, flowering quince, and mountain laurel. Spanish moss grows in the coastal regions, and kudzu vines, originally from Asia, are plentiful. The state lists 58 protected plants, of which 23—including buckthorn, golden seal, spiderlily, fringed campion, and starflower—are endangered.

Prominent among Georgia animals is the white-tailed (Virginia) deer, found in some 50 counties. Other common mammals include the black bear, muskrat, mink, and three species of squirrel: fox, gray, and flying. No fewer than 160 bird species breed in Georgia, among them the mockingbird, brown thrasher (the state bird), and numerous sparrows. There are 79 species of reptile, including such poisonous snakes as the rattler and copperhead.

The state's 63 amphibian species consist mainly of various salamanders, frogs, and toads. The most popular freshwater game fish are trout, bream, bass, and catfish. Dolphins, porpoises, shrimp, oysters, and blue crabs are found off the Georgia coast.

Rare or threatened animals include the indigo snake and Georgia's blind cave salamander. The state protects 23 species of wildlife, among them the colonial and Sherman's pocket gophers, right and humpback whales, manatee, brown pelican, American alligator, three species of sea turtles, shortnose sturgeon, and southern cave fish.

5 ENVIRONMENTAL PROTECTION

Georgia's greatest environmental problems are an increasingly scarce water supply, water pollution, and hazardous waste sites. In 1972, at the prodding of Governor Jimmy Carter, the general assembly created the Environmental Protection Division (EPD), which administers 21 state environmental laws, most of them passed during the 1970s. The EPD's Emergency Response Team is on call 24 hours a day to assist in environmental emergencies and averages about 2,000 calls per year. In 1994, there were 13 hazardous waste sites in the state.

6 POPULATION

Georgia ranked 11th among the 50 states in 1990 with a population of 6,478,216. The estimated population for 1995 was 7,102,000. With a median age of 26.7, Georgia residents were somewhat younger than the national average. The population density was 112 persons per square mile (43 persons per square kilometer) in 1990.

About 65% of all Georgians lived in urban areas in 1990, and 35% in rural areas. The state's four largest cities in 1992 were Atlanta, 394,848; Columbus, 186,369; Savannah, 138,908; and Macon, 107,257. The Atlanta metropolitan area had an approximate population of 2,834,000.

7 ETHNIC GROUPS

Most Georgians are of English or Scotch-Irish descent. Between 1970 and 1990, the number of Georgians from Asia or the Pacific Islands increased from 8,838 to 76,000. By 1990, 6,284 Vietnamese had resettled in Georgia. Black citizens composed 27% of the total population and numbered 1,747,000 in 1990. There were only 13,000 Native Americans in Georgia in 1990.

8 LANGUAGES

Except for the South Midland speech of the extreme northern up-country, Georgia English is typically Southern. However, a highly unusual variety of regional differences makes a strong contrast between northern up-country and southern low-country speech. In such words as *care* and *stairs*, for example, many up-country speakers have a vowel like that in *cat*, while many low-country speakers have a vowel like that in *pane*.

A distinctive variety of black English, called Gullah, is spoken in the islands off the Georgia and South Carolina coast, to which Creole-speaking slaves escaped from the mainland during the 17th and 18th centuries. Many personal names stem directly from West African languages.

About 5.7 million Georgians speak only English at home. Other languages spoken at home, and the number of people who speak them, include Spanish (122,295); German (29,480); French (34,422); and Korean (13,433).

9 RELIGIONS

There are approximately 3,450,000 known Protestants in Georgia. The leading denominations are the Southern Baptist Convention, 1,582,000; United Methodist, 530,000; Presbyterian, 101,000; Church of God (Cleveland, Tenn.), 96,000; and Episcopal, 63,000. In 1990, Georgia has 210,000 Roman Catholics and an estimated 73,000 Jews.

10 TRANSPORTATION

Due to competition from the trucking industry, Class I rail trackage declined to 3,828 rail miles (6,159 kilometers) in 1992, and as of 1991, CSX and Norfolk Southern were the only Class I railroads operating within the state. As of 1992, Amtrak operated five long-distance trains through the state. In 1979, Atlanta inaugurated the first heavy rail mass-transit system in the state, including the South's first subway.

Georgia's old intracoastal waterway carries about one million tons of shipping annually and is also used by pleasure craft and fishing vessels. Savannah's modern port facilities handled 13,325,692 million tons of cargo in 1991. The coastal cities of

Photo credit: Metro Atlanta Chamber of Commerce.

Atlanta skyline.

Brunswick and St. Marys also have deep-water docks.

In the 1920s, Georgia became the gateway to Florida for motorists. During the 1980s, Atlanta invested $1.4 billion in a major freeway expansion program. In 1993, Georgia had 110,879 miles (178,404 kilometers) of public roads and 5,632,425 registered motor vehicles. Hartsfield International Airport (Atlanta) is the hub of air traffic in the Southeast; it boarded 18,392,449 passengers and handled 228,772 tons of freight and mail in 1991. In 1991 there were 240 private and 135 public airports in Georgia.

when Republican Barry Goldwater won the state. The state's 12 electoral votes went to independent candidate George C. Wallace in 1968 and Republican Richard Nixon in 1972. In 1976, Georgia's native son Jimmy Carter returned the state to the Democratic camp in presidential balloting.

Democratic nominee Bill Clinton and Republican incumbent George Bush each won 43% of the vote in the 1992 presidential election, while Independent Ross Perot won 13%. Zell Miller, a Democrat, won the gubernatorial race in 1990 and was reelected in 1994. Democrat Sam Nunn was elected to his fourth term in the Senate in 1990. Georgia's other Senator in 1994 was Paul Coverdell, elected in 1992 in a special run-off election. Congressman Newt Gingrich was instrumental in guiding the Republicans to control of both the House and the Senate in the 1994 elections. Following the election, Gingrich became the first Republican Speaker of the House in 40 years.

14 LOCAL GOVERNMENT

Georgia has 157 counties, 536 municipal governments, and 442 special districts. In 1965, the legislature passed a home-rule law permitting local governments to amend their own charters. The traditional and most common form of municipal government is the mayor-council form. But city managers are employed by some communities, and a few make use of the commission system.

15 JUDICIAL SYSTEM

Georgia's highest court is the supreme court, consisting of a chief justice, presiding justice, and five associate justices. Georgia's general trial courts are the superior courts, which have exclusive jurisdiction in cases of divorce and land title, and

Georgia Presidential Vote by Political Parties, 1948–92

YEAR	GEORGIA WINNER	DEMOCRAT	REPUBLICAN	STATES' RIGHTS DEMOCRAT	PROGRESSIVE
1948	*Truman (D)	254,646	76,691	85,136	1,636
1952	Stevenson (D)	456,823	198,961		
1956	Stevenson (D)	444,6878	222,778		
1960	*Kennedy (D)	458,638	274,472		
1964	Goldwater (R)	522,163	616,584		
1968	Wallace (AI)	334,440	380,111	535,550	
1972	*Nixon (R)	289,529	881,490		
1976	*Carter (D)	979,409	483,743	**1,071	1,1681
				LIBERTARIAN	
1980	Carter (D)	890,955	654,168	15,627	
1984	*Reagan (R)	706,628	1,068,722	1521	
					NEW ALL.
1988	*Bush (R)	714,792	1,081,331	8,435	5,099
					IND. (Perot)
1992	*Clinton (D)	1,008,966	995,252	7,110	309,657

* Won US presidential election.

** Write-in votes.

Photo credit: Metro Atlanta Chamber of Commerce.

Georgia's capitol in Atlanta.

in major criminal cases. Cases from local courts can be carried to the court of appeals. Each county has a probate court; there are also separate juvenile courts. The prison population in Georgia numbered 27,783 by the end of 1993. According to the FBI Crime Index, the crime rate per 100,000 inhabitants for 1994 was 6,010.3.

16 MIGRATION

The greatest population shifts during the 20th century have been from country to town and, after World War I, of black Georgians to northern cities. From 1985 to 1990, Georgia's net gain through migration was greater than that of any other state except California and Florida. From 1980 to 1990, the proportion of native-born residents in Georgia fell from 71% to 64.5%.

17 ECONOMY

Georgia's economy underwent drastic changes as a result of World War II. The raising of poultry and livestock became more important than crop cultivation, and manufacturing replaced agriculture as the chief source of income. Georgia is a leader in the making of paper products, tufted textiles products, processed chickens, naval stores, lumber, and transportation equipment.

Textile manufacturing, Georgia's oldest industry, remains its most important source of income. However, that area has grown slowly in recent years, while most durable-goods industries, such as electrical machinery and appliances, have grown rapidly. The state economy suffered in the national recession of the early 1980s but performed better during the expansion of the latter part of the decade than the nation as a whole. Service industries grew dramatically, particularly health and business as well as finance, insurance, and real estate.

18 INCOME

The per capita (per person) income of Georgians has been low historically, at least since the Civil War. Georgia's per capita income rose to $20,198 in 1994, boosting the state's national rank to 29th. In 1993, about 13.5% of all state residents were living below the poverty level.

19 INDUSTRY

Georgia had 9,771 manufacturing firms in 1992. The transport equipment, chemical, food-processing, apparel, and forest-products industries today rival textile industries in economic importance. The state's most famous product was created in 1886, when druggist John S. Pemberton developed the formula for what became Coca-Cola, the world's most widely known commercial product. In 1994, 13 of the nations' 500 largest industrial corporations listed by *Fortune* magazine had headquarters in Georgia.

20 LABOR

Georgia's civilian labor force was estimated at 3,566,000 in 1994. Of this total, 5.2% were unemployed. The most remarkable change in the labor force since World War II has been the rising proportion of women, whose share increased from less than 28% in 1940 to an estimated 57.9% in 1992.

The trend during the 1970s and early 1980s was toward increased employment in service industries and toward multiple job-holding. Employment in agriculture, the leading industry prior to World War II, continued its long-term decline. The mining, construction, and manufacturing industries registered employment increases but declined in importance relative to such sectors as trade and government.

Georgia has not been hospitable to union organizers. In 1994, 8% of all workers were union members. As of 1993, there were six national labor unions operating in Georgia.

21 AGRICULTURE

In 1994, Georgia's farm marketings totaled $4.7 billion (14th in the US). Georgia ranked first in the production of peanuts and pecans. Peanuts accounted for 11.3% of agricultural receipts in 1994.

Cotton was the mainstay of Georgia's economy through the early 20th century, and the state's plantations also grew corn, rice, tobacco, wheat, and sweet potatoes. World War I stimulated the cultivation of peanuts along with other crops. By the 1930s, tobacco and peanuts were challenging cotton for agricultural supremacy, and Georgia had also become an important producer of peaches, a product for which the "peach state" is still widely known.

Georgia's farmland area of 10 million acres (4 million hectares) represents 27.1% of its land area. Farm real estate debt in Georgia was estimated at $1.65 billion in 1994.

The following table shows acreage and production for leading crops in 1994:

CROP	HARVESTED ACRES (1,000)	PRODUCTION (1,000)
Peanuts	654.0	1,864,050 pounds
Cotton	875.0	1,550 bales*
Tobacco	37.0	80,660 pounds
Corn	540.0	57,240 bushels
Pecans	—	55,000 pounds
Soybeans	500.0	15,500 bushels
Peaches	21.0	175,000 pounds
Wheat	400.0	20,400 bushels

*One bale weighs about 480 pounds.

22 DOMESTICATED ANIMALS

Georgia's cash receipts from livestock and livestock products totaled almost $2.7 billion in 1994, or more than half of the total farm income. Georgia ranks second only to Arkansas in total cash receipts from chickens and broilers, and second to California in receipts from eggs.

At the close of 1994, Georgia farms had 1,560,000 cattle, and 1,020,000 hogs. Cows kept for milk production numbered 102,000 in 1995. Poultry farmers sold some $1.6 billion of broilers in 1994, equivalent to 35% of the state's agricultural receipts.

23 FISHING

Georgia's total commercial catch of fish and shellfish in 1992 was 17,620,000 pounds, valued at $22,957,000. Commercial fishing in Georgia involves more shellfish—mainly shrimp and crabs—than finfish, the most important of which are caught in the nets of shrimp trawlers. Leading finfish in 1991 were snappers, groupers, tilefish, and porgy. In 1991 the commercial shrimp harvest was 8.5 million pounds. Sports fishermen catch bass, catfish, jackfish, bluegill, crappie, perch, and trout. In 1991/92, over 2.2 million (177,852 pounds) coldwater species fish and roe (fish eggs) were distributed within the state by federal hatcheries.

24 FORESTRY

Georgia's forest area totals 24,136,737 acres (9,768,137 hectares). Forests cover 65% of the state's land area. The chief products of Georgia's timber industry are pine lumber and pine plywood for the building industry, hardwood lumber for the furniture industry, and pulp for the paper and box industry. In 1992, Georgia produced approximately 2.6 billion board feet of lumber and 7.5 million cords of pulpwood.

The two chief recreational forest areas are Chattahoochee National Forest, in the northern part of the state, and Oconee National Forest, in the central region. The state of Georgia has 872,479 acres (353,080 hectares) of National Forest System lands, 99% of which are within the boundaries of the two national forests.

25 MINING

The estimated value of nonfuel minerals produced in Georgia in 1994 was $1.53 billion, an all-time record high. Clays, valued at almost $1.2 billion, accounted for 75.8% of the total estimated value of minerals produced in Georgia. Kaolin, fuller's earth, and common clay and shale were mined. In 1994 the state was once again the national leader in quantity and value of both kaolin and fuller's earth.

Georgia also led the nation in value of iron oxide pigments and in quantity of granite dimension stone. The estimated quantity of dimension stone produced increased to 169,383 short tons. Crushed stone, Georgia's second leading mineral commodity, increased 5.5% to 43.6 million short tons, valued at $242.1 million. The state also ranked second nationally in the quantity and value of barite, which was used by the chemical and the industrial filler and pigments industries.

26 ENERGY AND POWER

Georgia is an energy-dependent state which produces only a small proportion of its energy needs, most of it through hydroelectric power. There are no commercially recoverable petroleum or natural-gas reserves, and the state's coal deposits are not of great importance. Georgia does have large amounts of timberland, however, and it has been estimated that 20–40% of the state's energy demands could be met by using wood that is currently wasted.

In 1992, Georgia's energy consumption per capita (per person) was 309.3 million Btu, slightly less than the national average. In that year, Georgia produced 95.7 billion kilowatt hours of electricity, over 66% from coal-fired power plants. Georgia's four nuclear power plants produced 28.4% of the total output. Petroleum accounted for 38% of all fuel used in Georgia in 1992, coal for 31%, and natural gas for 16%. Georgia's demonstrated coal reserves were approximately 3.6 million tons in 1992.

27 COMMERCE

Georgia ranked tenth among the 50 states in wholesale trade in 1991, with total sales of $113.8 billion. The state ranked 12th in retail trade in 1993, with sales totaling $54.3 billion. Georgia exported goods worth $7.7 billion in 1992, ranking 15th among the states.

28 PUBLIC FINANCE

Since the Georgia constitution forbids the state to spend more than it takes in from all sources, the governor attempts to reconcile the budget requests of the state department heads with the revenue predicted by economists for the coming fiscal year.

The total state revenues and expenditures for 1993 (actual) were: revenues, $16.5 billion; expenditures, $15.3 billion.

Georgia's state debt totaled more than $4.5 billion in 1993. Total state indebtedness in 1993 amounted to $655 per person.

29 TAXATION

Georgia was the last of the 13 original colonies to tax its citizens, but today its state tax structure is among the broadest in the US. It includes property and income taxes, as well as taxes on gasoline and tobacco. In 1951, Georgia enacted what at that time was the most all-inclusive sales tax in the US. This 4% tax is now the state's second-largest source of revenue. Georgians paid $28.2 billion in federal taxes in 1992.

30 HEALTH

Heart disease, cancer, and cerebrovascular disease are the leading causes of death in Georgia. In 1993, there were 159 community hospitals in Georgia with 26,500 beds. The average hospital expense in 1993 was $775 per inpatient day and $5,554 per stay, in each case below the US average. In 1993, Georgia had 12,456 nonfederal doctors and 43,300 registered nurses. Atlanta has been the site of the federal Centers for Disease Control since 1973. Over 18% of Georgians do not have health insurance.

31 HOUSING

Post–World War II housing developments provided Georgia families with modern, affordable dwellings. The home-loan guarantee programs of the Federal Housing

Administration and the Veterans Administration made modest down payments, low interest rates, and long-term financing the norm in Georgia.

Between 1940 and 1970, the number of housing units in the state doubled to 1,470,754. In July 1993, there were an estimated 2,784,000 housing units in Georgia. The median cost for housing to owners with a mortgage was $737 per month in 1990, and $182 per month for those without a mortgage. The median monthly rent of renter-occupied housing was $433.

32 EDUCATION

In 1993, expenditures per student amounted to $4,730, ranking 36th in the nation. Georgia has made great strides in education in recent decades. In 1990, 71% of the population age 25 or older had a high school diploma. Some 203,000 Georgians were enrolled in college compared to 30,000 in 1960. The state offers full-day kindergarten statewide, and preschool for disadvantaged four-year-olds. In 1993, Georgia public schools enrolled 1,205,357 students, of whom 403,977 were in grades 8 to 12.

Georgia had 111 institutions of higher learning, 66 public and 45 private, with a total of 251,810 students in 1990/91. Thirty-two public colleges are components of the University System of Georgia. The largest of these is the University of Georgia (Athens), with a 1990/91 enrollment of 28,395. The largest private university is Emory University (Atlanta), with 10,367 students in 1992/93.

33 ARTS

During the 20th century, Atlanta has replaced Savannah as the major art center of Georgia, while Athens, the seat of the University of Georgia, has continued to share in the cultural life of the university. The state has eight major art museums, as well as numerous private galleries. The Atlanta Art Association exhibits the work of contemporary Georgia artists. Georgia's Art Bus Program delivers art exhibits to Georgia communities, mostly in rural areas, for three-week periods.

The theater has enjoyed popular support since the first professional resident theater troupe began performing in Augusta in 1790. Atlanta has a resident theater, and there are community theaters in some 30 cities and counties.

Georgia has at least 11 symphony orchestras, ranging from the Atlanta Symphony to community and college ensembles throughout the state. Atlanta and Augusta have professional ballet touring companies, and Augusta has a professional opera company. Macon and Atlanta have become major recording centers, especially for popular music. The north Georgia mountain communities retain their traditional folk music. From 1987 to 1991, the state of Georgia generated $29,241,204 from federal and state sources for support of the arts.

34 LIBRARIES AND MUSEUMS

In 1995, the Georgia public library system included 34 regional and 20 county systems, each operating under its own board. The holdings of all public libraries totaled

13,448,065 volumes in 1992, and the combined circulation was 27,350,186 volumes. The University of Georgia had by far the largest academic collection, including 3,048,491 books.

Georgia has at least 135 museums, including the Telfair Academy of Arts and Sciences in Savannah, the Georgia State Museum of Science and Industry in Atlanta, and the Columbus Museum of Arts and Sciences. Atlanta's Cyclorama depicts the 1864 Battle of Atlanta.

Georgia abounds in historic sites. Sites administered by the National Park Service include the Chickamauga battlefield, Kennesaw Mountain battlefield, Fort Pulaski National Monument, and Andersonville prison camp near Americus, all associated with the Civil War, as well as the Fort Frederica National Monument, an 18th-century English barracks on St. Simons Island. The Martin Luther King, Jr., National Historic Site was established in Atlanta in 1980. Also in Atlanta is former President Jimmy Carter's library, museum, and conference center complex.

35 COMMUNICATIONS

As of March 1993, there were 2,378,000 Georgian residences (93.5%) with telephones. That same year, Georgia had 374 radio stations, 183 AM and 191 FM. There were 36 commercial and 9 educational television stations in 1993. Fifteen large cable television systems were operating in 1993. On 1 June 1980, Atlanta businessman Ted Turner inaugurated the independent Cable News Network, (CNN). By the late 1980s, CNN had become well-known worldwide.

36 PRESS

In 1817, the *Savannah Gazette* became the state's first daily. After the Native American linguist Sequoyah gave the Cherokee a written language, Elias Boudinot gave them a newspaper, the *Cherokee Phoenix,* in 1828. Georgia authorities suppressed the paper in 1835, and Boudinot joined his tribe's tragic migration westward.

As of 1994, Georgia had 16 morning dailies and 4 Sunday newspapers. Leading newspapers with their 1994 daily circulations are: the *Atlanta Journal* (533,306); the *Atlanta Constitution* (329,582); the *Macon Telegraph* (75,307); and the *Augusta Chronicle* (71,442).

Periodicals published in Georgia in 1994 included *Golf World, Atlanta Weekly, Robotics World,* and *Southern Accents.* Among the nation's better-known scholarly presses is the University of Georgia Press (Athens), which publishes the *Georgia Review.*

37 TOURISM, TRAVEL, AND RECREATION

Georgia's travel industry earned $9.6 billion in 1990; tourists spent nearly $26.3 million per day. Besides national forests and parks, major tourist attractions include the Okefenokee Swamp in southern Georgia; Stone Mountain near Atlanta; former President Jimmy Carter's home in Plains; the birthplace, church, and gravesite of Martin Luther King, Jr., in Atlanta; and the historic squares and riverfront of Savannah. The varied attractions of the Golden Isles include fashionable Sea Island. Georgia has long been a hunters' paradise.

Photo credit: Metro Atlanta Chamber of Commerce.

Georgia Dome in Atlanta.

Waynesboro calls itself the "bird dog capital of the world," and Thomasville in South Georgia is a mecca for quail hunters.

38 SPORTS

There are three major league professional sports teams in Georgia. Atlanta-Fulton County Stadium, completed in 1965 at a cost of over $18 million, serves as the home field for two professional teams: Major League Baseball's Atlanta Braves and the Atlanta Falcons of the National Football League. The Braves won the World Series in 1995. The Omni International Sports Complex houses the Atlanta Hawks of the National Basketball Association. The Atlanta 500 is one of the Winston Cup Grand National auto races. The Masters Golf Tournament has been played at the Augusta National Golf Club since 1934.

Football is the king of college sports. The University of Georgia Bulldogs play in the Southeastern Conference, and Georgia Tech's "Rambling Wrecks" compete in the Atlantic Coast Conference. Professional fishing is one of the fastest-growing sports in the state. A popular summer pastime is rafting. Atlanta will host the 1996 Summer Olympic Games.

39 FAMOUS GEORGIANS

James Earl "Jimmy" Carter (b.1924), born in Plains, was the first Georgian to serve as president of the US. He was governor of

Photo credit: Courtesy, Jimmy Carter Library.

Jimmy Carter, who was elected president of the United States in 1976, was born in Plains, Georgia. He was governor of Georgia from 1971 to 1975.

Revolutionary War hero James Jackson (b.England, 1757–1806) organized the Democratic-Republican Party (today's Democratic Party) in Georgia. Confederate General Joseph Wheeler (1836–1906) became a major general in the US Army during the Spanish-American War. Other Civil War generals included W. H. T. Walker (1816–64), Thomas R. R. Cobb (1823–62), who also codified Georgia's laws, and John B. Gordon (1832–1904), later a US senator and governor of the state.

Among Georgia's notable Native Americans were Osceola (1800–38), who led his Seminole into the Florida swamps rather than move west; Sequoyah (b.Tennessee, 1773–1843), who framed an alphabet for the Cherokee; and John Ross (Coowescoowe, b.Tennessee, 1790–1866), the first president of the Cherokee republic.

Distinguished black Georgians include civil-rights activists William Edward Burghardt (W.E.B.) DuBois (b.Massachusetts, 1868–1963). One of the best-known Georgians was Martin Luther King, Jr. (1929–68), born in Atlanta, leader of the March on Washington in 1963, and winner of the Nobel Peace Prize in 1964. Black Muslim leader Elijah Muhammad (Elijah Poole, 1897–1975) was also a Georgian. Other prominent black leaders include Atlanta Mayor and former UN Ambassador Andrew Young (b.Louisiana, 1932), former Atlanta Mayor Maynard Jackson (b.Texas, 1938), and Georgia Senator Julian Bond (b.Tennessee, 1940).

the state (1971–75) before being elected to the White House in 1976. Clarence Thomas, Supreme Court Justice appointed to the court during the Bush Administration, was born 23 June 1948 in Savannah, Georgia. Dean Rusk (b.1909) was secretary of state in the Kennedy and Johnson administrations. Notable US senators in recent years were Herman Talmadge (b.1913), and Sam Nunn (b.1938). A Georgia member of Congress, Newt Gingrich (b. Pennsylvania 1943), became Speaker of the US House of Representatives in 1994.

Famous Georgia authors include Joel Chandler Harris (1848–1908), Conrad Aiken (1889–1973), Erskine Caldwell (1903–87), Carson McCullers (1917–67), James Dickey (b.1923), and Flannery O'Connor (1925–64). Also notable is Margaret Mitchell (1900–49), whose Pulitzer Prize-winning *Gone With the Wind* (1936) typifies Georgia to many readers.

Entertainment celebrities include songwriter Johnny Mercer (1909–76); comedian Oliver Hardy (1877–1961); musicians Ray Charles (Ray Charles Robinson, b.1930), James Brown (b.1933), Little Richard (Richard Penniman, b.1935), Otis Redding (1941–67), Gladys Knight (b.1944), Brenda Lee (b.1944), and Amy Grant (b.1961); and actors Melvyn Douglas (1901–81), Joanne Woodward (b.1930), and Burt Reynolds (b.1936).

Major sports figures include baseball's "Georgia peach," Tyrus Raymond "Ty" Cobb (1886–1961); Jack Roosevelt "Jackie" Robinson (1919–72), the first black man to be inducted into the Baseball Hall of Fame; and Robert Tyre "Bobby" Jones (1902–71), winner of the "grand slam" of four major golf tournaments in 1930.

Robert E. "Ted" Turner (b.Ohio, 1939), who formed the Cable News Network (CNN), owns the Atlanta Hawks and the Atlanta Braves and skippered the *Courageous* to victory in the America's Cup yacht races in 1977.

40 BIBLIOGRAPHY

Coleman, Kenneth, et al. *A History of Georgia.* Athens: University of Georgia Press, 1977.

King, Coretta Scott. *My Life with Martin Luther King.* New York: Holt, Rinehart & Winston, 1970.

Lane, Mills. *The People's Georgia: An Illustrated Social History.* Savannah: Beehive Press, 1975.

HAWAII

State of Hawaii

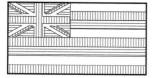

ORIGIN OF STATE NAME: Unknown. The name may stem from Hawaii Loa, traditional discoverer of the islands, or from Hawaiki, the traditional Polynesian homeland.

NICKNAME: The Aloha State.

CAPITAL: Honolulu.

ENTERED UNION: 21 August 1959 (50th).

SONG: "Hawaii Ponoi."

MOTTO: *Ua mau ke ea o ka aina i ka pono* (The life of the land is perpetuated in righteousness).

COAT OF ARMS: The heraldic shield of the Hawaiian kingdom is flanked by the figures of Kamehameha I, who united the islands, and Liberty, holding the Hawaiian flag. Below the shield is a phoenix surrounded by taro leaves, banana foliage, and sprays of maidenhair fern.

FLAG: Eight horizontal stripes, alternately white, red, and blue, represent the major islands, with the British Union Jack (reflecting the years that the islands were under British protection) in the upper left-hand corner.

OFFICIAL SEAL: Same as coat of arms, with the words "State of Hawaii 1959" above and the state motto below.

BIRD: Nene (Hawaiian goose).

FLOWER: Pua aloalo (hibiscus).

TREE: Kukui (candlenut).

ISLAND EMBLEMS: Each of the eight major islands has its own color and emblem.

　HAWAII: red; lehua (ohia blossom).

　KALHOOLAWE: gray; hinahina (beach heliotrope).

　KAUAI: purple; mokihana (fruit capsule of the *Pelea anisata)*.

　LANAI: yellow; kaunaoa *(Cuscuta sandwichiana)*.

　MAUI: pink; lokelani (pink cottage rose).

　MOLOKAI: green; kukui (candlenut) blossom.

　NIIHAU: white; white pupa shell.

　OAHU: yellow; ilima *(Sida fallax)*.

TIME: 2 AM Hawaii-Aleutian Standard Time = noon GMT.

1 LOCATION AND SIZE

The State of Hawaii is an island group situated in the northern Pacific Ocean, about 2,400 miles (3,900 kilometers) west-southwest of San Francisco. The smallest of the five states on the Pacific Ocean, Hawaii ranks 47th in size among the 50 states. The 132 Hawaiian Islands have a total area of 6,470 square miles (16,758 square kilometers). The island chain extends over 1,576 miles (2,536 kilometers) north-south and 1,425 miles (2,293 kilometers) east-west. The collective coastline of the islands is 750 miles (1,207 kilometers).

2 TOPOGRAPHY

The 8 major and 124 minor islands that make up the State of Hawaii were formed by volcanic eruptions. Mauna Loa, on the island of Hawaii, is the world's largest active volcano, at a height of 13,675 feet (4,168 meters). The largest natural lake in the state is Halulu (182 acres—74 hectares) on Niihau. The longest rivers are Kaukonahua Stream (33 miles—53 kilometers) on Oahu, and Wailuku River (32 miles—51 kilometers) on Hawaii.

3 CLIMATE

Hawaii has a tropical climate cooled by trade winds. Normal daily temperatures in Honolulu average 72°F (22°C) in February and 78°F (26°C) in August. The record high for the state is 100°F (38°C), and the record low is 12°F (−11°C). Rainfall is extremely variable. Mt. Waialeale, on Kauai, said to be the rainiest place on earth, has a mean annual total of 496 inches (1,234 centimeters), while the driest areas average under 10 inches (25 centimeters). The highest tidal wave (tsunami) in the state's history reached 56 feet (17 meters).

4 PLANTS AND ANIMALS

Of 2,200 species and subspecies of plants, more than half are endangered, threatened, or extinct. The only land mammal native to the islands is the Hawaiian hoary bat, now endangered. Listed as threatened are Newell's shearwater and the green sea

Hawaii Population Profile

Estimated 1995 population:	1,221,000
Population change, 1980–90:	14.9%
Leading ancestry group:	Japanese
Second leading group:	Filipino
Foreign born population:	14.7%
Hispanic origin†:	7.3%
Population by race:	
White:	33.4%
Black:	2.5%
Native American:	0.5%
Asian/Pacific Islander:	61.8%
Other:	1.8%

Population by Age Group

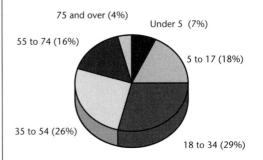

Top Cities with Populations Over 25,000

City	Population	National rank	% change 1980–90
Honolulu	371,320	43	0.1

Notes: †A person of Hispanic origin may be of any race. NA indicates that data are not available.
Sources: Economic and Statistics Administration, Bureau of the Census. *Statistical Abstract of the United States, 1994–95.* Washington, DC: Government Printing Office, 1995; Courtenay M. Slater and George E. Hall. *1995 County and City Extra: Annual Metro, City and County Data Book.* Lanham, MD: Bernan Press, 1995.

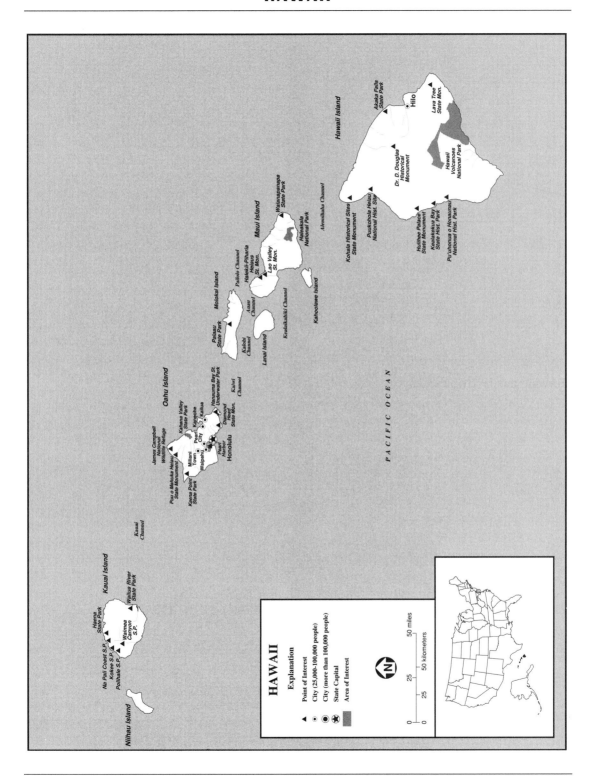

Hawaii Island

Akaka Falls
State Park

Hilo

Lava Tree
State Mon.

Dr. D. Douglas
Historical
Monument

Hawaii
Volcanoes
National Park

Kohala Historical Sites
State Monument

Puukohola Heiau
National Hist. Site

Hulihee Palace
State Monument

Kealakekua Bay
State Hist. Park

Puuhonua o Honaunau
National Hist. Park

Alenuihaha Channel

Walanapanape
State Park

Haleakala
National Park

Maui Island

Lao Valley
St. Mon.

Halekii-Pihana
Heiau
St. Mon.

Pailolo Channel

Molokai Island

Auau
Channel

Kaholawe Island

Kealakahiki Channel

Palaau
State Park

Kalohi
Channel

Lanai Island

Kaiwi
Channel

PACIFIC OCEAN

Oahu Island

Hanauma Bay St.
Underwater Park

Kohana Valley
State Park

Kaneohe

Kailua

Diamond
Head
State Mon.

James Campbell
National
Wildlife Refuge

Puu o Mahuka Heiau
State Monument

Mililani
Town

Pearl
City

Pearl
Harbor

Honolulu

Waipahu

Keena Point
State Park

Kauai
Channel

Kauai Island

Haena
State Park

Wailua River
State Park

Na Pali Coast S.P.

Kokee S.P.

Polihale S.P.

Waimea
Canyon
S.P.

Niihau Island

HAWAII

Explanation

Point of Interest

City (25,000-100,000 people)

City (more than 100,000 people)

State Capital

Area of Interest

N

50 miles

50 kilometers

25

25

0

0

Photo credit: Corel Corporation.

An area of devastation near the Kiluaea Crater. Although destructive at times, Hawaii's volcanoes are also beneficial. Not only do they add new land to the island chain, but they also form a soil is that is high in nutrients.

turtle. The nene (the state bird), once close to extinction, now numbers in the hundreds and is on the increase.

5 ENVIRONMENTAL PROTECTION

Noise pollution requirements in Honolulu are among the strictest in the US, and air and water purity levels are well within federal standards. In 1992, there were 13 municipal landfills and 2 hazardous waste sites.

6 POPULATION

According to the 1990 census, Hawaii had a population of 1,108,229, 39th among the 50 states. The estimated population for

1995 was 1,221,000. The Census Bureau projects a population of 1,362,000 in 2000. Almost four-fifths of the population lives on Oahu. The state had a population density of about 173 persons per square mile (about 66 persons per square kilometer) in 1990. Honolulu, by far the largest city, had a 1992 population of 371,320.

7 ETHNIC GROUPS

Of the state's 1.1 million residents, 685,000 are Asian or Pacific Islanders; 370,000 are white; about 81,000 are Hispanic; 27,000 are black; and 5,000 are Native American, Eskimo, or Aleut. Ethnic Hawaiians have been increasingly intent on preserving their cultural identity.

8 LANGUAGES

The Hawaiian legacy is apparent in the state's English. Newcomers soon add to their vocabulary *aloha* (love, good-bye), *haole* (white foreigner), *malihini* (newcomer), *ukulele, muumuu,* and other common native words. Most native-born residents of Hawaiian ancestry speak one of several varieties of Hawaiian pidgin, a common language with elements of Hawaiian, English, and other Asian and Pacific languages. Approximately 75% of Hawaiians speak only English at home. Other languages spoken at home, and the number of speakers, include Japanese (69,587); Tagalog (55,341); and Chinese (26,366).

9 RELIGIONS

An estimated 232,700 Hawaiians consider themselves Roman Catholics, and 158,047 view themselves as Protestants. Mormons (Church of Jesus Christ of Latter-day Saints) number about 38,000.

10 TRANSPORTATION

Hawaii's only operating railroad is the Lahaina, Kaanapali & Pacific on Maui, with six miles (ten kilometers) of track. Oahu and Hawaii islands have public bus systems. By the end of 1992, Hawaii had 4,106 miles (6,606 kilometers) of roads and streets. There were 659,365 passenger cars registered in 1993, along with 99,885 trucks and 4,241 buses.

All scheduled inter-island passenger traffic and most trans-Pacific travel is by air. In 1991, the state had 48 aircraft facilities—33 airports and 15 heliports. The busiest air terminal, Honolulu International Airport, accounted for about 63% of the state's boarded passengers and was 15th highest in the nation at 8,772,316.

11 HISTORY

The Western world learned of the Hawaiian islands in 1778, when an English navigator, Captain James Cook, sighted Oahu. At that time, each island was ruled by a hereditary chief under a caste system called *kapu*. Contact with European sailors and traders exposed the Polynesians to smallpox, venereal disease, liquor, firearms, and Western technology—and fatally weakened the *kapu* system. Within 40 years of Cook's arrival, one of the island chiefs, Kamehameha (r.1810–19), had conquered Maui and Oahu and established a royal dynasty in what became known as the Kingdom of Hawaii. His son, Liholiho, was proclaimed Kamehameha II in 1819.

After the death of Kamehameha II in 1824, his brother, Kauikeaouli, was proclaimed King Kamehameha III. His reign saw the establishment of public schools, the first sugar plantation, and a two-chamber legislature. Hawaii's first written constitution was adopted in 1840, and in 1848, a land reform called the Great Mahele abolished the feudal land system, fostering the expansion of sugar plantations. The 1840s and 1850s saw recognition of the kingdom from the US, Britain, and France. The following decades witnessed the arrival of Chinese contract laborers and the increasing influence of American sugar planters.

In 1893, the reigning monarch, Queen Liliuokalani, was overthrown in an American-led revolution that produced a provisional government under the leadership of Sanford B. Dole. After unsuccessfully requesting annexation by the US, Hawaii's government drafted a new constitution and on 4 July 1894 proclaimed the Republic of Hawaii. After the Spanish-American War, which fueled expansionist feelings in the US and pointed up the nation's strategic interests in the Pacific, the US annexed Hawaii, effective June 1900.

Notable in the territorial period were a steady US military buildup; the creation of a pineapple-canning industry; the growth of tourism (spurred in 1936 by the inauguration of commercial air service); and a rising desire for statehood. The Japanese attack on Pearl Harbor on 7 December 1941, crippling the US Pacific fleet and causing some 4,000 casualties, quickly turned Hawaii into an armed camp under martial law.

Hawaiians pressed for statehood after World War II, but Congress was reluctant, partly because of racial hostility and partly because of fears that Hawaii's powerful International Longshoremen's and Warehousemen's Union was Communist-controlled. Not until 21 August 1959, after Alaska became the 49th state, did Hawaii become the 50th. Since then, defense and tourism have been the mainstays of Hawaii's economy, with the state playing an increasingly important role as an economic, educational, and cultural bridge between the US and the nations of Asia and the Pacific.

12 STATE GOVERNMENT

Hawaii has a two-chamber legislature of 25 senators and 51 representatives. The governor and lieutenant governor are elected for four-year terms and must be of the same political party. They are the only elected officers of the executive branch, except for members of the Board of Education. There are 17 executive departments, each under the supervision of the governor and headed by a single appointed executive.

13 POLITICAL PARTIES

Before statehood, the Republican Party dominated the political scene. Since the 1960s, however, Hawaii has been solidly Democratic. As of 1994, Hawaii's governor, the majorities of both houses of the state legislature, its senators, and its two US Representatives were all Democrats. Democrat Bill Clinton won 48% of the vote in the presidential election in 1992, while Republican incumbent George Bush garnered 37% and Independent Ross Perot received 14%. As of 1994, 18 women served in the state legislature.

Hawaii Presidential Vote by Major Political Parties, 1960–92

YEAR	HAWAII WINNER	DEMOCRAT	REPUBLICAN
1960	*Kennedy (D)	92,410	92,295
1964	*Johnson (D)	163,249	44,022
1968	Humphrey (D)	141,324	91,425
1972	*Nixon (R)	101,433	168,933
1976	*Carter (D)	147,375	140,003
1980	Carter (D)	135,879	130,112
1984	*Reagan (R)	147,154	185,050
1988	Dukakis (D)	192,364	158,625
1992**	*Clinton (D)	179,310	136,822

* Won US presidential election.
**Independent candidate Ross Perot received 53,003 votes.

14 LOCAL GOVERNMENT

The state is divided into four principal counties—Hawaii, Maui, Honolulu, and Kauai—and a fifth county of Kalawao (administered by the state Department of Health), consisting of that part of Molokai more commonly known as the Kalaupapa Settlement, primarily for the care and treatment of persons suffering from leprosy. Since there are no further subdivisions, the counties provide some services traditionally performed in other states by cities, towns, and villages. On the other hand, the state government provides many functions normally performed by counties on the mainland. Each of the four principal counties has an elected council and a mayor.

15 JUDICIAL SYSTEM

The supreme court, the highest in the state, consists of a chief justice and four associate justices. The state is divided into four judicial circuits with 21 circuit court judges and 3 intermediate appeals court judges. Circuit courts are the main trial courts, having jurisdiction in most civil and criminal cases. District courts function as inferior courts within each judicial circuit; district court judges may also preside over family court proceedings. Hawaii also has a land court and a tax appeal court. Hawaii's crime rate in 1994 per 100,000 totaled 6,680.5. There were 3,129 persons in the state's jails and prisons at the end of 1993.

16 MIGRATION

Since the early 1970s, about 40,000 mainland Americans have come each year to live

Photo credit: Corel Corporation.

Hawaii's famous Waikiki Beach on the island of Oahu. Income generated from tourism is important to Hawaii's economy.

in Hawaii. More than half are military personnel and their dependents, on temporary residence during their term of military service. Residents born within Hawaii made up 56.1% of the population in 1990.

17 ECONOMY

Tourism remains Hawaii's leading employer, revenue producer, and growth area. However, agricultural diversification—including the cultivation of flowers and nursery products, papaya, and macadamia nuts—fish farming, manganese nodule mining, and film and television

A pineapple crop ready for harvest. Pineapple and sugarcane dominate Hawaiian agriculture.

production have broadened the state's economic base.

18 INCOME

Average per capita (per person) income in Hawaii in 1994 was $24,042 (6th in the US). In 1993, 8% of all Hawaii residents were below the federal poverty level.

19 INDUSTRIES

Food and food products account for about one-third of the total annual value of shipments by manufacturers. Other major industries are clothing; stone, clay, and glass products; fabricated metals; and shipbuilding.

20 LABOR

The civilian labor force in 1994 averaged 583,000, and there was an unemployment rate of 6.1%. Some 28% of all workers were union members in 1994.

21 AGRICULTURE

Export crops—especially sugarcane and pineapple—dominate Hawaiian agriculture, which had farm receipts exceeding $498.1 million in 1994. Sugar and pineapple sales accounted for 31.9% and 15.8%, respectively, of total farm receipts in 1994. Crop production for 1994 included sugarcane, 5,619,000 tons; pineapples, 365,000 tons; and macadamia nuts,

50,000,000 pounds. In 1994, sugarcane acreage amounted to 66,500 acres (26,913 hectares), down from 226,580 acres (91,697 hectares) in 1973. The Kona district is the only place in the US where coffee is grown commercially; production totaled 4,600,000 pounds in 1994.

22 DOMESTICATED ANIMALS

Livestock products accounted for 15.3% of Hawaii's farm income in 1994. Sales of dairy products accounted for 6.3% of agricultural receipts in 1994. At the end of 1994, Hawaii had 175,000 cattle, 35,000 hogs, and about 981,000 chickens.

23 FISHING

Although expanding, Hawaii's commercial catch remains surprisingly small: 27.8 million pounds, worth $70.2 million, in 1992. The most important fish caught in 1991 were swordfish, accounting for 33% of the total value, followed by bigeye tuna (23%). Sport fishing is extremely popular, with bass, bluegill, tuna, and marlin among the most sought-after varieties.

24 FORESTRY

As of 1994, Hawaii had 1,748,000 acres (716,680 hectares) of forestland and water reserves. Production of lumber and plywood falls far short of local demand. Specialty woods include eucalyptus robusta, used for making pallets for shipping, and blue gum eucalyptus, converted to chips for use by papermakers in Japan.

25 MINING

The value of Hawaii's nonfuel mineral production in 1994 was estimated at $137 million. Crushed stone, construction sand and gravel, and portland cement were the principal mineral commodities produced. Modest masonry cement and gemstone production was also reported. Mineral production in Hawaii is mainly for local construction usage.

26 ENERGY AND POWER

Lacking native fossil fuels and nuclear installations, Hawaii depends on imported petroleum for 98% of its energy needs. Only a tiny fraction of Hawaii's electric production comes from alternative energy sources. In 1993, electric power production totaled 6.1 billion kilowatt hours.

27 COMMERCE

In 1992, sales from wholesale trade amounted to $8 billion. Retail sales amounted to $13.2 billion in 1993. Service establishment receipts totaled $8 billion. Foreign imports to Hawaii totaled 2.1 billion in 1992, while exports exceeded $600 million.

28 PUBLIC FINANCE

Hawaii's biennial budget is the responsibility of the Department of Budget and Finance. The operating revenues for the 1992/93 fiscal year were $3,902.0 million, and the expenditures were $4,118.5 million.

The debt of the Hawaii state government at the end of fiscal 1993 was $4.9 billion, or $4,193 per capita (per person).

Contestants participating in the May Day Hula Contest, an event held in Princeville, Kauai.

29 TAXATION

Hawaii's per capita (per person) tax burden is one of the highest in the US. There are personal income taxes, a capital gains tax, a business income tax, a broad-based general excise tax, and a 4% tax on retail sales of goods and services. Taxes on estates, fuel, liquor, and tobacco are also imposed, and the property tax is a major source of county income. Hawaii's total federal tax burden in 1992 was $4.5 billion.

30 HEALTH

Death rates from heart diseases, cancer, cerebrovascular diseases, accidents, and suicide are all below national rates. However, Hawaii ranks second among the states in the frequency of smoking-attributed deaths. In 1993, Hawaii had 20 community hospitals, with 2,900 beds. As of 1993 there were 2,728 nonfederal physicians and surgeons in Hawaii. Average hospital expense in 1993 was $823 per inpatient day.

31 HOUSING

In 1993 there were an estimated 416,000 housing units. Hawaii had a greater proportion of condominiums (20.8%) than any other state in 1990. In 1993, 6,624 new housing units were authorized (30% multi-unit dwellings), with a value of

$678.4 million. Renters throughout Hawaii had a median monthly cost of $650, higher than in any other state.

32 EDUCATION

Education has developed rapidly in Hawaii: 92% of all state residents 25 years of age or older had completed high school in 1993. Hawaii is the only state with a single, unified public school system. In 1993/94 there were 241 public schools with 11,457 teachers and 179,876 students. In addition, 121 private schools had 33,220 pupils. The University of Hawaii's three campuses—Manoa (by far the largest), Hilo, and West Oahu—had 50,229 students in fall 1993, while Hawaii's six community colleges enrolled 26,563.

33 ARTS

Performance facilities in Honolulu include the Neal Blaisdell Center, the John F. Kennedy Theater at the University of Hawaii, and the Waikiki Shell for outdoor concerts. Oahu cultural institutions include the Honolulu Symphony Orchestra, the Honolulu Community Theater, Honolulu Theater for Youth, Windward Theater Guild, and the Polynesian Cultural Center. From 1987 to 1991, the state of Hawaii generated $40,151,129 in federal state funds for the development of its arts programs.

34 LIBRARIES AND MUSEUMS

The Hawaii state library system had 47 facilities in 1991–92, with a combined book stock of 2,857,090. During the same year, the University of Hawaii library system had over 2.3 million volumes. Hawaii

Photo credit: Corel Corporation.

A surfer rides the wave at Sunset Beach.

has 35 major museums and cultural attractions. Among the most popular sites are the USS *Arizona* Memorial at Pearl Harbor; Kahuku Sugar Mill; and the Honolulu Academy of Arts.

35 COMMUNICATIONS

In March 1993, 93.5% of Hawaii's 407,000 occupied housing units had telephones. Hawaii had 27 AM radio stations and 33 FM stations as of 1994, as well as 22 television stations. Two large cable television systems were operating in 1993.

36 PRESS

In 1993, Hawaii had six English daily newspapers: the *Honolulu Advertiser,*

Honolulu Star-Bulletin, Hawaii Tribune-Herald, Maui News, West Hawaii Today, and *The Garden Island.* The combined average circulation of the daily papers in 1993 was 241,467 Monday through Saturday, and 255,692 on Sunday.

37 TOURISM, TRAVEL, AND RECREATION

Jet air service has fueled the Hawaii travel boom in recent decades. As of 1992, tourists staying at least one night in Hawaii spent almost $9.6 billion, exclusive of transpacific air fare. Over 2,700,000 visitors come annually from foreign countries. Visitors come for scuba diving, snorkeling, swimming, and sailing; for the hula, luau, lei, and other distinctive island pleasures; for the tropical climate and magnificent scenic beauty; and for a remarkable variety of recreational facilities, including national and state parks, historic sites, public golf courses, and 1,600 recognized surfing sites.

38 SPORTS

Hawaii has no major league professional sports team. The Pro Bowl (the National Football League's all-star game) is played in Honolulu on the weekend following the Super Bowl. Hawaii is also the site of the annual Duke Kahanamoku and Makaha surfing meets and the world-famous Ironman Triathlon competition.

39 FAMOUS HAWAIIANS

Hawaii's best-known federal officeholder is Daniel K. Inouye (b.1924), a US senator since 1962 and the first person of Japanese ancestry ever elected to Congress. George R. Ariyoshi (b.1926), who was elected governor of Hawaii in 1974, was the first Japanese-American to serve as chief executive of a state.

Commanding figures in Hawaiian history are King Kamehameha I (1758?–1819), who unified the islands through conquest, and Kamehameha III (Kauikeaouli, 1813–54), who transformed Hawaii into a constitutional monarchy. Sanford B. Dole (1844–1926) led a revolutionary movement that overthrew Queen Liliuokalani (1838–1917) and ultimately secured annexation by the US.

Don Ho (b.1930) is the most prominent Hawaiian-born entertainer; singer-actress Bette Midler (b.1945) was also born on the islands. Duke Kahanamoku (1889–1968) held the Olympic 100-meter free-style swimming record for almost 20 years.

40 BIBLIOGRAPHY

Fuchs, Lawrence H. *Hawaii Pono: A Social History.* San Diego: Harcourt Brace Jovanovich, 1984.
Joesting, Edward. *Hawaii: An Uncommon History.* New York: Norton, 1972.
Wenkam, Robert. *Hawaii.* Chicago: Rand McNally, 1972.

IDAHO

State of Idaho

ORIGIN OF STATE NAME: Apparently coined by a lobbyist-politician, George M. Willing, who claimed the word came from an Indian term meaning "gem of the mountains."

NICKNAME: The Gem State.

CAPITAL: Boise.

ENTERED UNION: 3 July 1890 (43d).

SONG: "Here We Have Idaho."

MOTTO: *Esto perpetua* (May it endure forever).

FLAG: On a blue field with gilt fringe, the state seal appears in the center with the words "State of Idaho" on a red band below.

OFFICIAL SEAL: With cornucopias at their feet, a female figure (holding the scales of justice in one hand and a pike supporting a liberty cap in the other) and a miner (with pick and shovel) stand on either side of a shield depicting mountains, rivers, forests, and a farm; the shield rests on a sheaf of grain and is surmounted by the head of a stag above whose antlers is a scroll with the state motto. The words "Great Seal of the State of Idaho" surround the whole.

BIRD: Mountain bluebird.

FLOWER: Syringa.

TREE: Western white pine.

GEM: Star garnet.

HORSE: Appaloosa.

TIME: 5 AM MST = noon GMT; 4 AM PST = noon GMT.

1 LOCATION AND SIZE

Idaho is the smallest of the eight Rocky Mountain states and 13th in size among the 50 states. The total area of Idaho is 83,564 square miles (216,431 square kilometers). Idaho extends a maximum of 305 miles (491 kilometers) east-west and 479 miles (771 kilometers) north-south. Its total boundary length is 1,787 miles (2,876 kilometers).

2 TOPOGRAPHY

Idaho is extremely mountainous. Its northern two-thirds consists of a mountain massif (a single block of the earth's crust) broken only by valleys and by the Big Camas and Palouse Country prairies. The Snake River Plain extends east–west across Idaho from Yellowstone National Park to the Boise area, curving around the southern end of the mountain mass. A forested high-mountain area juts into the southeastern corner; the rest of Idaho's southern edge consists mostly of low, dry mountains. More than 150 peaks rise above 10,000 feet (3,000 meters), of which the highest is Mt. Borah, at 12,662 feet (3,859 meters).

The largest lakes are Pend Oreille (180 square miles—466 square kilometers), Coeur d'Alene, and Priest in the panhandle, and Bear on the Utah border. The Snake River that dominates southern Idaho is one of the longest in the US, extending 1,038 miles (1,671 kilometers) across Wyoming, Idaho, and Washington. The Salmon, Clearwater, Kootenai, Bear, Boise, and Payette are other major rivers.

3 CLIMATE

The four seasons are distinct in Idaho but do not occur at the same time in all parts of the state. Mean temperatures in Boise range from 30°F (–1°C) in January to 75°F (24°C) in July. The record low temperature is –60°F (–51°C); the record high, 118°F (48°C). Precipitation in southern Idaho averages 13 inches (33 centimeters) per year; in the north, over 30 inches (76 centimeters).

4 PLANTS AND ANIMALS

Idaho has some 3,000 native plants. Evergreens include Douglas fir and western white pine (the state tree). Oak/mountain mahogany and ponderosa pine are among the other main forest types. Syringa is the state flower. Game mammals include the elk, mountain sheep, antelope, black bear, moose, mule deer and white-tailed deer. Pheasant, partridge, quail, and forest grouse are the main game birds, and there are trout, salmon, and bass in Idaho's lakes and streams. The grizzly bear is listed as threatened, while the woodland caribou, bald eagle, Arctic and American and peregrine falcons are endangered.

Idaho Population Profile

Estimated 1995 population:	1,156,000
Population change, 1980–90:	6.7%
Leading ancestry group:	English
Second leading group:	German
Foreign born population:	2.9%
Hispanic origin†:	5.3%
Population by race:	
White:	94.4%
Black:	0.3%
Native American:	1.4%
Asian/Pacific Islander:	0.9%
Other:	3.0%

Population by Age Group

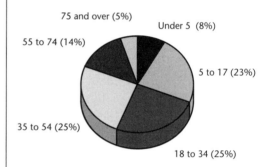

75 and over (5%)
Under 5 (8%)
55 to 74 (14%)
5 to 17 (23%)
35 to 54 (25%)
18 to 34 (25%)

Top Cities with Populations Over 25,000

City	Population	National rank	% change 1980–90
Boise	135,506	140	22.7
Idaho Falls	48,226	551	11.0
Pocatello	47,914	554	–0.6
Nampa	31,416	891	13.0
Twin Falls	29,684	940	5.3
Lewiston	29,119	953	0.3

Notes: †A person of Hispanic origin may be of any race. NA indicates that data are not available.
Sources: Economic and Statistics Administration, Bureau of the Census. *Statistical Abstract of the United States, 1994–95.* Washington, DC: Government Printing Office, 1995; Courtenay M. Slater and George E. Hall. *1995 County and City Extra: Annual Metro, City and County Data Book.* Lanham, MD: Bernan Press, 1995.

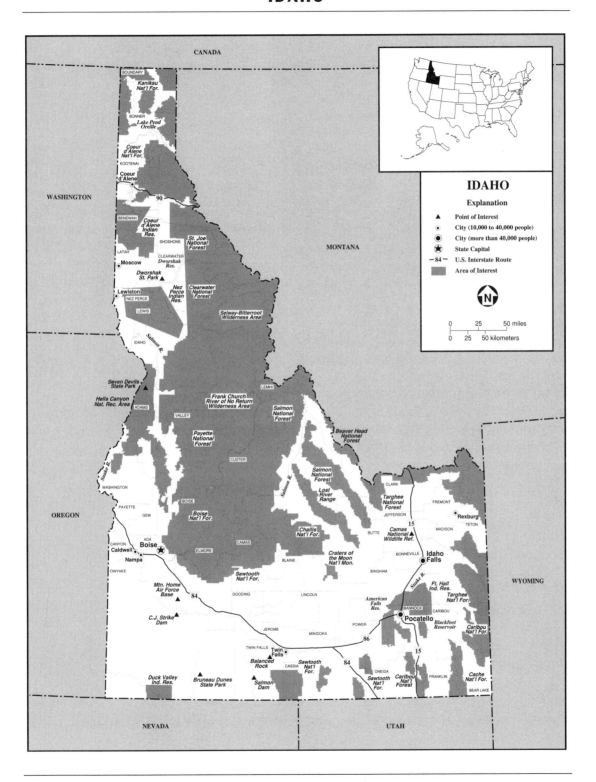

Mt. Borah, Idaho's highest peak.

5 ENVIRONMENTAL PROTECTION

Air quality improved greatly between 1978 and 1993. Emissions have dropped to the point that no carbon monoxide violations have occurred for four years. Water quality is generally good. Most of the existing problems stem from runoff from agricultural lands. Since 1953, nuclear waste has been buried at the Idaho National Engineering Laboratory west of Idaho Falls or discharged in liquid form into the underground aquifer. As of 1994, Idaho had ten hazardous waste sites.

6 POPULATION

Idaho's population at the 1990 census was 1,006,749—42d among the 50 states. The estimated population for 1995 was 1,156,000. The population projection for 2000 is 1,290,000. Boise's 1992 population was 135,506; Idaho Falls was next with 48,226; and Pocatello with 47,914.

7 ETHNIC GROUPS

The 1990 census included 14,000 Native Americans. There is a very small population of African Americans (about 3,000 in 1990) and a somewhat larger number (9,000) of Asian-Pacific peoples, over 3,800 of them Japanese. There were 53,000 persons of Hispanic origin in Idaho, and a very visible Basque community in the Boise area.

8 LANGUAGES

In Idaho, English is a merger of Northern and North Midland features, with certain Northern pronunciations marking the panhandle. More than 93% of the people spoke only English at home in 1990. Spanish speakers numbered 37,081.

9 RELIGIONS

The Church of Jesus Christ of Latter-day Saints (Mormon) has been the leading religion in Idaho since 1860; with about a quarter of the population, the number of Mormons in Idaho is second only to that in Utah. Catholicism predominates north of Boise. According to 1990 estimates, Idaho has about 268,060 Mormons, 13,303 members of various Lutheran denominations, and 20,979 United Methodists. In 1990 there were 232,780 Roman Catholics and an estimated 320 Jews.

10 TRANSPORTATION

In 1993, Idaho had 58,835 miles (94,666 kilometers) of public roads and streets. There were 1,023,179 registered vehicles—including 636,250 automobiles, 383,557 trucks, and 3,372 buses—in 1993. There were 1,884 rail miles (3,031 kilometers) of Class I track used by the five railroads operating within the state in 1992. Amtrak provides limited passenger service to several cities; the number of Idaho riders in 1991/92 was 37,926. Boise's modern airport boarded 547,723 passengers during 1991. A Snake River port at Lewiston links Idaho with the Pacific via navigable waterways in Washington State.

11 HISTORY

The Shoshone, Northern Paiute, Salishan, and Shapwailutan tribal families were living in the area now known as Idaho when fur trappers and missionaries arrived in the early 1800s. The Oregon Trail opened in 1842, but for two decades people used it only to cross Idaho, not to settle there. In 1860 Mormons from Utah established Franklin, Idaho's first permanent settlement, and began farming. Gold was discovered that summer in northern Idaho. A gold rush, lasting several years, led directly to the organizing of the Idaho Territory on 10 July 1863.

Idaho's population nearly doubled between 1870 and 1880. The threat to Native American hunting and fishing grounds posed by growing white settlement touched off a series of wars in the late 1870s, the most famous being the Nez Percé War. With a population of 88,548 in 1890, Idaho was eligible to enter the Union, becoming the 43d state on 3 July.

From 1895 onward, federal land and irrigation projects fostered rapid economic growth. The modern timber industry began in 1906 with the completion of one of the nation's largest sawmills at Potlatch. By World War I, agriculture was a leading enterprise. Between the wars, Idaho suffered first from a farm depression in the 1920s, then from the nationwide Great Depression of the 1930s. After the war, an agri-industrial base was created, with fertilizers and potato-processing leading the way. In recent decades, population expansion and the push for economic growth have collided with a new interest in the environment, creating controversies over land-use planning, mineral development, and water supply and dam construction.

12 STATE GOVERNMENT

The legislature, consisting of a 42-seat senate and an 84-member house of representatives, meets regularly for 60–90 days a year. The executive branch is headed by the governor, lieutenant governor, and five other elected officials. The governor can sign or veto a bill or let it become law without his signature. Vetoes may be overridden by a two-thirds vote of each legislative house.

13 POLITICAL PARTIES

Idahoans usually vote Republican in presidential elections. However, while the state has become increasingly conservative politically since the early 1960s, only Democrats were elected governor during 1970–92. In 1992 Republican George Bush received 42% of the vote while Democrat Bill Clinton won 28% of the vote, and Independent Ross Perot captured 27%.

Elected governor in November 1994, Republican Phil Batt ended 24 years of Democratic control of that office. Following the November 1994 elections, the state legislature had 23 Republicans and 12 Democrats in the state senate and 50 Republicans and 20 Democrats in the state house. Idaho's US Representatives in 1994, Helen Chenoweth and Mike Crapo, were both Republican. Its senators, Larry Craig (elected in 1990) and Dirk

Kempthorne (elected in 1992) were also both Republicans.

Idaho Presidential Vote by Major Political Parties, 1948–92

Year	Idaho Winner	Democrat	Republican
1948	*Truman (D)	107,370	101,514
1952	*Eisenhower (R)	395,081	180,707
1956	*Eisenhower (R)	105,868	166,979
1960	Nixon (R)	138,853	161,597
1964	*Johnson (D)	148,920	143,557
1968	*Nixon (R)	389,273	165,369
1972	*Nixon (R)	380,826	199,384
1976	Ford (R)	126,549	204,151
1980	*Reagan (R)	110,192	290,699
1984	*Reagan (R)	108,510	297,523
1988	*Bush (R)	147,272	253,881
1992**	Bush (R)	137,013	202,645

* Won US presidential election.
** Independent candidate Ross Perot received 130,395 votes.

14 LOCAL GOVERNMENT

As of 1992, Idaho had 44 counties, 199 municipal governments, 116 school districts, and 745 special districts. Most counties elect three commissioners and other officers. Nearly all cities have an elected mayor and a council of four to six members.

15 JUDICIAL SYSTEM

Idaho's highest court, the supreme court, consists of five justices. There is a three-member court of appeals. The district court is the main trial court in civil and criminal matters, while magistrates' courts handle traffic, misdemeanor, and minor civil cases and preliminary hearings in felony cases. Idaho's crime rates are low in almost every category. The total rate in 1994 was 4,077 per 100,000. In 1993 there were 2,606 inmates in state and federal prisons.

Photo credit: Mary J. Davis.

Skyline view of Boise, Idaho's state capital.

16 MIGRATION

Since 1960, immigrants have come largely from California. Idaho suffered a net loss from migration of 109,000 persons between 1940 and 1970, but had a net gain of 110,000 persons in the 1970s. During the 1980s, Idaho had a net loss of 28,000 persons from migration, but this trend was largely offset by a steady migration into Idaho during the early 1990s.

17 ECONOMY

Currently, agriculture, mining, forest products, and food processing comprise Idaho's largest industries. The early 1980s brought a national recession to Idaho. Recovery, which required a restructuring of Idaho's mining, forest products, and agricultural industries, has come slowly. In some areas of the economy, the labor force has shrunk permanently. Modernization in lumber and wood products eliminated hundreds of jobs. Disputes with the federal government over the management of federal lands—66% of Idaho's public land—remain central to discussion of Idaho's economic policy.

18 INCOME

Per capita (per person) income in Idaho in 1994 was $18,406, 39th in the US. Total personal income rose to $20.9 billion in the same year. Some 13.1% of all state residents were below the federal poverty level in 1993.

19 INDUSTRY

Resource industries—food processing, chemical manufacturing, and lumber production—form the backbone of manufacturing in Idaho. Some northern California computer companies, including Hewlett Packard, have opened or expanded plants in Idaho. Electronics manufacturers headquartered in Idaho include Advanced Input Devices and Micron Technology.

20 LABOR

Idaho's average civilian labor force was 591,000 in 1994. Unemployment averaged 5.6% in 1994. Nonagricultural employment in 1993 amounted to 437,200, of which manufacturing accounted for 69,300; construction, 23,800; food processing, 18,700; lumber and wood products, 14,300; and mining, 2,200. Some 8.5% of all workers were union members as of 1994.

21 AGRICULTURE

Farm marketings were about $2.9 billion in 1994, when Idaho led the US in potato production. In 1994, the state produced over 13.4 trillion pounds of potatoes. About three-fourths of the crop is processed into frozen french fries, instant mashed potatoes, and other products. Other leading crops were hay, 4,438,000 tons; wheat, 100,280,000 bushels; and barley, 54,000,000 bushels.

22 DOMESTICATED ANIMALS

By the close of 1994 there were about 1,780,000 beef cattle, 220,000 dairy cows, 270,000 sheep, 58,000 hogs, and 1,300,000 chickens on the state's farms and ranches. Cattle products made up 22% of agricultural receipts in 1994, and dairy products accounted for 15.4%.

23 FISHING

Sport fishermen catch trout, salmon, bass, and 33 other game-fish species. Idaho hatcheries ship close to six million fish annually, mostly trout and salmon.

24 FORESTRY

As of 1993, Idaho forests covered 21,727,000 acres (8,793,000 hectares), or 41% of the land area. Idaho forests are used increasingly for skiing, hunting, and other recreation, as well as for timber and pulp. The total lumber production is nearly 2 billion board feet annually. Shipments of lumber and wood products in 1993 were valued at $897.8 million.

25 MINING

The estimated value of nonfuel mineral production for Idaho in 1994 was $343 million. The state's mineral production includes: pumice, 37.8 million metric tons; sand and gravel for construction, 12 million short tons; phosphate rock, 5.7 million metric tons; gold, 4,759 kilograms; and crushed stone, 4.4 million short tons.

26 ENERGY AND POWER

In 1993, electric power production (over 99.9% hydroelectric) totaled 9 billion kilowatt hours. About half of Idaho's irrigation depends on electric pumping, and electrical energy consumption regularly exceeds the state's supply. Idaho's large size, widespread and relatively rural population, and lack of public transportation

Photo credit: James W. Davis.

Thousands of acres of irrigated Idaho potatoes are grown on the Snake River Plain.

foster reliance on motor vehicles and imported petroleum products. Hot water from thermal springs is used to heat a few buildings in Boise.

27 COMMERCE

In 1992 Idaho's wholesale establishments registered nearly $9 billion in sales. Retail sales exceeded $8 billion in 1993, a 10% increase over 1992. Service establishment receipts totaled almost $4 billion. Boise is the headquarters of the Albertson's supermarket chain, a large retailer with over $10 billion in sales annually.

28 PUBLIC FINANCE

Idaho's annual budget, prepared by the Division of Financial Management, is submitted by the governor to the legislature for amendment and approval. Revenues for 1994/95 were estimated at $2,968.8 million and expenditures at $2,968.8 million.

29 TAXATION

As of 1994, the personal income tax ranged from 2% to 8.2%, the corporate income tax was 8%, and the general sales tax was 5%. The state also levies taxes on inheritances, alcoholic beverages, cigarettes and tobacco products, motor fuels, insurance premiums, hotel/motel rooms and campgrounds, ores mined and extracted, oil and gas produced, and electric utilities. Property taxes are the only major source of local revenue. In 1992, Idaho paid federal taxes totaling $3.5 billion.

30 HEALTH

Death rates in Idaho from accidents and adverse effects, motor vehicle accidents, and suicide are above the respective national rates. Death rates for heart diseases, cancer, and cerebrovascular diseases, however, are below their corresponding national rates. In all, 41 community hospitals had 3,400 beds in 1993. The average expense for hospital care provided in 1993 was $659 per inpatient day, among the lowest in the US. There were 1,428 nonfederal physicians and 5,702 nurses in 1993. Almost 15% of Idahoans were without health insurance in 1993.

31 HOUSING

Single-family housing predominates in Idaho. In 1993 there were an estimated 436,000 housing units. The median monthly expense for owner-occupied housing by mortgage holders ($561) and median gross monthly rent ($330) were below the national averages. In 1993, 11,567 new private units worth $928.5 million were authorized.

32 EDUCATION

Idaho's state and local per-pupil expenditure on education, $4,025 in 1993, is one of the lowest among the states. However, nearly 80% of Idahoans over 25 are high school graduates, well above the national average.

As of fall 1993, public educational institutions enrolled 128,339 elementary school students and 108,435 secondary school students. Idaho's 11 institutions of higher learning had 58,668 students in the fall of 1993. The leading public higher educational institutions are the University of Idaho at Moscow; Idaho State University (Pocatello); Boise State University; and Lewis-Clark State College in Lewiston. There are two public community colleges and five private institutions.

33 ARTS

The Boise Philharmonic is Idaho's leading professional orchestra. Other symphony orchestras are in Coeur d'Alene, Moscow, Pocatello, and Twin Falls. Boise and Moscow have seasonal theaters. The Idaho Commission on the Arts and Humanities, founded in 1966, offers grants to support both creative and performing artists. From 1987 to 1991, arts programs in Idaho received $4,555,900 from federal and state sources.

34 LIBRARIES AND MUSEUMS

Idaho's 107 public libraries have a combined book stock of nearly 2,914,960 volumes and a total circulation of more than 6,247,000. The largest public library system is the Boise Public Library and Information Center. The leading academic library is at the University of Idaho (Moscow). The state also has 28 museums, notably the Boise Art Museum, Idaho State Historical Museum (Boise), and the Idaho Museum of Natural History (Pocatello).

35 COMMUNICATIONS

As of March 1993, 94.8% of Idaho's 392,000 occupied housing units had telephones. As of 1993, the state had 96

Photo credit: Mary J. Davis.

Skiing is one of Idaho's many winter sports.

operating radio stations (42 AM, 54 FM) and 11 commercial and 6 noncommercial educational television stations. Two large cable systems serviced the state in 1993.

36 PRESS

Idaho had 12 daily newspapers in 1994, and 9 Sunday papers. There were 49 weeklies. The most widely read newspaper was the (morning) *Idaho Statesman,* published in Boise, with a circulation of 60,333 daily and 80,471 on Sundays as of September 1994.

37 TOURISM, TRAVEL, AND RECREATION

Tourists come to Idaho primarily for outdoor recreation—river trips, skiing, camping, hunting, fishing, and hiking. There are 19 ski resorts, of which by far the most famous is Sun Valley. Tourist attractions include the Craters of the Moon National Monument, the Nez Percé National Historical Park, and two US parks.

38 SPORTS

Idaho has no major league professional team, although the Atlanta Braves have a farm team in Idaho Falls, and the California Angels have a farm team in Boise. In college sports, the Idaho State Bengals and the University of Idaho Vandals play Division I basketball in the Big Sky Conference. World chariot racing championships have been held at Pocatello, as are the National Circuit Rodeo Finals.

39 FAMOUS IDAHOANS

Leading federal officeholders born in Idaho include Ezra Taft Benson (b.1899), US secretary of agriculture from 1953 to 1961, and Cecil D. Andrus (b.Oregon, 1931), governor of Idaho from 1971 to 1977 and secretary of the interior from 1977 to 1981. Republican William E. Borah (b.Illinois, 1865–1940) served in the US Senate from 1907 until his death, chairing the foreign relations committee for 16 years. Senator Frank Church (1924–84) became chairman of the same committee in 1979; however, he was defeated in his bid for a fifth term in 1980. Important state officeholders were the nation's first Jewish governor, Moses Alexander (b.Germany,

1853–1932), and New Deal governor C. Ben Ross (1876–1946).

Idaho was the birthplace of poet Ezra Pound (1885–1972). Nobel Prize-winning novelist Ernest Hemingway (b.Illinois, 1899–1961) is buried at Ketchum. Gutzon Borglum (1871–1941), the sculptor who carved the Mt. Rushmore National Memorial in South Dakota, was an Idaho native. Baseball slugger Harmon Killebrew (b.1936) and football star Jerry Kramer (b.1936) are Idaho's leading sports personalities.

40 BIBLIOGRAPHY

Etulain, Richard W., and Merwin Swanson. *Idaho History: A Bibliography*. Pocatello: Idaho State University Press, 1975.

Peterson, F. Ross. *Idaho: A Bicentennial History*. New York: Norton, 1976.

Young, Virgil. *The Story of Idaho*. Moscow: University of Idaho Press, 1984.

ILLINOIS

State of Illinois

ILLINOIS

ORIGIN OF STATE NAME: French derivative of *Iliniwek*, meaning "tribe of superior men," a Native American group formerly in the region.

NICKNAME: The Prairie State.

SLOGAN: Land of Lincoln.

CAPITAL: Springfield.

ENTERED UNION: 3 December 1818 (21st).

SONG: "Illinois."

MOTTO: State Sovereignty–National Union.

FLAG: The inner portion of the state seal and the word "Illinois" on a white field.

OFFICIAL SEAL: An American eagle perched on a boulder holds in its beak a banner bearing the state motto; below the eagle is a shield resting on an olive branch. Also depicted are the prairie, the sun rising over a distant eastern horizon, and, on the boulder, the dates 1818 and 1868, the years of the seal's introduction and revision, respectively. The words "Seal of the State of Illinois Aug. 26th 1818" surround the whole.

ANIMAL: White-tailed deer.

BIRD: Cardinal.

FISH: Bluegill.

FLOWER: Violet.

TREE: White oak.

MINERAL: Fluorite.

INSECT: Monarch butterfly.

TIME: 6 AM CST = noon GMT.

1 LOCATION AND SIZE

Illinois ranks 24th in size among the 50 states. Its area totals 56,345 square miles (145,934 square kilometers). Illinois extends 211 miles (340 kilometers) east-west; its maximum north-south extension is 381 miles (613 kilometers). Its boundaries total 1,297 miles (2,088 kilometers).

2 TOPOGRAPHY

Illinois is predominantly flat. Lying wholly within the Central Plains, the state's physical features are uniform, relieved mainly by rolling hills in the northwest and throughout the southern third of the state. The highest natural point, Charles Mound, is only 1,235 feet (376 meters) above sea level—far lower than Chicago's towering skyscrapers. The low point is 279 feet (85 meters) above sea level. Most of the state's 2,000 lakes of 6 acres (2.4 hectares) or more were created by dams. The most important rivers are the Illinois, the Wabash, the Ohio, and the Mississippi. Illinois has three manmade lakes. The artificial Lake Carlyle (41 square miles—106 square kilometers) is the largest body of inland water.

3 CLIMATE

Illinois has a temperate climate, with cold, snowy winters and hot, humid summers. The seasons are sharply differentiated by region: mean winter temperatures are 22°F (–6°C) in the north and 37°F (3°C) in the south. Mean summer temperatures are 70°F (21°C) in the north and 77°F (25°C) in the south. The record high, 117°F (47°C), was set at East St. Louis on 14 July 1954; the record low, –35°F (–37°C), was registered at Mt. Carroll on 22 January 1930. Average annual precipitation is 36 inches (91 centimeters). An annual snowfall of 37 inches (94 centimeters) is normal for northern Illinois, decreasing to 24 inches (61 centimeters) or less in the central and southern regions.

4 PLANTS AND ANIMALS

About 90% of the oak and hickory forests that once were common in the north have been cut down for fuel and lumber. In the forests that do remain, mostly in the south, typical trees are black oak, sugar maple, box elder, and slippery elm. Characteristic wildflowers are the Chase aster, lupine, and primrose violet. The small-whorled pogonia is endangered.

The bison, elk, bear, and wolves that once roamed freely have long since vanished. Deer are abundant and among the state's fur-bearing mammals are also opossum, raccoon, mink, and muskrat. More than 350 birds have been identified, with such game birds as ruffed grouse,

Illinois Population Profile

Estimated 1995 population:	11,853,000
Population change, 1980–90:	<0.5%
Leading ancestry group:	German
Second leading group:	Irish
Foreign born population:	8.3%
Hispanic origin†:	7.9%
Population by race:	
White:	78.3%
Black:	14.8%
Native American:	0.2%
Asian/Pacific Islander:	2.5%
Other:	4.2%

Population by Age Group

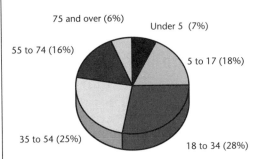

75 and over (6%)
Under 5 (7%)
55 to 74 (16%)
5 to 17 (18%)
35 to 54 (25%)
18 to 34 (28%)

Top Cities with Populations Over 25,000

City	Population	National rank	% change 1980–90
Chicago	2,768,483	3	–7.4
Rockford	141,679	126	–0.2
Peoria	113,983	164	–8.6
Springfield	106,429	185	5.6
Aurora	105,929	189	22.5
Naperville	91,928	228	101.6
Decatur	84,273	263	–10.8
Elgin	81,108	276	20.7
Joliet	78,917	287	–1.4
Arlington Heights	76,518	299	14.1

Notes: †A person of Hispanic origin may be of any race. NA indicates that data are not available.
Sources: Economic and Statistics Administration, Bureau of the Census. Statistical Abstract of the United States, 1994–95. Washington, DC: Government Printing Office, 1995; Courtenay M. Slater and George E. Hall. 1995 County and City Extra: Annual Metro, City and County Data Book. Lanham, MD: Bernan Press, 1995.

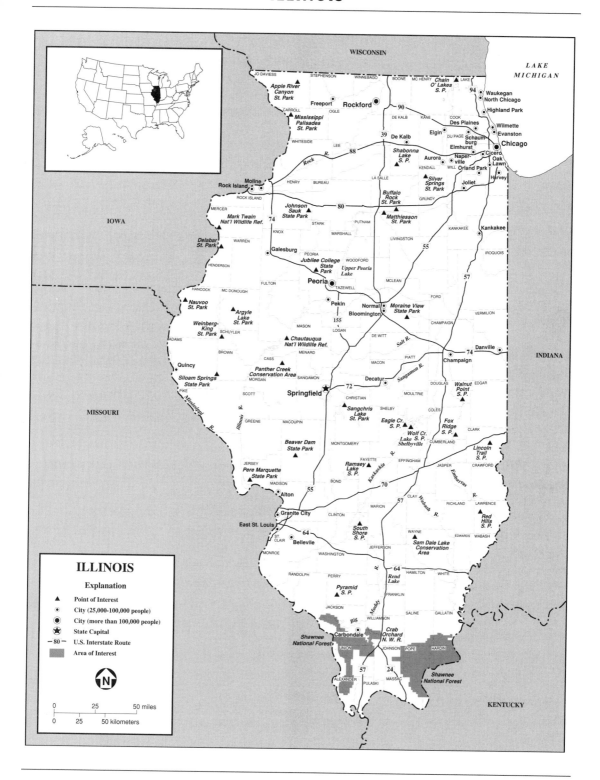

ILLINOIS

Explanation

▲ Point of Interest
• City (25,000-100,000 people)
◉ City (more than 100,000 people)
✪ State Capital
—80— U.S. Interstate Route
▨ Area of Interest

N

0   25   50 miles
0   25   50 kilometers

Photo credit: William Semple.

Chicago waterfront from Olive Park.

wild turkey, and bobwhite quail especially prized. Other native birds are the cardinal (the state bird), horned lark, and blue jay. Mallard and black ducks are common, and several subspecies of the Canada goose are also found. Coho salmon were introduced into Lake Michigan in the 1960s, thus reviving sport fishing. Other endangered species include the gray and Indiana bats, eastern woodrat, and white-tailed jackrabbit.

5 ENVIRONMENTAL PROTECTION

The 1970s saw a noticeable improvement in environmental quality. Dirty air became less common—though clean-air requirements crippled the state's high-sulfur coal industry. The Illinois EPA maintains more than 200 air-monitoring stations and conducts about 3,000 facility inspections each year. Since Illinois produces about six million tons of hazardous wastes annually (second only to New Jersey), the state agency tries to pinpoint and clean up abandoned hazardous waste sites. Thanks to that program, 64 sites were cleaned up as of 1993.

6 POPULATION

At the 1990 census, Illinois ranked 6th among the 50 states, with a population of 11,430,602, or 205.6 persons per square mile (79 persons square kilometer). The estimated population for 1995 was 11,853,000. The projected population for the year 2000 is 12,168,000. The age distribution of the state's population in 1990 closely mirrored the national pattern, with 25% under age 18 and 21% aged 55 or older.

By 1990, 83% of the population lived in metropolitan areas. With a population of 8,066,000 in 1990, Greater Chicago was the third-largest metropolitan area in the nation and accounted for just over 70% of the total state population. The state's other major metropolitan areas, with their 1990 populations, were Peoria, 339,172; and Rockford, 283,719. The largest city in 1992 was Chicago, with 2,768,483 residents, followed by Rockford, 141,679; Peoria, 113,983; Springfield, 106,429; and Aurora, 105,929.

7 ETHNIC GROUPS

In 1990, Illinois had 22,000 Native Americans and 1,694,000 blacks. In 1990, the number of Illinoisans of Hispanic origin was 904,000, chiefly in Chicago. There were 557,536 persons of Mexican origin, 121,871 Puerto Ricans, and 14,625 Cubans. Most of the remainder came from other Caribbean and Latin American countries. In 1990 there were 44,077 Chinese in Illinois, 26,579 Japanese, 66,984 Filipinos, 42,167 Koreans, and 8,550 Vietnamese.

Members of non-British European ethnic groups are prevalent in all the state's major cities and in many farming areas. In 1990, the most common European countries of origin were Poland (80,594), Germany (39,920), Italy (33,812), the former

Yugoslavia (20,953), and the former Soviet Union (19,507). There were also significant numbers of Scandinavians, Irish, Lithuanians, Serbs, and East European Jews. Most ethnic groups in Illinois maintain their own newspapers, clubs, festivals, and houses of worship.

8 LANGUAGES

A number of place-names—Illinois itself, Chicago, Peoria, Kankakee, and Ottawa— attest to the early presence of various Algonkian-speaking tribes. Excepting the Chicago metropolitan area and the extreme northwestern corner of Illinois, the northern quarter of the state is dominated by Northern speech, while settlement from Pennsylvania and Ohio led to a mix of Northern and North Midland speech in central Illinois. Migration from South Midland areas in Indiana and Kentucky affected basic speech in the southern third of Illinois, known as Egypt.

Metropolitan Chicago has experienced such complex in-migration that, although it still has a basic Northern/North Midland mix, elements of almost all varieties of English appear somewhere. Educational policies were reassessed in the 1970s, when the state legislature mandated bilingual classes for immigrant children, especially Spanish speakers. In 1990, English was spoken at home by 85.8% of all state residents five years of age and older. Speakers of other languages included Spanish, 728,380; Polish, 143,480; German, 84,625; and Italian, 66,903.

Photo credit: William Semple.

Chicago River harbor locks and lighthouse.

has been of central importance in the state's economic development. The state has access to the east by way of the major rivers and the Great Lakes system. Most of the nation's rail lines converge on Illinois. Chicago has been one of the main US railroad centers since the late 19th century. Interstate highways also cross the state, and Chicago's central location has made it a major transfer point for airline connections.

Chicago is the hub of Amtrak's passenger service, which operated approximately 30 train routes through Illinois in 1992. The total number of riders through the state's 35 stations amounted to 3,025,960 that year. There were 42 railroad companies operating 7,714 route miles (12,738 kilometers) of track within the state at the end of 1992. In 1991, the state ranked first in rail carloads handled, total tons carried by rail, and total railroad employment.

Mass transit is of special importance to the Chicago metropolitan area. Buses and commuter railroads are essential to daily movement. Chicago's commuter railroads use a combination of underground and elevated tracks. However, the number of riders declines every year, as fewer people work in the central city and more choose the privacy and convenience of travel by automobile. Outside Chicago, bus service, Amtrak, and commuter flights are still available in many of the larger cities.

In 1993, 136,965 miles (220,280 kilometers) of public roadway served 8,070,464 registered vehicles—including 6,650,165 automobiles and 1,404,308 trucks. The Interstate Highway System

9 RELIGIONS

Today, the largest Christian denomination is the Roman Catholic Church, with 3,611,000 members. The largest Protestant denomination is the United Methodist Church, with 440,000 members, followed by the Lutheran Church–Missouri Synod, 223,000; Southern Baptist Convention, 293,000; Presbyterian Church, 158,000; and United Church of Christ, 185,000. The Jewish population was estimated at over 269,000.

10 TRANSPORTATION

The fact that Illinois is intersected by several long-distance transportation routes

Photo credit: William Semple.

View under elevated transit line, Wabash St.

totaled 2,053 miles (3,303 kilometers) in the state as of 31 December 1992.

Barge traffic along the Mississippi, Ohio, and Illinois rivers remains important, especially for the shipment of grain. The Port of Chicago is the largest on the Great Lakes, handling 21.7 million tons of cargo in 1991, mostly grain and iron ore. With 25,872,241 arriving and departing travelers in 1991, Chicago's O'Hare International was the busiest airport in the country. With 687 airports and 231 heliports, Illinois is also an important center for general aviation. There were 25,653 licensed pilots and 6,543 operating aircraft in the state in 1991.

11 HISTORY

When European explorers arrived in Illinois in the 17th century, the region was inhabited by Algonkian-speaking tribes, including the Kickapoo, Sauk, Potawatomi, Ojibwa, and Peoria. Constant warfare with tribes from neighboring areas, plus disease and alcohol introduced by European fur traders and settlers, combined to devastate the tribal population. Defeat of the tribes in the Black Hawk War (1832) led to a series of treaties that removed all of the Native Americans to lands across the Mississippi River.

The first permanent European settlement in Illinois was a mission built by French Catholic priests at Cahokia, near present-day St. Louis, in 1699. In 1765, under the Treaty of Paris that ended the French and Indian War, the British took control of the Illinois country but established no settlements of their own. During the American Revolution, troops from Virginia captured the small British forts at Cahokia and Kaskaskia in 1778, after which Virginia governed Illinois as its own territory. In 1787, Illinois became part of the newly organized Northwest Territory, and in 1800, it was included in the Indiana Territory.

Statehood

Nine years later the Illinois Territory, including the present state of Wisconsin, was created, and a territorial legislature was formed in 1812. During the War of 1812, British and Native American forces combined in a last attempt to push back American expansion into the Illinois country, and much fighting took place in the area. On 3 December 1818, Illinois was formally admitted to the Union as the 21st state. The capital was moved from Vandalia to Springfield in 1839.

The withdrawal of British influence after the War of 1812 and the final defeat of the Native American tribes in the Black Hawk War of 1832 opened the fertile prairies to white settlers from the south, especially Kentucky. Despite a heavy state debt resulting from the collapse of ambitious financial development schemes in the 1830s, the arrival after 1840 of energetic Yankee pioneers, attracted by the rich soil and excellent water routes, guaranteed rapid growth.

During the Civil War, Illinois sent half its young men to the battlefield and supplied the Union armies with huge amounts of food, feed, and horses. The wartime administration of Republican Governor Richard Yates guaranteed full support for the policies of Abraham Lincoln, who had been prominent in Illinois political life since the 1840s and had been nominated for the presidency in 1860 at a Republican convention held in Chicago.

Economic and population growth quickened after 1865, and Chicago became the principal city of the Midwest. Responding to opportunities presented by the coming of the railroads, hundreds of small towns and cities built banks, grain elevators, retail shops, small factories, stately courthouses, and schools, in an abundance of civic pride.

During the second half of the 19th century, Illinois was a center of the American labor movement. Workers joined the Knights of Labor in the 1870s and 1880s and fought for child-labor laws and the eight-hour day. Union organizing led to several spectacular incidents, including the Haymarket riot in 1886 and the violent Pullman strike in 1894. After the great fire of 1871 destroyed Chicago's downtown section, the city's wealthy elite dedicated itself to rebuilding Chicago and making it one of the great metropolises of the world. Immense steel mills, meat-packing plants, and factories sprang up, and growth was tremendous in the merchandising, banking, and transportation fields.

Twentieth Century

The first three decades of the 20th century witnessed almost unbroken prosperity in all sections except Egypt, the downstate region where poor soil and the decline of the coal industry produced widespread poverty. The slums of Chicago were poor, too, because most of the hundreds of thousands of new immigrants arrived nearly penniless. After 1920, however, large-scale immigration ended and the immigrants achieved steady upward mobility, based on hard work, savings, and education. During the Prohibition era, a vast organized crime empire rose to prominence, giving Chicago and Joliet a reputation for gangsterism, violence, and corruption.

The Great Depression of the 1930s affected the state unevenly, with agriculture hit first and recovering first. Industries began shutting down in 1930 and did not fully recover until massive military contracts during World War II restored full prosperity. The depression destroyed the credibility of the pro-business Republican regime that had run the state since 1856, as blacks, white ethnics, and factory workers responded enthusiastically to Franklin Roosevelt's New Deal.

The goals of personal security and prosperity dominated Illinois life in the postwar period. However, events in the 1960s and 1970s—assassinations, the Viet Nam war, the race riots, and the violence that accompanied the 1968 Democratic National Convention in Chicago—coupled with a new awareness of such issues as poverty and environmental pollution, helped reshape attitudes in Illinois. This transformation was perhaps best shown in Chicago, where voters elected Jane Byrne the city's first woman mayor in 1979 and chose Harold Washington as its first black mayor in 1983.

The economy of Illinois, like other "rust belt" states, suffered a severe recession in the early 1980s. Hit hard by foreign competition, producers of steel, machine tools, and automobiles engaged in massive layoffs. By the end of the decade, the economy had begun to rebound, but many industrial jobs were permanently lost, as industries sought to improve their efficiency and productivity through automation. In 1990, the unemployment rate in Illinois was 7.2%, in contrast to the national average of 5.2%.

In 1992, the 60-mile maze of tunnels beneath downtown Chicago ruptured, filling basements with up to 30 feet of water, and forcing the temporary closure of the Chicago Board of Trade and City Hall. A year later, flooding of the Mississippi and Illinois rivers caused $1.5 billion of damage in the western part of the state and forced 12,800 people to evacuate their homes.

12 STATE GOVERNMENT

Under the 1970 constitution, as amended, the upper house of the general assembly consists of a senate of 59 members who are elected to four-year terms on a two-year cycle. In November 1980, Illinois voters chose to reduce the size of house membership from 177 to 118 (two representatives from each district). The executive officers elected statewide are the governor and lieutenant governor (who run jointly), secretary of state, treasurer, comptroller, and attorney general. Each serves a four-year term and is eligible for reelection.

Bills passed by both houses of the legislature become law if signed by the governor; if left unsigned for 60 days while the legislature is in session or 90 days after it adjourns; or if vetoed by the governor but passed again by three-fifths of the elected members of each house. Constitutional amendments require a three-fifths vote by the legislature for placement on the ballot. Either a simple majority of those voting in the election or three-fifths of those voting on the amendment is sufficient for ratification.

13 POLITICAL PARTIES

Politically, Illinois is a closely balanced state, with a slight Republican predominance from 1860 to 1930 giving way to a highly competitive situation statewide.

The party balance changed with the rise of the powerful Cook County Democratic organization in the 1930s. Built by Mayor Anton Cermak and continued from 1955 to 1976 by six-term Mayor Richard J. Daley, the Chicago "Democratic machine" totally controlled the city, dominated the state party, and exerted enormous power at the national level. However, the machine lost its clout with the election in 1979 of independent Democrat Jane Byrne as Chicago's first woman mayor, and again in 1983 when Harold Washington became its first black mayor. Although Richard Daley's son, also named Richard Daley, won the mayoralty in 1989, the machine has never recovered the power it once enjoyed.

There is no party registration requirement. As of the November 1994 elections, Republicans held the governorship, Democrats held both US Senate seats, and each party had 10 of the 20 US House seats. In those elections, the once-powerful chair of the House Ways and Means Committee, Dan Rostenkowski, was defeated by a relative unknown, Michael P. Flanagan. The Republicans fared well in the state legislature where they not only retained control of the senate but also took control of the house.

14 LOCAL GOVERNMENT

Illinois has more units of local government (most with property-taxing power) than any other state. In 1992 there were 102 counties, 1,282 municipalities, 1,433 townships, 997 school districts, and 2,995 special districts. Chicago is governed by an elected mayor, clerk, treasurer, and city council composed of 50 aldermen. Other cities may choose either the commission or aldermanic system: most are administered by nonpartisan city managers.

Illinois Presidential Vote by Political Parties, 1948–92

Year	Illinois Winner	Democrat	Republican	Socialist Labor	Prohibition	Communist
1948	*Truman (D)	1,994,715	1,961,103	3,118	11,959	—
1952	*Eisenhower (R)	2,013,920	2,457,327	9,363	—	—
1956	*Eisenhower (R)	1,775,682	2,623,327	8,342	—	—
1960	*Kennedy (D)	2,377,846	2,368,988	10,560	—	—
1964	*Johnson (D)	2,796,833	1,905,946	—	—	—
					American Ind.	
1968	*Nixon (R)	2,039,814	2,174,774	13,878	390,958	—
					American	
1972	*Nixon (R)	1,913,472	2,788,179	12,344	2,471	4,541
					Libertarian	
1976	Ford (R)	2,271,295	2,364,269	2,422	8,057	9,250
				Citizens		
1980	*Reagan (R)	1,981,413	2,358,094	10,692	38,939	9,711
1984	*Reagan (R)	2,086,499	2,707,103	2,716	10,086	—
1988	*Bush (R)	2,215,940	2,310,939	10,276	14,944	—
				New Alliance		Ind. (Perot)
1992	*Clinton (D)	2,453,350	1,734,096	5,267	9,218	840,515

* Won US presidential election.

15 JUDICIAL SYSTEM

The state's highest court is the supreme court, consisting of seven justices elected by judicial districts for ten-year terms. The supreme court has appeals jurisdiction generally, and original jurisdiction in certain cases. The chief justice, assisted by an administrative director, has administrative and supervisory authority over all other courts. The appeals court is divided into five districts. Appeals judges hear appeals from the 22 circuit courts, which handle civil and criminal cases.

As of 1994 the number of crimes in Illinois was 661,150, for a rate of 5,625.9 per 100,000 population. Illinois had 34,495 prisoners in 1993.

16 MIGRATION

Immigration from Europe became significant in the 1840s and continued in a heavy stream for about 80 years. Before 1890, most of the new arrivals came from Germany, Ireland, Britain, and Scandinavia. These groups continued to arrive after 1890, but they were soon outnumbered by heavy immigration from southern and eastern Europe. Concern for the welfare of these newcomers led to the establishment by Jane Addams in Chicago of Hull House (1889), which served as a social center, shelter, and advocate for immigrants, and launched the settlement movement in America.

The outbreak of World War I interrupted the flow of European immigrants but also increased the economy's demand for unskilled labor. The migration of blacks from states south of Illinois played an important role in meeting the demand for labor during both world wars. After World War II, the further collapse of the cotton labor market drove hundreds of thousands more blacks to Chicago and other northern cities. The major intrastate migration pattern has been from farms to towns. From 1985 to 1990, the net loss from migration came to 139,360. Some 69% of all state residents had been born in Illinois as of 1990.

17 ECONOMY

Since 1950, the importance of manufacturing has declined, but a very strong shift into services—government, medicine, education, law, finance, and business—has underpinned the state's economic vigor. In the 1970s heavy industrial competition from Japan wreaked havoc in the state's steel, television, and automotive industries, while Illinois's high-wage, high-cost business climate encouraged the migration of factories to the South. Meat-packing, once the most famous industry in Illinois, dwindled after the closing of the Chicago stockyards in 1972.

Chicago remained the nation's chief merchandising center during the early 1980s, and an influx of huge international banks boosted the city's financial strength. Currently, Illinois' major industries include primary and secondary metals; industrial and farm equipment; electric equipment and appliances; electronic components; food processing; and printing equipment.

18 INCOME

Illinois is a rich state and has been for the last century. Its $23,607 in per capita (per person) income ranked ninth in 1994. Its 1994 total personal income was $277.4 billion. In 1993, 13.6% of the population lived below the poverty level.

19 INDUSTRY

Manufacturing in Illinois, concentrated in but not limited to Chicago, has always been diverse. Of the major industries, food and food products contributed 18%; non-electrical machinery, 12%; petroleum and coal products, 6%; electric and electronic equipment, 8%; chemicals and allied products, 11%; fabricated metal products, 8%; printing and publishing, 8%; and primary metal industries, 6%. Leading industrial corporations headquartered in Illinois in 1993 included Amoco (Chicago), Sara Lee, and Caterpillar Tractor (Peoria).

20 LABOR

In 1994, the Illinois labor force numbered 6,000,000 persons, of whom 5,660,000 were employed. Some 340,000 were unemployed, for an unemployment rate of 5.7%.

Today, labor unions are powerful in Chicago but relatively weak downstate. In 1994, 19.9% of workers belonged to unions. There were 22 national labor unions operating in the state in 1993.

21 AGRICULTURE

Total agricultural income in 1994 reached $8.2 billion in Illinois, fifth behind California, Texas, Iowa, and Nebraska. Crops accounted for nearly 75% of the value of farm marketings, with soybeans and corn the leading cash commodities.

The number of farms reached a peak at 264,000 in 1900 and began declining rapidly after World War II, down to 77,000 in 1994. Total acreage in farming was 27.3 million acres (11 million hectares) in 1992, or 76.6% of the state's land area. The farm population, which averaged 1.2 million persons from 1880 to 1900, declined to 197,000 in 1994.

The major agricultural region is the corn belt, covering all of central and about half of northern Illinois. Among the 50 states, Illinois ranked second only to Iowa in production of corn and soybeans in 1994. The following table shows output of leading field crops in that year:

CROP	VOLUME (MILLION BUSHELS)
Corn for grain	1,786.2
Soybeans	438.4
Hay (million tons)	3.2
Wheat	50.4
Sorghum for grain	17.8
Oats	5.5

22 DOMESTICATED ANIMALS

Livestock is raised almost everywhere in Illinois, but production is concentrated especially in the west-central region. In 1994, livestock marketings and products were valued at $2 billion. In 1994, Illinois farms had 5,350,000 hogs and 1,820,000 head of cattle. Hog production contributed 11.4% to the state's agricultural receipts in 1994; cattle production; 8.3%; and dairy products, 4%. The dairy belt covers part of northern Illinois, providing milk for several cheese factories.

23 FISHING

Commercial fishing is insignificant in Illinois: only 187,000 pounds of fish, valued at $367,000, made up the commercial catch in 1992, down from 229,000 pounds and $377,000 in 1991. Sport fishing is of modest importance in southern Illinois and in Lake Michigan. Some 450 lakes and ponds and 200 streams and rivers are open to the public.

24 FORESTRY

Forestland covering 4,260,000 acres (1,720,000 hectares) comprises about 12% of the state's land area. The majority of Illinois' forests are located in the southern one-third of the state. The Shawnee National Forest encompasses over 270,000 acres (109,269 hectares). Lumbering produced 100 million board feet of lumber in 1982 and annually contributes more than $2 billion to the state's economy.

25 MINING

The value of nonfuel mineral production for Illinois in 1994 was estimated to be $770 million. The state's five leading nonfuel mineral commodities are crushed stone, portland cement, construction sand and gravel, industrial sand, and clay.

Illinois is the only state with reported fluorspar production in the United States, and the state continues to lead in the production of tripoli, contributing more than 70% of the tripoli mined in the United States. Tripoli, a microcrystalline silicate, is used as an abrasive and as a filler and extender.

26 ENERGY AND POWER

Illinois is one of the nation's leading energy producers and consumers. Electric power production totaled 140 billion kilowatt hours (third in the US) in 1993. Consumption of electrical energy in 1991 amounted to 3,487 trillion Btu, of which industry accounted for 35%; residences, 25%; commercial establishments, 19%; and transportation, 21%. Coal-fired plants account for about 42% of the state's power production; nuclear power is also important, particularly for the generation of electricity in the Chicago area.

In 1992, Illinois ranked fourth in natural-gas usage, with 976.3 billion cubic feet delivered to 3.6 million customers. Petroleum production, though steadily declining, totaled 17 million barrels in 1993; reserves were 128 million barrels. Illinois ranked fifth in the US in bituminous coal production in 1992, with 59.4 million tons. Bituminous coal reserves were estimated at 78.1 billion tons.

27 COMMERCE

Chicago is the leading wholesaling center of the Midwest. The state's 24,000 wholesale establishments employ over 320,000 people (fourth in the US) and have sales of over $219 billion. Chicago is an especially important trade center for furniture, housewares, and apparel. The state's 64,000 retail stores employ 820,000 people and record yearly sales in excess of $96 billion. Leading Illinois-based retailing companies include Sears, Roebuck, with nationwide sales of $52.4 billion; McDonald's, $7.1 billion; and Walgreen's, $7.5 billion. Service establishments in

Illinois record annual receipts in excess of $64 billion. Illinois ranked eighth among the states in exports with an estimated $15.3 billion in 1992.

28 PUBLIC FINANCE

Among the larger states, Illinois is known for its low taxes and conservative fiscal policy. Revenues for fiscal year 1993/94 (estimated) were $26,549 million, and appropriations were $30,277 million. In 1993, the state's debt approached $20 billion, or $1,702 per capita (per person).

29 TAXATION

Illinoisans have fiercely resisted the imposition of new and higher taxes. Total state revenue from 1991 sources was $25.1 billion. As of 1994, the state personal income tax was a flat 3%. The corporate income tax was 7.3% and the sales tax 6.25%. Excise taxes included charges on cigarettes and on gasoline. In 1992, Illinois ranked 7th among the states in per capita (per person) federal tax payments, averaging $5,694.1. The federal government collected $65.8 billion in Illinois for 1992, and sent back $44.4 billion.

30 HEALTH

Health conditions in Illinois do not meet the national norm. Although the infant mortality rate fell from 21.5 (per 1,000 live births) in 1970 to 10.7 in 1991, it did not decline as rapidly as elsewhere. Today, Illinois ranks above the national average in deaths due to heart disease, cancer, and cerebrovascular disease, but below the average in accidents and suicide.

Chicago serves as a diagnostic and treatment center for patients throughout the Midwest. With 208 facilities (many quite large) and 44,000 beds, Illinois community hospitals recorded 1,467,000 admissions in 1993. The average expense of hospitals per admission in 1993 was $6,318 per stay and $912 per inpatient day, both above the US average. In 1993, the state had 26,800 nonfederal physicians and 93,000 nurses. Over 12% of Illinoisans do not have health insurance.

31 HOUSING

In 1993 there were an estimated 4,595,000 housing units in Illinois. In 1993, more than 44,700 new units valued at nearly $4.5 billion were authorized. The median monthly cost for owners with a mortgage in 1990 was $767, and $241 for owners without a mortgage. The same costs in the greater Chicago area of Illinois were $889 and $284, respectively. The median monthly rent in 1990 throughout the state was $445; in the greater Chicago area it was $491.

32 EDUCATION

In 1993, Illinois had slightly higher literacy levels than the national averages. In 1990, 76.2% of the Illinois adult population held high school diplomas, with nearly 21% continuing their education for a bachelor's degree or higher.

In 1994/95, Illinois had 2,597 public elementary schools, 587 junior high schools, and 645 high schools. Enrollment in 1994/95 was 1,365,876 at the elementary level and 550,296 at the secondary level. Over 35% of all public school

Photo credit: Grant H. Kessler.

Residents enjoy a friendly chat in a small farming community in Fulton County. With three-fourths of the state's land area devoted to farming, Illinois is a major agricultural region.

students are minorities. The per pupil average expenditure on primary and secondary education is $5,399.

Nonpublic schools, dominated by Chicago's extensive Roman Catholic school system, have shown a slight decrease in enrollment since the early 1980s. In 1992/93, total nonpublic enrollment in Illinois private schools was 315,595.

Illinois institutions of higher education have always been of the highest caliber, with 186 public and private universities having a total fall 1993 enrollment of 740,185 (public enrollment, 197,377; community colleges, 354,717; private, 188,091). The state appropriated a $2.4 billion budget for colleges and universities

in 1994/95. The largest system, the University of Illinois, operates three major campuses—Champaign-Urbana, Chicago, and Springfield. Illinois maintains a flourishing network of 49 community colleges.

Major private universities include the University of Chicago, Northwestern University (Evanston), Illinois Institute of Technology (Chicago), and Loyola University (Chicago). Each maintains undergraduate and research programs, as well as nationally recognized professional schools.

33 ARTS

Chicago emerged in the late 19th century as the leading arts center of the Midwest, and it continues to hold this premier position. From 1987 to 1991, the State of Illinois generated $70,147,655 from federal and state sources to develop its art programs.

Architecture is the outstanding art form in Illinois, especially Chicago—where the first skyscrapers were built in the 1880s. Chicago has been a mecca for modern commercial and residential architects ever since the fire of 1871. The Art Institute of Chicago, incorporated in 1879, is the leading art museum in the state. Its French Impressionist collection is especially noteworthy.

Theater groups abound—notably in Chicago, where the Second City comedy troupe and the Steppenwolf Theatre are located. The Chicago Symphony Orchestra boasts world stature. Opera flourished in Chicago in the early 20th century, and was reborn through the founding of the Lyric Opera in 1954. Chicago's most original musical contribution was jazz, imported from the South by black musicians in the 1920s. Such jazz greats as Louis Armstrong, Jelly Roll Morton, and Benny Goodman all worked or learned their craft in the jazz houses of the city's South Side.

The seamy side of Chicago has fascinated writers throughout the 20th century. Among well-known American novels set in Chicago are two muckraking works, Frank Norris's *The Pit* (1903) and Upton Sinclair's *The Jungle* (1906), as well as James T. Farrell's *Studs Lonigan* (1935) and Saul Bellow's *The Adventures of Augie March* (1953). Famous American plays associated with Chicago are *The Front Page* (1928), by Ben Hecht and Charles MacArthur, and *A Raisin in the Sun* (1959), by Lorraine Hansberry.

34 LIBRARIES AND MUSEUMS

Libraries and library science are particularly strong in Illinois. In 1995 there were 620 public libraries, with a combined book stock of over 32,500,000. The facilities in Peoria, Oak Park, Evanston, Rockford, Quincy, and the Harold Washington Library Center in Chicago are noteworthy. The outstanding libraries of the University of Illinois (Champaign–Urbana) and the University of Chicago constitute the state's leading research facilities, together with the Newberry Library in Chicago.

Illinois has 263 museums and historic sites. Chicago's Field Museum of Natural History, founded in 1893, has sponsored numerous worldwide expeditions in the course of acquiring some 13 million anthropological, zoological, botanical, and geological specimens. The Museum of Science and Industry, near the University of Chicago, attracts five million visitors a year, mostly children, to see its exhibits of industrial technology.

Just about every town has one or more historic sites authenticated by the state. The most popular is New Salem, near Springfield, where Abraham Lincoln lived from 1831 to 1837. Its reconstruction, begun by press magnate William Randolph Hearst in 1906, includes one original cabin and numerous replicas.

35 COMMUNICATIONS

Illinois has an extensive communications system. The state's households with telephones numbered about 4,268,000 in March 1993, or 93.7% of all households. Illinois had 134 AM and 247 FM commercial radio stations in 1993, when 38 commercial television stations and 10 educational stations served the state. The state's 25 large cable systems have brought good television reception, even to the rural areas. The National Center for Supercomputing Applications at the University of Illinois (Champaign–Urbana) is involved in software development for the Internet.

36 PRESS

As of 1994, Illinois had 21 morning newspapers, 50 evening dailies, and 27 Sunday papers. The Illinois editions of St. Louis newspapers are also widely read. The state's leading dailies with their 1994 daily circulations are the *Chicago Tribune* (733,775); the *Chicago Sun-Times* (557,780); the *Peoria Journal Star* (88,957); and the *Rockford Register Star* (73,719). The most popular magazines published in Chicago are *Playboy* and *Ebony*.

37 TOURISM, TRAVEL, AND RECREATION

The tourist industry is of special importance to Chicago, the nation's leading convention center. The city's chief tourist attractions are its museums, restaurants, and shops. Chicago also boasts the tallest building in the US, the Sears Tower, 110 stories and 1,454 feet (443 meters) high.

For the state as a whole, tourism generated $14 billion in revenue in 1990. There are 42 state parks, 4 state forests, 36,659 campsites, and 25 state recreation places; the total number of visitors was 34.6 million in 1991. The Lincoln Home National Historic Site in Springfield is a popular tourist attraction.

Swimming, bicycling, hiking, camping, horseback riding, fishing, and motorboating are the most popular recreational activities. Even more popular than hunting is wildlife observation, an activity that engages nearly three million Illinoisans annually.

38 SPORTS

Illinois has five major league professional sports teams, all of which play in Chicago: the Cubs and the White Sox of Major League Baseball, the Bears of the National Football League, the Bulls of the National Basketball Association, and the Blackhawks of the National Hockey League.

The Bulls established a remarkable basketball dynasty fueled by the play of Michael Jordan, perhaps the best athlete in the history of basketball, winning NBA Championships in 1991, 1992, and 1993. They were the first basketball team to win three consecutive championships since the Boston Celtics set the probably unbreakable record of eight consecutive titles from 1959 to 1966.

In collegiate sports, the emphasis is on basketball and football. The University of Illinois and Northwestern University compete in the Big Ten Conference. The Depaul University Blue Demons of the Great

Photo credit: Grant H. Kessler.

Biographer/poet Carl Sandburg's birthplace in Galesburg, Illinois.

Midwest Conference consistently rank high among college basketball teams.

[39] FAMOUS ILLINOISANS

Abraham Lincoln (b.Kentucky, 1809–65), 16th president of the US, is the outstanding figure in Illinois history, having lived and built his political career in the state between 1830 and 1861. The only Illinois native to be elected president is Ronald Reagan (b.1911), who left the state after graduating from Eureka College to pursue his film and political careers in California. Ulysses S. Grant (b.Ohio, 1822–85), the nation's 18th president, lived in Galena on the eve of the Civil War. Adlai E. Stevenson (b.Kentucky, 1835–1914), founder of a political dynasty, served as US vice-president from 1893 to 1897, but was defeated for the same office in 1900. His grandson, also named Adlai E. Stevenson (b.California, 1900–65), served as governor of Illinois from 1949 to 1953, was the Democratic presidential nominee in 1952 and 1956, and ended his career as US ambassador to the United Nations. William Jennings Bryan (1860–1925), a leader of the free-silver and Populist movements, was the Democratic presidential nominee in 1896, 1900, and 1908. John B. Anderson (b.1922), Republican congressman for 20 years, was an independent presidential candidate in 1980.

US Supreme Court justices associated with Illinois include Chicago-born Arthur Goldberg (b.1908), who also served as secretary of labor and succeeded Stevenson as UN ambassador; Harry A. Blackmun (b.1908); and John Paul Stevens (b.1920). Richard J. Daley (1902–76) was Democratic boss and mayor of Chicago from 1955 to 1976. Jane Byrne (b.1934), a Daley protégé, became the city's first female mayor in 1979; she was succeeded in 1983 by Harold Washington (1922–87), the city's first black mayor. Richard Michael Daley (b. 1942), son of Richard J. Daley, also became mayor.

An outstanding Illinoisan was Jane Addams (1860–1935), founder of Hull House (1889), author, reformer, prohibitionist, feminist, and tireless worker for world peace who shared the Nobel Peace Prize in 1931. Feminist leader Betty Friedan (b. 1921) founded the National Organization for Women in 1966. Winners of the Nobel Prize in physics include Albert Michelson (b.Germany, 1852–1931) and Enrico Fermi (b.Italy, 1901–54). A Nobel award in literature went to Saul Bellow (b.Canada, 1915), and the economics prize was given to Milton Friedman (b.New York, 1912), leader of the so-called Chicago school of economists. Jerome Friedman (b. 1930) was a 1990 co-recipient of the Nobel Prize for physics, and Harry M. Markowitz (b.1927) won the Nobel prize for economics in 1990.

Some of the most influential Illinoisans have been religious leaders, and many of them also exercised social and political influence. Notable are Mother Frances Xavier Cabrini (b.Italy, 1850–1917), the first American to be canonized as a Catholic saint; Bishop Fulton J. Sheen (1895–1979), influential spokesman for the Roman Catholic Church; Elijah Muhammad (Elijah Poole, b.Georgia, 1897–1975), leader of the Black Muslim movement; and Jesse Jackson (b.North Carolina, 1941), civil rights leader and one of the most prominent black spokespersons of the 1980s.

Outstanding business and professional leaders who lived in Illinois include John Deere (b.Vermont, 1804–86), industrialist and inventor of the steel plow; railroad car inventor George Pullman (b.New York 1831–97); merchant Marshall Field (b.Massachusetts, 1834–1906); sporting-goods manufacturer Albert G. Spalding (1850–1915); breakfast-food manufacturer Charles W. Post (1854–1911); lawyer Clarence Darrow (b.Ohio, 1857–1938); and meat packer Oscar Mayer (1888–1965).

Artists who worked for significant periods in Illinois (usually in Chicago) include architects Frank Lloyd Wright (b.Wisconsin, 1869–1959) and Ludwig Mies van der Rohe (b.Germany, 1886–1969). Important writers include novelists John Dos Passos (1896–1970) and Ernest Hemingway (1899–1961). Poets include Edgar Lee Masters (b.Kansas, 1869–1950); Carl Sandburg (1878–1967); Nicholas Vachel Lindsay (1879–1931); Archibald MacLeish (1892–1982), also Librarian of Congress and assistant secretary of state; Gwendolyn Brooks (b.Kansas, 1917), the first black woman to win a Pulitzer Prize; and Ray Bradbury (b.1920). Robert Butler (b.

1945), 1993 winner of the Pulitzer Prize for fiction, was born in Granite City.

Performing artists connected with the state include opera stars Sherrill Milnes (b.1935); clarinetist Benny Goodman (1909–86); singers Mel Torme (b.1925) and Grace Slick (b.1939); musician Ray Charles (b.1918); comedians Jack Benny (Benjamin Kubelsky, 1894–1974), Bob Newhart (b.1929), and Richard Pryor (b.1940); and a long list of stage and screen stars, including Gloria Swanson (1899–1983), Karl Malden (Malden Sekulovich, b.1913), Jason Robards, Jr. (b.1922), Charlton Heston (b.1922), Rock Hudson (Roy Fitzgerald, 1925–85), Bruce Dern (b.1936), and Raquel Welch (Raquel Tejeda, b.1942).

Dominant figures in the Illinois sports world include Ernest "Ernie" Banks (b.Texas, 1931) of the Chicago Cubs; Robert "Bobby" Hull (b.Canada, 1939) of the Chicago Black Hawks; owner George Halas (1895–83) and running back Walter Payton (b.Mississippi, 1954) of the Chicago Bears; and Michael Jordan (b.New York, 1963) of the Chicago Bulls.

40 BIBLIOGRAPHY

Illinois, State of. Department of Commerce and Community Affairs. *Illinois Data Book*, Springfield. 1994.

Illinois, State of. Secretary of State. *Illinois Blue Book*. Springfield.

Jensen, Richard J. *Illinois: A Bicentennial History.* New York: Norton, 1978.

Glossary

ALPINE: generally refers to the Alps or other mountains; can also refer to a mountainous zone above the timberline.

ANCESTRY: based on how people refer to themselves, and refers to a person's ethnic origin, descent, heritage, or place of birth of the person or the person's parents or ancestors before their arrival in the United States. The Census Bureau accepted "American" as a unique ethnicity if it was given alone, with an unclear response (such as "mixed" or "adopted"), or with names of particular states.

ANTEBELLUM: before the US Civil War.

AQUEDUCT: a large pipe or channel that carries water over a distance, or a raised structure that supports such a channel or pipe.

AQUIFER: an underground layer of porous rock, sand, or gravel that holds water.

BLUE LAWS: laws forbidding certain practices (e.g., conducting business, gaming, drinking liquor), especially on Sundays.

BROILERS: a bird (especially a young chicken) that can be cooked by broiling.

BTU: The amount of heat required to raise one pound of water one degree Fahrenheit.

CAPITAL BUDGET: a financial plan for acquiring and improving buildings or land, paid for by the sale of bonds.

CAPITAL PUNISHMENT: punishment by death.

CIVILIAN LABOR FORCE: all persons 16 years of age or older who are not in the armed forces and who are now holding a job, have been temporarily laid off, are waiting to be reassigned to a new position, or are unemployed but actively looking for work.

CLASS I RAILROAD: a railroad having gross annual revenues of $83.5 million or more in 1983.

COMMERCIAL BANK: a bank that offers to businesses and individuals a variety of banking services, including the right of withdrawal by check.

COMPACT: a formal agreement, covenant, or understanding between two or more parties.

CONSOLIDATED BUDGET: a financial plan that includes the general budget, federal funds, and all special funds.

CONSTANT DOLLARS: money values calculated so as to eliminate the effect of inflation on prices and income.

CONTERMINOUS US: refers to the "lower 48" states of the continental US that are enclosed within a common boundary.

CONTINENTAL CLIMATE: the climate typical of the US interior, having distinct seasons, a wide range of daily and annual temperatures, and dry, sunny summers.

COUNCIL-MANAGER SYSTEM: a system of local government under which a professional administrator is hired by an elected council to carry out its laws and policies.

CREDIT UNION: a cooperative body that raises funds from its members by the sale of shares and makes loans to its members at relatively low interest rates.

CURRENT DOLLARS: money values that reflect prevailing prices, without excluding the effects of inflation.

DEMAND DEPOSIT: a bank deposit that can be withdrawn by the depositor with no advance notice to the bank.

ELECTORAL VOTES: the votes that a state may cast for president, equal to the combined total of its US senators and representatives and nearly always cast entirely on behalf of the candidate who won the most votes in that state on Election Day.

ENDANGERED SPECIES: a type of plant or animal threatened with extinction in all or part of its natural range.

FEDERAL POVERTY LEVEL: a level of money income below which a person or family qualifies for US government aid.

FISCAL YEAR: a 12-month period for accounting purposes.

FOOD STAMPS: coupons issued by the government to low-income persons for food purchases at local stores.

GENERAL BUDGET: a financial plan based on a government's normal revenues and operating expenses, excluding special funds.

GENERAL COASTLINE: a measurement of the general outline of the US seacoast. See also TIDAL SHORELINE.

GREAT AWAKENING: during the mid–18th century, a Protestant religious revival in North America, especially New England.

GROSS STATE PRODUCT: the total value of goods and services produced in the state.

GROWING SEASON: the period between the last 32°F (0°C) temperature in spring and the first

32°F (0°C) temperature in autumn.

HISPANIC: a person who originates from Spain or from Spanish-speaking countries of South and Central America, Mexico, Puerto Rico, and Cuba.

HOME-RULE CHARTER: a document stating how and in what respects a city, town, or county may govern itself.

HUNDREDWEIGHT: a unit of weight that equals 100 pounds in the US and 112 pounds in Britain.

INPATIENT: a patient who is housed and fed—in addition to being treated—in a hospital.

INSTALLED CAPACITY: the maximum possible output of electric power at any given time.

MASSIF: a central mountain mass or the dominant part of a range of mountains.

MAYOR-COUNCIL SYSTEM: a system of local government under which an elected council serves as a legislature and an elected mayor is the chief administrator.

MEDICAID: a federal-state program that helps defray the hospital and medical costs of needy persons.

MEDICARE: a program of hospital and medical insurance for the elderly, administered by the federal government.

METRIC TON: a unit of weight that equals 1,000 kilograms (2,204.62 pounds).

METROPOLITAN AREA: in most cases, a city and its surrounding suburbs.

MONTANE: refers to a zone in mountainous areas in which large coniferous trees, in a cool moist setting, are the main features.

NO-FAULT INSURANCE: an automobile insurance plan that allows an accident victim to receive payment from an insurance company without having to prove who was responsible for the accident.

NONFEDERAL PHYSICIAN: a medical doctor who is not employed by the federal US government.

NORTHERN, NORTH MIDLAND: major US dialect regions.

OMBUDSMAN: a public official empowered to hear and investigate complaints by private citizens about government agencies.

PER CAPITA: per person.

PERSONAL INCOME: refers to the income an individual receives from employment, or to the total incomes that all individuals receive from their employment in a sector of business (such as personal incomes in the retail trade).

PIEDMONT: refers to the base of mountains.

POCKET VETO: a method by which a state governor (or the US president) may kill a bill by taking no action on it before the legislature adjourns.

PROVED RESERVES: the quantity of a recoverable mineral resource (such as oil or natural gas) that is still in the ground.

PUBLIC DEBT: the amount owed by a government.

RELIGIOUS ADHERENTS: the followers of a religious group, including (but not confined to) the full, confirmed, or communicant members of that group.

RETAIL TRADE: the sale of goods directly to the consumer.

REVENUE SHARING: the distribution of federal tax receipts to state and local governments.

RIGHT-TO-WORK LAW: a measure outlawing any attempt to require union membership as a condition of employment.

SAVINGS AND LOAN ASSOCIATION: a bank that invests the savings of depositors primarily in home mortgage loans.

SECESSION: the act of withdrawal, such as a state that withdrew from the Union in the US Civil War.

SERVICE INDUSTRIES: industries that provide services (e.g., health, legal, automotive repair) for individuals, businesses, and others.

SHORT TON: a unit of weight that equals 2,000 pounds.

SOCIAL SECURITY: as commonly understood, the federal system of old age, survivors, and disability insurance.

SOUTHERN, SOUTH MIDLAND: major US dialect regions.

SUBALPINE: generally refers to high mountainous areas just beneath the timberline; can also more specifically refer to the lower slopes of the Alps mountains.

SUNBELT: the southernmost states of the US, extending from Florida to California.

SUPPLEMENTAL SECURITY INCOME: a federally administered program of aid to the aged, blind, and disabled.

TIDAL SHORELINE: a detailed measurement of the US seacoast that includes sounds, bays, other outlets, and offshore islands.

TIME DEPOSIT: a bank deposit that may be withdrawn only at the end of a specified time period or upon advance notice to the bank.

VALUE ADDED BY MANUFACTURE: the difference, measured in dollars, between the value of finished goods and the cost of the materials needed to produce them.

WHOLESALE TRADE: the sale of goods, usually in large quantities, for ultimate resale to consumers.

Abbreviations & Acronyms

AD—Anno Domini
AFDC—aid to families with dependent children
AFL–CIO—American Federation of Labor–Congress of Industrial Organizations
AI—American Independent
AM—before noon
AM—amplitude modulation
American Ind.—American Independent Party
Amtrak—National Railroad Passenger Corp.
b.—born
BC—Before Christ
Btu—British thermal unit(s)
bu—bushel(s)
c.—circa (about)
c—Celsius (Centigrade)
CIA—Central Intelligence Agency
cm—centimeter(s)
Co.—company
comp.—compiler
Conrail—Consolidated Rail Corp.
Corp.—corporation
CST—Central Standard Time
cu—cubic
cwt—hundredweight(s)
d.—died
D—Democrat
e—evening
E—east
ed.—edition, editor
e.g.—exempli gratia (for example)
EPA—Environmental Protection Agency
est.—estimated
EST—Eastern Standard Time
et al.—et alii (and others)
etc.—et cetera (and so on)
F—Fahrenheit
FBI—Federal Bureau of Investigation
FCC—Federal Communications Commission
FM—frequency modulation
Ft.—fort
ft—foot, feet
GDP—gross domestic products
gm—gram
GMT—Greenwich Mean Time
GNP—gross national product
GRT—gross registered tons
Hist.—Historic

I—interstate (highway)
i.e.—id est (that is)
in—inch(es)
Inc.—incorporated
Jct.—junction
K—kindergarten
kg—kilogram(s)
km—kilometer(s)
km/hr—kilometers per hour
kw—kilowatt(s)
kwh—kilowatt-hour(s)
lb—pound(s)
m—meter(s); morning
m^3—cubic meter(s)
mi—mile(s)
Mon.—monument
mph—miles per hour
MST—Mountain Standard Time
Mt.—mount
Mtn.—mountain
mw—megawatt(s)
N—north
NA—not available
Natl.—National
NATO—North Atlantic Treaty Organization
NCAA—National Collegiate Athletic Association
n.d.—no date
NEA—National Education Association or National Endowment for the Arts
N.F.—National Forest
N.W.R.—National Wildlife Refuge
oz—ounce(s)
PM—after noon
PST—Pacific Standard Time
r.—reigned
R—Republican
Ra.—range
Res.—reservoir, reservation
rev. ed.—revised edition
s—south
S—Sunday
Soc.—Socialist
sq—square
St.—saint
SRD—States' Rights Democrat
UN—United Nations
US—United States

NAMES OF STATES AND OTHER SELECTED AREAS

	Standard Abbreviation(s)	Postal Abbreviation
Alabama	Ala.	AL
Alaska	*	AK
Arizona	Ariz.	AZ
Arkansas	Ark.	AR
California	Calif.	CA
Colorado	Colo.	CO
Connecticut	Conn.	CN
Delaware	Del.	DE
District of Columbia	D.C.	DC
Florida	Fla.	FL
Georgia	Ga.	GA
Hawaii	*	HI
Idaho	*	ID
Illinois	Ill.	IL
Indiana	Ind.	IN
Iowa	*	IA
Kansas	Kans. (Kan.)	KS
Kentucky	Ky.	KY
Louisiana	La.	LA
Maine	Me.	ME
Maryland	Md.	MD
Massachusetts	Mass.	MA
Michigan	Mich.	MI
Minnesota	Minn.	MN
Mississippi	Miss.	MS
Missouri	Mo.	MO
Montana	Mont.	MT
Nebraska	Nebr. (Neb.)	NE
Nevada	Nev.	NV
New Hampshire	N.H.	NH
New Jersey	N.J.	NJ
New Mexico	N.Mex.(N.M.)	NM
New York	N.Y.	NY
North Carolina	N.C.	NC
North Dakota	N.Dak. (N.D.)	ND
Ohio	*	OH
Oklahoma	Okla.	OK
Oregon	Oreg. (Ore.)	OR
Pennsylvania	Pa.	PA
Puerto Rico	P.R.	PR
Rhode Island	R.I.	RI
South Carolina	S.C.	SC
South Dakota	S.Dak. (S.D.)	SD
Tennessee	Tenn.	TN
Texas	Tex.	TX
Utah	*	UT
Vermont	Vt.	VT
Virginia	Va.	VA
Virgin Islands	V.I.	VI
Washington	Wash.	WA
West Virginia	W.Va.	WV
Wisconsin	Wis.	WI
Wyoming	Wyo.	WY

*No standard abbreviation